Singing a Hindu Nation

SINGING A HINDU NATION

Marathi Devotional Performance and Nationalism

Anna C. Schultz

OXFORD
UNIVERSITY PRESS

OXFORD
UNIVERSITY PRESS

Oxford University Press is a department of the
University of Oxford. It furthers the University's objective
of excellence in research, scholarship, and education
by publishing worldwide

Oxford New York
Auckland Cape Town Dar es Salaam Hong Kong Karachi
Kuala Lumpur Madrid Melbourne Mexico City Nairobi
New Delhi Shanghai Taipei Toronto

With offices in
Argentina Austria Brazil Chile Czech Republic France Greece
Guatemala Hungary Italy Japan Poland Portugal Singapore
South Korea Switzerland Thailand Turkey Ukraine Vietnam

Oxford is a registered trade mark of Oxford University Press
in the Uk and certain other countries

Published in the United States of America by
Oxford University Press
198 Madison Avenue, New York, New York 10016

Library of Congress Cataloging-in-Publication Data
Schultz, Anna C.
Singing a Hindu Nation: Marathi devotional performance and nationalism / Anna C. Schultz.
p. cm.
Includes bibliographical references and index.
ISBN 978-0-19-973082-7 (hardcover : alk. paper)—ISBN 978-0-19-973083-4
(pbk. : alk. paper) 1. Sacred vocal music—India—Maharashtra—History and criticism.
2. Maratha (Indic people)—Songs and music—History and criticism.
3. Patriotic music—India—Maharashtra—History and criticism. I. Title.
ML3748.7.M37S38 2012
782.3'450095479—dc23 2012006976
Publication of this book was supported by the AMS 75 PAYS Endowment of the American
Musicological Society, funded in part by the National Endowment for the Humanities and the
Andrew W. Mellon Foundation.

1 3 5 7 9 8 6 4 2

Printed in the United States of America
on acid-free paper

For my parents, Peggy and Jerold Schultz

CONTENTS

Acknowledgments ix
Notes on Transliteration and Orthography xiii
About the Companion Website xiv

1. Standing on Nārad's Mat: Nationalism and Hindu Performance in Western India *3*

PART I: Marathi Kīrtan and Modernity Before 1947

2. Nāradīya Kīrtan for "Modern Educated Graduates" *21*
3. Rāṣṭrīya Kīrtan: Resisting Modernity, Devotionalizing Nationalism *50*

PART II: Nationalist Kīrtan Within and Beyond the Post-Colonial State

4. "From 'Self Rule' to 'Good Rule'": Nationalism and Kīrtan after Independence *79*
5. The Re-Institutionalization of Marathi Kīrtan *102*

PART III: Performing a Hindu Nation

6. Performance, Genre, and Politics in Rāṣṭrīya Kīrtan *135*
7. Sudhatai Dhamankar: Embedded Embodiments *156*
8. Yogeshwar Upasani: The Collision of Genres and Collusion of Participants *174*
9. Conclusion *189*

Notes *195*
References *207*
Glossary *215*
Index *223*

ACKNOWLEDGMENTS

Ever since this project began fourteen years ago in the aisles of the University of Illinois library, I have been nurtured by the help of more people than I could possibly name. Without the scores of once-strangers-now-friends in India who fed my curiosity about kīrtan, without a network of colleagues to indulge my thoughts on topics that must have seemed immeasurably arcane, and without friends to tame the frustrations of a first book, there would be no *Singing a Hindu Nation*.

My parents are the source of my love of India. They had been in Pune for nine months when I arrived to spend the summer with them in 1990. During those blissful months, I learned the quiet rhythm of a life filled with people—friends dropping by for tea, schoolchildren running after my mother, "Peggy Teacher," a gardener who spent more time in our apartment than in the garden. My mother taught me to welcome this sociability and to embrace the vibrant city, and my father reminded me that even urban landscapes are home to birds, trees, fruits, and snakes.

This experience led me to join the Associated Colleges of the Midwest (ACM) study abroad program in Pune in 1992. On and before that trip, Philip Engblom taught the best introductory language course I have ever had, and Eleanor Zelliot became an intellectual force in my life. Throughout these two decades, her warmth, incisive critiques, and devotion to Maharashtrian social life have fed and inspired me. During my ACM period, I was also fortunate enough to stay with Sharmila, Jaywardhan, and Aishwarya Shaligram. I have been a "tai" to Jay and Aishwarya for as long as they remember, and I can always count on the hospitality and love of my second family when I'm in Pune.

When kīrtan became my obsession and I found my way back to India for fieldwork, I was received with incredible warmth and a spirit of collaboration. My deepest gratitude goes to my kīrtan teacher and mentor, Vaman Vasudeo Kolhatkar. Two to three times per week, he patiently taught me songs, philosophy, and kīrtan history in his "Temple of Mathematics." His sharp wit and intelligence incited me to hear alternative tales in the stories and songs of others. The hours I spent with him and his wife, engaging in unhurried but animated discussion about philosophy and performance, are some of my life's precious moments. His wife, Dyotana Kaku, has an excellent command of raga and of English, and she deftly identified ragas and provided precise translations of esoteric Marathi terms. Indeed, the entire family has helped me with this project, especially my dear friends Ratnadha and Varada Kolhatkar, the youngest daughters in the Kolhatkar family.

Innumerable kīrtankārs, scholars, audience members, and organizations aided my research and enriched my days in Maharashtra. Wherever I went, doors were opened, tea was offered, ideas were debated, songs were sung, and stories were shared. The late G. N. Koparkar and his disciple Sudhatai Dhamankar welcomed me to their special events and daily activities at Tapodham Ashram and graciously responded to my many questions. I am particularly grateful to Mrs. Dhamankar for teaching me kīrtan songs and for allowing me to record and share one of her performances in Pandharpur. Charudatta Aphale is probably Pune's busiest rāṣṭrīya kīrtankār, but he and Shubhangitai always made time to talk with me and fill my stomach with puraṇpoḷī. The late B. R. Ghaisas was a patient teacher to me and many other students in the Harikīrtanottejak Sabhā Kīrtan School at Nārad Maṅdir. Moreshwarbuwa Joshi, a leader in the Akhil Bhāratīya Kīrtan Kula, was helpful and enthusiastic, and Dr. Ramchandra Dekhane taught me to appreciate the humor of kīrtan. Manjushree Khadilkar sings with extraordinary skill, and she and her late husband Shrikant Khadilkar showed me how wonderful kīrtan can be when song is prioritized.

In Pandharpur, Dr. Dadamaharaj Manmadkar shared with me an alternative vision of what rāṣṭrīya kīrtan has been and could be. I cherished the hours I spent talking to parrots and eating modak with his wife and her sister, Shaila Maushi. Also in Pandharpur, Jaytumbi Maharaj Sayyid shared her unique perspectives on being female, Muslim, and a vārkarī, and Ramdas Maharaj Jadhav unlocked some of the mysteries behind the visionary Kaikadi Maharaj Math.

I also benefited greatly from many conversations with and performances by V. K. Wagh, Yogeshwar Upasani, Naraharibuva Appamarjane, Dr. Dilip Dabir, Shrikrishna Vaman Sinnarkarbuva, Shreeyash Badave, Rohini Joshi, Yogeshwar Upasani, Narendrabuwa Hate, Vasudeo Burse, Lilatai Gole, Mangalabai Kulkarni, Gita Mahabar, Milinda Badave, Dattadas Ghag, Tarabai Deshpande, Smita Deshpande, Vijay Appamarjane, the family of Govinda Khare, V. K. Wagh, Manjiri Kelkar, the Shankaracarya of Karveer Pith, Dnyaneshwar Tandale, and many others.

Several scholars in Pune helped me to place my experiences with kīrtankārs in a wider perspective, including Dr. Yeshwant Pathak, the late Dr. Ashok Ranade, Dr. Digvijay Vaidya (my patient, talented singing teacher), Prof. Gayatri Chatterjee, and Dr. Sadanand More. I am particularly grateful to V. L. Manjul, a scholar of Marathi literature, librarian, son of a kīrtankār in Pandharpur, and former chairperson of the All Indian Kīrtan Organization.

A number of organizations provided assistance, including the Akhil Bhāratīya Kīrtan Kula, the Akhil Bhāratīya Kīrtan Sansthā, the Gadge Maharaj Mission, Tapodhām Pratiṣṭhān, the Pune Marathi Granthalaya, *Kesari* newspaper, and the University of Bombay. I am grateful to have learned from so many brilliant kīrtankārs, scholars, and kīrtan families, but my thoughts at times diverged from what they taught me. I trust that they will forgive me for any shortcomings, and I hope that readers will understand that these interpretations are mine alone.

Much of my time for this project has been spent translating kīrtans, often with the assistance of others. I thank the translators and transcribers who suffered through the painful crackling of poor cassette recordings to assist me. Sunila Ranade, Manisha Bhagwat, and Vaishali Joshi were diligent and precise. Vidya Marathe, my friend and Marathi teacher, was also a dedicated translator. Sharvari Nadkarni, a physicist, surprised me with her subtle understandings of language and her attention to detail. Jaywardhan Shaligram and Jashan Bhumkar were of great assistance in the later stages of this research.

Philip Bohlman has been an inspiration since serving as my M.A. advisor at the University of Chicago, and over the past few years has emerged as my colleague in the music of Maharashtra. While I was working on my Ph.D. at the University of Illinois, Bruno Nettl, Rajeshwari Pandharipande, and Thomas Turino carefully read my dissertation; their insightful comments guided me even years later as I reshaped and rewrote the dissertation to create this book. My advisor, Charles Capwell, has mentored me in every phase of this project and has constantly challenged me to write with clarity and vibrancy.

Several people helped me make the transition from fieldwork to writing, having been with me during both phases of this project. Adheesh Sathaye and Christian Novetzke provided challenging and thoughtful reflections on many parts of this book, and Adheesh read and provided detailed feedback on the first three chapters of this book. His keen eye for orthography led me to correct several glaring errors of transliteration. Many friends have provided feedback on presentations and articles that found new shape in this book. I am particularly grateful Zoe Sherinian, Davesh Soneji, Regula Qureshi, Michael Nijhawan, Peter Manuel, Sumit Guha, Anne Feldhaus, Scott Marcus, Matthew Allen, Stefan Fiol, Justin Scarimbalo, Matt Rahaim, Shalini Ayyagari, Tim Cooley, Aneesh Pradhan, Bali Sahota, and Ladona Martin-Frost.

Since I began this project fourteen years ago, I have been fortunate to have had the support and inspiration of the best colleagues, teachers, and students at the University of Illinois, Ithaca College, University of Minnesota, and Stanford University. At Illinois, Joanna Bosse, Chris Scales, Rebecca Bryant, Tulsi Dharmarajan, Indranil Dutta, Tony Perman, Stefan Fiol, and Donna Buchanan have been fantastic scholarly interlocutors and wonderful friends. In Ithaca, I relished the opportunity to share ideas—many of which have appeared in this dissertation—with Lee-Ellen Marvin and Barbara Johnson.

In Minnesota, Kelley Harness, Pooja Goswami, Bali Sahota, Arun Saldanha, Gloria Raheja, Diya Larasati, Rick Asher, Melinda Russell, Matt Rahaim, and Chuen-Fung Wong were truly engaging colleagues. Sumanth Gopinath read many drafts of my articles and papers, and provided some of the most valuable feedback I have received on this project. My students Alison Adrian, Kylah Aull, Kevin Schwandt, Aniruddha Dutta, Matthew Mihalka, David McCarthy, Lars Christensen, Jenni Kotting, Brian Schmidt, Justin Schell, and especially Emily McManus have contributed key insights to this project. In my newest home at Stanford University, Jesse Rodin, Daphna Davidson, Charles Kronengold, Carol Vernallis, Mark Applebaum, Joan Friedman, Albert Cohen, Betty Cohen, Jarek Kapuscinski, Thomas Blom Hansen, Sangeeta Mediratta, and Jisha cheered me on, read and listened to my work, and tolerated my absences during the final burst of writing energy.

The research for this project was made possible with grants and fellowships from the University of Illinois, the Nelle Seignor Fund, Fulbright-Hays, and the American Association of University Women. I am also grateful to the Society for Ethnomusicology for allowing me to use two articles previously published in the journal, *Ethnomusicology*. These articles have been revised and expanded as Chapters 7 and 8 in this book.

My dear friends Claire Colton and Pooja Goswami, my parents Peggy and Jerold Schultz, and my husband Mark Nye have been my most avid cheerleaders. I am infinitely grateful to have their loving support. When I went to India to do the dissertation research that led to this book, my husband Mark was there, and when I returned in 1999, he was with me again. He has arranged his professional life so that he can be with me for fieldwork. Thankfully, this is not only because he wants to be with me, but also because he shares my love of Indian music, ethnography, and the varieties of human sociability. Mark has been a true partner in my life and in this project. You'll see his photos in these pages and you'll hear his technical skills in my recordings. He has read and critiqued almost everything I have written. He is the love of my life and more support than I could possibly hope for.

NOTES ON TRANSLITERATION AND ORTHOGRAPHY

Each word of Indian origin is italicized in its first usage, but is not italicized for subsequent usages. Marathi words in this dissertation are transliterated following the conventions of IAST (International Alphabet of Sanskrit Transliteration). The names of people and places are transliterated without the use of diacritics, since most of these proper nouns have conventional Romanized spellings. The names of saints (from the seventeenth century and earlier) and deities are transliterated following the IAST system.

ABOUT THE COMPANION WEBSITE

www.oup.com/us/singingahindunation

You are encouraged to listen to the musical examples found on the password-protected companion website to *Singing a Hindu Nation*. These are field recordings of kīrtan performances discussed in the text, most of them made by the author at temples and concert venues in Maharashtra, India. Because kīrtan is a performance art that is meant to be heard, listening to the examples will enhance your engagement with kīrtan and the themes of this book. These recorded examples are referenced throughout the text with Oxford's symbol .

User name: Music3
Password: Book3234

Singing a Hindu Nation

1

Standing on Nārad's Mat

Nationalism and Hindu Performance in Western India

143. In the first watch of Brahmadev's day fourteen Indras were born. All these fell into prison. Such were the wonderful deeds of fate. 144. On a certain day the son of Brahmadev, the storehouse of all knowledge and bhakti, by name Narad, a noble Vaishnava, suddenly appeared. 145. The moment the fourteen rishis saw him they made him a namaskar. The celestrial rishi with a smiling face began singing full of love.

—Mahipati, *Ch. XXII*

In this passage by the eighteenth-century Marathi hagiographer Mahipati, Nārad is an ideal scholar, singer, and devotee worshipped by fourteen divine kings. Like Nārad, Marathi *nāradīya kīrtankārs* (performers of kīrtan) are learned Brahmans with expertise in ethics and philosophy who express their profound devotion in song and dare to teach those with political power. The similarity is more than coincidental—nāradīya kīrtan is named for Rishi Nārad, and when a kīrtankār sings a prayer of invocation, he has sonically defined the temple space on which he stands as "Nārad's mat." He is not dressed as Nārad nor is he depicting Nārad in any way, but as a singer, scholar, and devotee, he is embodying the *essence* of Nārad. Richard Schechner describes a North Indian performer who portrays Nārad in the *Rāmlīla*[1] in a way that translates perfectly to Marathi kīrtan: "This man is not Narad-Muni, but he is also not not Narad Muni: he performs in the field between a negative and a double negative, a field of limitless potential, free as it is from both the person (not) and the person impersonated (not not)" (Schechner 1985: 123). The power of Marathi kīrtan resides in this realm between not and not-not, and a kīrtankār's ability to inspire listeners devotionally and politically depends on what happens in that "field of limitless potential."

This book is concerned with the performance of nationalism through a subgenre of nāradīya kīrtan known as *rāṣṭrīya* (nationalist) kīrtan, charting the nationalist interventions of Marathi kīrtankārs from the anticolonial nationalist movement through the consolidation of Hindutva politics at the turn of the millennium. It attempts to complicate historiographies that equate the nationalist with the national and relegate regional leaders to the role of political messenger. Nationalist movements are effective when they can present a seamless and sometimes totalizing narrative, but this seamlessness belies a much more complicated, variegated, and fractured landscape. The subjects of this book are part of that landscape—they are neither the nationalist elite of party-driven politics nor performers whose "nationalism" (read nationalist sentiment) can be found in the symbolic appropriation of nativisms. In other words, this project demonstrates that performers can be nationalist actors in ways that exceed the symbolic expression of nation-ness while steadfastly avoiding politics in the most restricted sense. They are important local leaders who seem insignificant on the national stage, but in combination with those conducting parallel projects in other parts of India, they comprise the bewildering, contested landscape of Indian nationalism.

Religious identities have become intimately connected with modern Indian politics, and this study of the musical, rhetorical, and contextual structures of rāṣṭrīya kīrtan seeks to help explain how the devotional becomes political and why it can motivate people to action. Rāṣṭrīya kīrtan has been especially successful in combining the devotional and the political because of its ritual context, its participatory nature, and the capacity of music to juxtapose vastly different signs and genres in ways that make their connections seem natural and desirable. I focus on the *mechanisms* by which kīrtan listeners develop devotion to the nation and on how that devotion is used by kīrtankārs for political ends.

The privileging of politics over religion reflects my own bias; most rāṣṭrīya kīrtankārs consider their primary goals to be spiritual and devotional. My bias stems largely from a preexisting interest in Indian politics, but I can't deny my secular-left suspicion that religion is being used as a tool to propagandize conservative political agendas. All of this has been tempered by my anthropological impulse to take seriously the claims of the teachers and consultants who told me that they are nationalists *and* divorced from politics in the restricted sense of the word. Thus, I consider the landscape of nationalism from the perspective of a loose network of regional preacher-performers who have recently become co-opted by centralized, tightly organized political parties and organizations such as the RSS[2] and VHP.[3] Powerful coalitions have emerged from the complex dialectic between central bodies that rally behind religious symbolism and rāṣṭrīya kīrtankārs who interpret nationalist ideas as devotion. I hope to approach an understanding of how nationalism has become domesticated by people whose motivations are personal and devotional, and whose sphere of influence is both political and regional.

RELIGION, REGIONAL CONSCIOUSNESS, AND THE NATION

One of the goals of this book is to illustrate how nation and state are imagined and performed through regional idioms in local contexts. The idea for this project was sparked in 1996 after I read V. D. Divekar's chapter on Marathi rāṣṭrīya kīrtankārs in Makrand Mehta's collection, *Regional Roots of Indian Nationalism* (Divekar 1990). Mehta's collection theorizes against the grain of scholarship that constructs regionalism as a response *to* nationalism or as a reaction *against* nationalism. By looking at regional roots *of* nationalism, the authors attend to the work of nationalist leaders whose political sentiments emerged outside of "Western political and intellectual values" (Mehta 1990: 5). While I would argue that it is difficult to draw a boundary between Western and Indian values in a context of colonial modernity and cultural translation, I am sympathetic to an approach that emphasizes the diversity and regional character of nationalism(s) in India. Liberal European philosophies of nationalism entered the subcontinent not always via a *national* language and idiom, but through many regional languages and idioms with their own histories and memories. Indeed, millions of people were inspired to participate in the Indian nationalist movement through the Marathi language, Marathi songs, Marathi literature, and Marathi historical narrative.

Maharashtra was a fluid and disputed concept during the anti-colonial movement and until the 1960 formation of the modern Marathi linguistic state of Maharashtra according to the boundary proposed by the Samyukta Maharashtra Samiti (United Maharashtra Committee). A sense of unified Marathi[4] history, however, extends back to the early seventeenth century, when Shivaji Bhonsle established a Maratha[5] state that endured until the official onset of British rule in 1818 (Deshpande 2007: 1). Indeed, there were Marathi-speaking kingdoms as far back as the twelfth century, and the term "Maharashtra" has been in use for 1,500 years (Feldhaus 2003: 8). As Anne Feldhaus has demonstrated, of the many religious geographies contributing to regional consciousness in Marathi-speaking areas, the one that overlaps most with the boundaries of the modern state of Maharashtra is that of the Maharashtrian *vārkarī* tradition that began with Saint Jñāneśvar in the thirteenth century (Feldhaus 2003: 216-221). The vārkarī saints (*sants*), who lived between the thirteenth and seventeenth centuries, composed songs in colloquial Marathi rather than Brahmanical Sanskrit and preached that people of all social categories should have access to profound spiritual experience. The core practice of the vārkarī tradition is a pilgrimage in which vārkarīs (members of the vārkarī sect) walk hundreds of miles each year to visit the town of Pandharpur and the temple of Viṭṭhala, singing songs of the vārkarī saints all the while.

The history of kīrtan in Maharashtra is deeply embedded in the vārkarī saint tradition. The saints are the originators of kīrtan in Maharashtra, stories of their activities occupy a central place in Marathi kīrtan, and their songs form the musical core of kīrtans. The vārkarī tradition, however, presents only one source of regional consciousness for most of the rāṣṭrīya kīrtankārs addressed in this study. Another lives in the memory of seventeenth-century Maharashtrian heroes—especially Shivaji—whose exploits have for centuries been extolled in sung historical ballads called *povāḍā*. Rāṣṭrīya kīrtan, born of colonial modernity and buttressed by the emotional potential of region-specific "religious-moral aphorisms" (Deshpande 2006: 30), elides povāḍā of Marathi heroes with storytelling of modern nationalists of the nineteenth and twentieth centuries and depictions of vārkarī saints. Rāṣṭrīya kīrtankārs additionally have varying degrees of training in traditional Brahman fields of Sanskrit knowledge and philosophy, they are fluent in a wide range of Marathi song genres beyond the vārkarī tradition, and they often have some expertise in Hindustani art music. When historical narratives meet vārkarī songs and the prestige of traditionally schooled Brahmans, Hindutva is experienced as a familiar, emotionally charged, and authoritative expression of regional devotion, which in turn shapes the actions of listeners involved in a modern nation.

HINDU NATIONALISM AND POLITICS AS DEVOTION

In India today, over sixty years after independence from the British, national sentiment is perhaps as strong as it ever has been. At the time of Indian independence, the Indian nation was still what Partha Nath Mukherjee (1999) calls a "crystallizing nation," and Congress Party leadership continued to rally support for their project of creating a unified, heterogeneous, and secular nation. More recently, this vision of the nation has been contested, and beginning in the 1980s Hindu nationalist parties and organizations steadily gained power, culminating in the Bharatiya Janata Party's (BJP) winning of Parliament in 1998. This transfer of power represents a distinct shift in nationalist discourse from civic-secular to religious-ethnic that has continued beyond the end of BJP rule in 2004. Rāṣṭrīya kīrtankārs have been part of this transformation and have contributed in a small way to the creation of Hindu national identity among Maharashtrians.

By stating that religion and politics are merged in rāṣṭrīya kīrtan, I do not mean to imply that they are necessarily distinct spheres, an issue addressed convincingly by Peter van der Veer:

> The notion that Hinduism has only recently been "politicized" is a false one. "Politicization" and "depoliticization" of something called "religion" are notions that belong to a discourse of modernity which invents a sharp distinction between two spheres of action: religion and politics. This is a discourse of secularization, developed in the European Enlightenment, which assigns religious faith to the private domain as a matter of personal beliefs without political consequences. (1994: 285)

Van der Veer argues that Hindu nationalism is a modern incarnation of the eighteenth-century European Enlightenment discourse of nationalism that "owes more to the colonial period than to the Gupta period" (1994: 303) but has followed a unique trajectory. Devotion and politics have operated in tandem since the fifth century, when Gupta kings supported temples and religious affairs and even compared themselves to Lord Rama (Van der Veer 1994). Though India's eighteenth- and early nineteenth-century nationalist movement was ostensibly secular, religious symbolism was integral to the creation of Indian national identity across a wide political spectrum, from Gandhi's invocation of an inclusive Rāmrājya to the conservative call to protect cows and Brahmans from foreign destruction.

Anti-colonial cosmopolitan elite leaders invoked the emotional resonance of Hindu religious signifiers while favoring a secularizable, eclectic, and inclusive Hindu identity. What began as a latent Hindu bias has been foregrounded in recent years. Hindu identity is now asserted not in the struggle against colonialism but as a response to the threat of American and European economic imperialism and to the empowerment of minority groups. Marathi rāṣṭrīya kīrtan is a particularly interesting medium through which to trace this change. Maharashtra, like Bengal, has been a major center for left-wing and right-wing nationalist activity, and many of the major Hindu nationalist parties and organizations, such as the Rāṣṭrīya Swayamsevak Sangh, the Hindu Mahasabha, and the Shiv Sena, have their roots in Maharashtra (Jaffrelot 1999). Also, many rāṣṭrīya kīrtankārs perform the same kīrtans as their parents or teachers, but the meanings assigned to those stories have been transformed through decades of sociopolitical change. As a kīrtankār told me, life stories about Hindu kings and soldiers were used before independence as inspirational metaphors to show the ability of indigenous rulers to fight against more powerful "foreign" rulers—either Mughal or British.[6] In recent kīrtans, however, the opposition is posited not as one between "native" and "foreigner," but as one between "Hindu" and "Muslim."

MUSIC ETHNOGRAPHY WITH HINDU NATIONALISTS

Music provides a key to understanding the affective power of rāṣṭrīya kīrtan, and my work responds to Turino's challenge for scholars to investigate the question, "why music?"—that is, what about music makes it such an integral part of nationalist movements (Turino 1999: 221)? Rāṣṭrīya kīrtankārs do not treat audience members as passive recipients of nationalist ideas but instead use music to lead audience members in physical and emotional *experiences* of nationalism. To try to understand some of the power of these musical/nationalist/devotional experiences, I talked to audiences and kīrtankārs about what they consider meaningful, observed responses during kīrtans, and traced the influence of kīrtan beyond actual performances. Kīrtan's nationalist efficacy owes much to its devotional context, its hagiographical and semi-historical storytelling, and its gestures, but music supplies one of the most important links in the affective chain. Music allows audience members to participate in the kīrtankār's version of religion and/or nationalism, and the eclectic repertoire of song genres can be ordered and contextualized in ways that suggest new modes of identity.

When I began fieldwork in Pune, India, in 1998 and again in 1999–2000, my interactions with informants/research associates/friends/acquaintances fell outside of models I had been expecting. I was prepared to treat my consultants with relativistic fairness while responding with my own ideas in a cross-cultural dialogue. Kīrtankārs express a wide range of political perspectives, and I found it easy to approach open-minded kīrtankārs with a similarly open mind, but my relativism was tested as I reflected on the words of Hindu nationalists. How should one fairly represent people whose majoritarian voices attempt to drown out alternative identities, and how can a fieldworker be completely honest when the open expression of his or her political views could lead to the end of fieldwork relationships? I struggled to find the right balance between honesty and silence so that I could maintain harmonious but authentic relationships. While I did not need to go "undercover," as some other ethnographers of Hindu nationalism have done (e.g., Sehgal 2007: 167–169), I was positioned uneasily on the edge of informed consent. Ultimately, though I did not seek to hide my political views from field associates, I also did not make a point of announcing my opinions, as this would this have greatly limited my opportunities for interaction. I have had to come to terms with the paradox that although I—like many ethnographers—do ethnography in part to foster tolerance for different lifeways, the people with whom I work may not share the same level of tolerance.

My position as a fieldworker working primarily with Hindu nationalists was an ambivalent and unusual one. Though the literature on Hindu nationalism is extensive, only very few works are ethnographically based (e.g., Hansen 2001, Mankekar 1999, McKean 1996, Sehgal 2007). The ethnomusicological literature in particular is almost entirely devoid of ethnographic studies of music and Hindu nationalism, but some excellent historical studies address the Hindu bias of Indic musicology (Bakhle 2005, Brown 2000, Capwell 2000, Lelyveld 1996, Qureshi 1991). Conducting fieldwork with

Hindu nationalists is complicated, but it can lead to nuanced understandings of how and why power structures are maintained and resisted. Nationalism and Hindu nationalism do not simply exist—they must be created—and rāṣṭrīya kīrtan is one medium through which this occurs. Despite the ethical messiness involved, I believe that it is important to study power not only from the position of the marginalized, but also from the perspective of those who seek to maintain established hierarchies. This may include functionaries of the state and it may, as in the case of rāṣṭrīya kīrtan, involve individuals operating as independent promoters of particular nationalist visions.

CULTURAL NATIONALISM, THE "INSIDE" SPHERE, AND INTELLIGENTSIA

While many political theorists base their studies on the writings of nationalist elite leaders and party politics, historian Partha Chatterjee looks beyond legislative politics to attend to what political theorists call "cultural nationalism" (Chatterjee 1993). John Hutchinson provides a concise description of the process of cultural nationalism:

> "Cultural nationalism" has as its primary concern the regeneration of the nation as a distinctive moral community. It is based on an organic conception, according to which the nation is a natural entity with unique cultural characteristics and homelands, so that to realize their humanity, its members must actively belong to their nation by participating in its way of life. (Hutchinson 2001: 40)

In a departure from the common thesis that cultural nationalism precedes political nationalism, Chatterjee proposes that the two occur simultaneously in anti-colonial nationalisms. He regards the Indian middle class's interest in the arts and spirituality as politics within a colonial context that frustrated overtly political acts. Chatterjee's discussions center on the Indian nationalist elite, cosmopolitans—primarily from high caste backgrounds—who were enculturated into post-Enlightenment ideas through British education and employment (Chatterjee 1993: 35–37). Chatterjee asserts that when the nationalist elite were divested of political and economic power, they constructed a dichotomy between the spiritual and artistic "inside" and the material, political, and economic "outside." They protected the "inside" as a sovereign realm undisturbed by the British while reforming it to fashion a spirituality that was "modern" but not Western. As they asserted their superiority and independence in matters of the "inside," they strove to erase any marks of difference from the British on the "outside," resisting the notion that they were unfit to rule themselves (Chatterjee 1993: 5–13). Chatterjee's discussion of the inside and the outside demonstrates how the nationalist elite internalized Orientalist assumptions regarding the "Spiritual East" while paradoxically using these assumptions to combat colonialism.

Chatterjee adequately describes the Indian nationalist elite, but I argue that nationalists of other classes imagined the nation without accepting this essentialist dichotomization of experience. Performers of rāṣṭrīya kīrtan—Brahmans who preached and sang to temple audiences about the nation and independence—contributed to the nationalist movement not by separating politics and religion but by transforming the political into a matter of devotion and spirituality. The most prominent anti-colonial nationalist elite leaders from Maharashtra included Gopalkrishna Gokhale, Justice M. G. Ranade, B. G. Tilak, and V. D. Savarkar, all of them Citpāvan Brahmans like most rāṣṭrīya kīrtankārs. Though kīrtankārs and all-India elite leaders belonged to the same caste, the conservatism of rāṣṭrīya kīrtankārs led them to mistrust post-Enlightenment ideas of progress and to construct a defense against the reformist hands of the more cosmopolitan nationalist elite. It would be inaccurate, however, to draw a sharp line between "traditional" kīrtankārs and "Westernized" Congress leaders, given that even the most traditionalist kīrtankārs had some Western-style education, and most Congress leaders had family members for whom Brahman performance or scholarship constituted a primary occupation. That said, the habitus of the colonial "middle class" was shaped through extensive British education and employment within the colonial administration, which presented a different intellectual landscape from that of Citpāvan Brahmans who earned their living through the historically Brahman practices of priesthood, Vedic memorization, or kīrtan.

Most political theorists agree that nationalism's leaders are drawn from the class of "intelligentsia," a term that is sometimes contrasted with and sometimes linked to the related class of "intellectuals" (Hutchinson 2001: 154–157; see also Chatterjee 1993, Gramsci 1971, Smith 1994). Anthony Smith, in his comprehensive discussion of the nationalist intelligentsia, wrote that the intelligentsia provide the primary initiative for nationalist movements but argued that the diversity of their social backgrounds, strategies, and ideologies lend unique personalities to various nationalist movements. He identified three general types of nationalist leaders: neo-traditionalists, who have encountered modernist ideas and rejected them in favor of traditional belief systems; assimilationists, who have completely accepted universalist Enlightenment ideas; and reformists, who have engaged in and seen the futility of joining a world order in which they are considered inadequate. Reformists turn "home" in attempts to locate the "eternal" truths of their indigenous religions and customs while ridding them of extraneous superstitions that do not mesh with ideas of progress and individual self-determination (Smith 1994: 113–121).

Scholars of non-European music and nationalism have emphasized the importance of reformist musicians, scholars, and composers, perhaps because their works are most readily available in objective form—scores, books, recordings—and because they operate in the more "national" of nationalist forums (e.g., Bakhle 2005, Largey 2006, Turino 2000). I argue that *both* reformists and neo-traditionalists have been profoundly influential for Indian nationalism. Smith mentions two Indian nationalists in his description of neo-traditionalism:

> In India... Tilak and Aurobindo were appealing to the masses in an attempt to revive the fortunes of Hinduism at a time when Christianity and westernization appeared to be eroding traditional faith, and they did so by politicizing the tradition and organizing the faithful into a modern-style crusade against alien unbelievers. (Smith 1994: 117)

Though B. G. Tilak was a neo-traditionalist according to Smith, he oscillated between both halves of Chatterjee's modernist binary. By contrast, Vasudeo S. Kolhaktar, a rāṣṭrīya kīrtankār born to a poor Citpāvan Brahman family in a small village on Maharashtra's Konkan Coast in the year 1904, was decidedly anti-reform and scorned Gandhi and Savarkar's attempts to alter Vedic tradition (Barve 1963: 1). Brahman rāṣṭrīya kīrtankārs like Kolhatkar are what Antonio Gramsci would have termed "traditional" intellectuals, that is, they belong to a social class specializing in teaching and scholarship. The nationalist elite leaders B. G. Tilak, M. G. Ranade, Gopalkrishna Gokhale, and V. D. Savarkar were also Citpāvan Brahmans, but while these men studied at colonial colleges, Kolhatkar received rigorous education in the *śāstras*[7] from a pandit in Sangli (Barve 1963: 1–5, Hay 1988: 101–104, 113–114, 140–142, 289–291). Having rejected a modernity that they experienced to varying degrees, colonial-era Brahman rāṣṭrīya kīrtankārs operated almost entirely outside of post-Enlightenment discourse.

Even today, many rāṣṭrīya kīrtankārs in Pune live in the older Brahman neighborhood of Sadashiv Peth and have been educated in Marathi medium schools, speaking minimal English but boasting extensive Sanskritic knowledge. In contrast, members of the more cosmopolitan Brahman elite gravitate toward new developments in suburban areas and speak the fluent English that comes with English-medium education. Many of today's Brahman rāṣṭrīya kīrtankārs are acutely aware of the new prestige awarded to secular Brahmans who pursue more lucrative occupations. The difference between these two groups, however, is a matter of degree rather than kind. The majority of rāṣṭrīya kīrtankārs today are cosmopolitans who hold middle-class jobs and do kīrtan part-time, or who have left middle-class jobs to devote their time more completely to kīrtan.[8] The recent effort of Hindutva groups to organize kīrtankārs and reframe kīrtans on concert stages has helped to articulate kīrtan's contemporary relevance for conservative Hindus of various classes.

The story of caste and class revealed through rāṣṭrīya kīrtan is, however, not limited to the urban high castes. One of Maharashtra's most prominent rāṣṭrīya kīrtankārs, Gadge Maharaj, was an illiterate farmer-turned-kīrtankār of the washerman caste. Preaching and singing in an earthy, conversational, and rurally accented style, Gadge Maharaj was an "organic intellectual," that is a thinker, organizer, and teacher for a particular social class (Gramsci 1971: 16, 3–23, 97, 349). Before Gandhi became an important figure in Indian politics, Gadge Maharaj traveled around Maharashtra preaching nonviolent resistance to the British and the importance of health, hygiene, and education. He later became a supporter of Gandhi, attended Congress meetings, and advocated his own brand of nationalism. His kīrtans were participatory events in which he asked the audience questions and encouraged them to sing with him. Like his kīrtans, Gadge Maharaj's political style was inclusive, and he challenged people to work together to make changes that were in the interest of both their local and national communities (Shirwadkar). While Gramsci uses the term "organic intellectual" to describe progressive leaders among the subaltern classes, he wrote that the "great amorphous, disintegrated mass of the peasantry" in Italy does not produce its own intellectuals because it is disengaged from the class struggle of industrial production[9] (Crehan 2002: 143–144). Marxist, Gramsci-inspired historians of South Asia have effectively demonstrated that Indian peasants, who constitute 72 percent of the citizenry,[10] have in fact created well-organized local movements related to issues of national importance (Guha and Spivak 1988). Similarly, the devotional practices of kīrtan and pilgrimage provided an organizational structure for peasant organic intellectuals.

Nationalism is a cosmopolitan concept, but not all nationalists are cosmopolitans living the schizophrenic lives suggested by Chatterjee. Theories of nationalism have been biased by an emphasis on the "outside" sphere of politics and economics, and though Chatterjee's incisive work suggests that modernist histories overlook some of the most critical aspects of anti-colonial nationalism, he also ignores the parallel nationalisms of those who are less cosmopolitan. These parallel nationalisms are the sites of my research on rāṣṭrīya kīrtan. Rāṣṭrīya kīrtankārs in the early to mid-century were from two social groups on the margins of a globalizing world: orthodox Brahmans and progressive low caste peasants, and they force us to make room for *both* organic and traditional intellectuals in our political theories. I hope to demonstrate not only how rāṣṭrīya kīrtankārs effectively led religious followers toward a free nation-state, but also how their spiritual, social, and personal goals colored their nationalist strategies. Rāṣṭrīya kīrtankārs later in the century consider themselves heirs of earlier rāṣṭrīya kīrtankārs, but recent kīrtans are characterized by a dichotomization of "inside" and "outside" in a manner more consistent with Chatterjee's model. In the later chapters of this book, I address changes in performance context, music, and rhetoric that have accompanied these social and political changes.

RE-THINKING REFORM IN THE MUSICOLOGY OF NATIONALISM

Over the past twenty years, ethnomusicological work on music and nationalism has emphasized musical reform and revival. Scholars address how states and nationalist elites co-opt "traditional" musics to represent a cosmopolitan vision of the nation and/or to suppress alternative identities (e.g., Austerlitz 1996, Guy 1999, Largey 2006, Rice 1994, Scruggs 1998, Sugarman 1999, Trumpener 2000, Turino 1993). According to Tamara Livingston, a commonality among these "music revivals" is "the overt cultural and political agenda expressed by the revivalists themselves," middle-class people dissatisfied with mainstream contemporary life[11] (Livingston 1999: 66). Some scholars also trace these nationalist projects into local and rural repertoires (Sugarman 1999, Turino 1993); but with a few exceptions (Buchanan 1995, Rice 1994, Turino 2000), musicologists rarely address the dialectic between nation-states and individuals, and instead view musicians as reacting against—rather than actively contributing to—nationalism. I believe that this neglect results from a sense that nationalist movements, though they may change over time, are characterized by fairly uniform approaches that begin with the programs of a few nationalist elite leaders.

Consistent with other musicological studies of nationalism, the South Asianist literature addresses issues of nationalist musical reform (e.g., Bakhle 2005, Capwell 1991, Lelyveld 1994, Subramaniam 1999, 2000, Weidman 2006). Particular attention has been paid to elite and middle-class revivalism, which changed middle-class attitudes toward South Asian music while delegitimizing Muslim and courtesan performers (Qureshi 1991). Most studies of Indian musical nationalism are historical and art music–based, and since art music has been a source of fascination for the Indian nationalist middle class, this emphasis has contributed to the notion that nationalism is primarily a middle-class phenomenon. That said, a handful of fieldwork-based studies have explored the effects of nationalism on devotional and folk music repertoires, reminding us that nationalism must obtain mass appeal to be successful, and Charles Capwell's work on the music of the Bengali Baul sect demonstrates the active nationalist role of marginal communities (Capwell 1987, 1988, 1991, 2000, Henry 1988, Singer 1972).

Like other studies of music and nationalism, this book addresses issues of folklorization and musical reform by nationalist elites, but it also suggests that noncosmopolitans actively contribute to nationalism in ways that subvert and reject reform. Rāṣṭrīya kīrtan is somewhat peculiar in that it did not *need* to be reformed serve nationalistic purposes. Like other arts that were revived in colonial India, kīrtan became institutionalized through schools and conferences in attempts to standardize and objectify kīrtan after Western models. But these attempts have been only partially successful because kīrtan's usefulness for nationalist purposes has been linked in large part to its temple context and position in the "inner" world seemingly untouched by the "degenerating" influences of the "material" and non-Hindu worlds.

MUSIC, EMOTION, AND PERFORMANCE

The orientation in scholarship on Indian (and Hindu) nationalism has been toward political parties and their ancillary "cultural" organizations, and artistic expressions of Hindutva have been analyzed primarily within the realm of secular public culture. That literature, in very broad terms, emphasizes the successes and failures of parties, and in the discursive realm, employs literary techniques for interpreting religious (and other cultural) signifiers in nationalist communication. By locating nationalism in the "outside" realm rather than in religious ritual and performance, little of the literature on nationalism incorporates theoretical insights from religious studies, performance studies, and ethnomusicology. My research focuses on nationalism in the religious sphere, which is not to say that Hinduism is the same as Hindu nationalism or that appropriations of Hinduism in political contexts are about something other than majoritarian politics, but simply that nationalism is experienced as religion in religious contexts and that research on Hindu religious experience and performance can help us to understand how it is meaningful and powerful.

A theme throughout the book is that musical performance is politically and spiritually integral to the power of kīrtan. My inspirations along these lines are drawn from semiotics, particularly Charles Peirce and ethnomusicologist Thomas Turino (Peirce 1955, Turino 1999); genre theory and intertextuality as articulated by Mikhail Bakhtin (1981, 1986), Richard Bauman (1992, 2004), and Julia Kristeva (Allen 2000); ethnography of embodiment à la anthropologist Thomas Csordas (1990) and ethnomusicologist Judith Becker (2004); religious studies scholarship of devotional embodiment (Cutler 1984, Prentiss 1999); and work by Richard Schechner (1985), Erving Goffman (1986), and other scholars of communication, frames, and the emergent experience of performance. I have cast the net widely because kīrtan is so many things at once: it is a complex semiotic system of rhetorical tropes and song genres, it is an embodied devotional experience, and it is a communicative event.

One of my arguments is that kīrtankārs use music to create a collective performance experience directed toward devotional embodiment. I use embodiment here both as it is used by scholars of Hinduism to refer to *bhakti* (devotion; devotional) songs about merging with the divine, and also to ethnographic work on the body as a site for the generation and inscription of culture (Csordas 1990, Cutler 1984, Prentiss 1999, Scheper-Hughes 1987). The body in rāṣṭrīya kīrtan is paradoxically a vehicle directed toward *loss* of bodily consciousness. Kīrtan lies somewhere between trance and theater, moving between the two poles as directed by the kīrtankār. Even performances that tend more toward theater are colored by the words of the Marathi saints whose songs evoke devotional embodiment. Moreover, kīrtan's ritual context frames the kīrtankār as an iconic representative of Nārad the preacher/singer, regardless of the topic of her songs and discourse. This contextual embodiment is distinct from her embodiment of the saints through song and storytelling.

Ethnographic work on embodiment served as a corrective to hermeneutic trends of the 1970s and '80s that described culture and ethnography as interpretive, symbolic processes (Geertz 1973). Anthropologists of embodiment in the 1990s and 2000s critiqued the mentalist and Eurocentric Cartesian dualism of symbolic anthropology, but as argued by Murphy Halliburton (2002), work on the body became so commonplace that there was almost an assumption that ethnographic subjects prioritize bodily experience. As Halliburton showed for Kerala, Marathi kīrtan encompasses a spectrum of attitudes toward the relationship between body and mind, and there is much to be gained from focusing on aesthetic symbolic systems as well as the body. Thomas Turino has merged both approaches by exploring semiotics in relation to emotion and identity. Indexicality provides a link between individual experience and cultural meaning; the song "Star-Spangled Banner" indexes patriotism through its association with contexts meant to inspire nationalist sentiment, but because each person's experience of those contexts is different, the anthem is tightly bound to memory and can have profound personal, emotional, and thus embodied resonance (Turino 1999). Many of the song genres in rāṣṭrīya kīrtan are chosen because of their strong indexical associations, and though these are felt in varied ways, I follow Bauman in arguing that performers actively but inconspicuously manage the interpretations of listeners (Bauman 1992).

I am inspired by close reading techniques from literary studies, performance theory, and folklore, but my analyses are grounded in an orientation toward musical sound that is sometimes missing from that work. As an ethnomusicologist, I listen carefully to how performers talk about musical aesthetics and improvisation, and I observe how particular rhythms, timbres, melodies, and performance styles are arranged within the larger narrative to communicate a philosophical concept, evoke the emotions of a memory, or encourage participation. Through the style in which they sing and the genres they choose to combine, kīrtankārs not only bring stories and philosophies vividly to life but they also create new meanings and align themselves with a range of religious, musical, and political lineages and organizations. Because each kīrtan is a unique experience performed by a singer with an individual style, I have devoted two chapters to single performances by different kīrtankārs, employing a different range of scholarship for each. The first considers how music contributes to experiences of devotional embodiment based on a conflation of performing and performed selves and a merging of nationalist and saintly identities. The second is inspired by literary theory and semiotics, and addresses how melody and rhythm are used to juxtapose signs with divergent meanings.

PLAN OF THE BOOK

Throughout the past century of rāṣṭrīya kīrtan performance, the relationship between rāṣṭrīya kīrtankārs and cosmopolitan elites has been in flux. Early rāṣṭrīya kīrtankārs eulogized the nationalist elite while narratively and musically transforming their actions into myth and devotion. This practice continues, but engagements between kīrtankārs, politicians, and political organizations have vacillated between collaboration, appropriation, mutual disregard, and parallel but distinct activities. The dialectic between region and nation and between kīrtankārs and nationalist elites/parties comprises a central theme of this book and is reflected in its structure on both a micro and macro level. The first two parts of the book are separated by the year of Indian Independence, which was accompanied by the violent Partition of India and Pakistan (1947). That year, 1947, was a turning point for rāṣṭrīya kīrtankārs because it forced them to imagine a nationalism that was no longer anti-state, and because it led to their increased insularity in the wake of the communal and caste conflicts that erupted with Partition. In the first part, I argue that earlier kīrtankārs staunchly defended the notion that nationalism belongs in the spiritual realm, while in the second part, I suggest that this trend was gradually reversed as Hindutva organizations recognized the usefulness of kīrtan for party politics. An undercurrent throughout the text that emerges most explicitly in Part III interrogates the role of music and performance in transforming listeners into devotees of the nation.

Chapter 2 charts the nineteenth-century consolidation of kīrtan practices into nāradīya kīrtan, a professional performance genre that became a target for cultural nationalist attempts at modernization through institutionalization, publishing, and thematic control. Nāradīya kīrtan was just one of the many art forms that attracted the reformist hands of the nationalist elite, but it stood apart from drama and classical music as a Hindu tradition performed by Brahmans who were "not Nārad" but "not not Nārad." Lokmanya Tilak, the Marathi Brahman who led the all-India nationalist movement in the 1900s and 1910s, extolled kīrtan's power to affect (Marathi-speaking) people and praised kīrtankārs' status as learned Brahmans with spiritual credibility. He advocated the telling of historical stories in nāradīya kīrtan, and urged kīrtankārs to reform their art to appeal to "modern educated graduates," that is, the class of people he saw leading the nationalist movement.

Chapter 3 demonstrates how the early twentieth-century subset of nāradīya kīrtankārs known as rāṣṭrīya kīrtankārs eulogized nationalist elites like Tilak while resisting their attempts to discipline and reform kīrtan. Instead, rāṣṭrīya kīrtankārs used performance, ritual, and pilgrimage to transform politics into religion and nationalists into saints. Through kīrtan, they enlisted support for violent and nonviolent nationalist resistance and became local leaders with unique philosophies and individual constituencies. In diverse ways, rāṣṭrīya kīrtankārs of the 1920s through 1940s all contributed to the broader anticolonial movement. Dattopant Patwardhan was a devoted follower of Tilak whose nationalist counternarratives were hidden in his inspiring kīrtans, Vasudeo Kolhatkar was more openly nonconforming, and Gadge Maharaj created a completely new style of rāṣṭrīya kīrtan inspired by rural idioms.

Chapter 4 follows Marathi kīrtan into the first decades after Independence, which had three major implications for rāṣṭrīya kīrtan. First, having achieved their primary goal, some rāṣṭrīya kīrtankārs switched from nationalist kīrtan to purely spiritual topics. Second, Independence was accompanied by the violent partition of India and Pakistan, and Hindu nationalist organizations including the RSS and the Hindu Mahasabha assigned blame for this to Mahatma Gandhi. When a Maharashtrian Brahman assassinated Gandhi, retaliatory measures led Brahmans to flee to cities and retreat into insular organizations. The Brahman rāṣṭrīya kīrtankārs who continued performing in the immediate wake of both Independence and partition were preaching to a smaller, marginal, and increasingly radicalized group. Third, the new Indian state extended support to arts—including rāṣṭrīya kīrtan—that had been considered mildly or threateningly subversive during the colonial era. Financial support was given to kīrtankārs like Kaikadi Maharaj, a low caste kīrtankār and follower of Gadge Baba whose popularity in the countryside was useful for incorporating rural people into the nation and popularizing Nehruvian socialist policies. Meanwhile, state funding became available for the founding of kīrtan universities in Pune, the goals of which were so out of sync with prevailing ideas regarding university education that they folded after just a few years.

By the 1990s, as Hindu nationalist power became consolidated in the form of regional and national parties, organizations, and coalitions, rāṣṭrīya kīrtan rapidly gained new popularity. A huge umbrella organization for Marathi kīrtan called the Akhil Bhāratīya Kīrtan Kula was established, and institutional connections between kīrtan and Hindutva organizations became increasingly entrenched. Chapter 5 addresses the social reorganization of the kīrtan community in light of these trends and the now-successful attempts to modernize kīrtan through institutions, conferences, and staging. The Akhil Bhāratīya Kīrtan Kula has developed a popular model for kīrtan presentation: by embedding kīrtans within larger events structurally similar to political functions and other secular rituals, they articulate kīrtan's contemporary nationalist relevance and have attracted new audiences. This chapter also presents an ethnographic account of institutional kīrtan pedagogy in the contemporary era, and argues that kīrtan schools have succeeded where universities failed because they offer schedules and employ pedagogies that suit the needs of hobbyist and part-time kīrtankārs. An additional implication of kīrtan schools is that they have opened kīrtan performance to women, who have in turn re-gendered aspects of kīrtan aesthetics and narrative.

Part III comprises three short chapters that focus more directly on the musical performance of nationalism and devotion. In Chapter 6, I discuss sonic references to *paṭhaḍi*, or performance tradition, and examine how pastness is narrativized, embodied, and politicized through a wide array of song genres with specific extra-kīrtan associations. Chapters 7 and 8 analyze two Hindu nationalist kīrtans recorded between 1998 and 2000 and attempt to identify what, musically, renders rāṣṭrīya kīrtans "nationalist" and how the interactions between genres and between singers and listeners produce powerful affective responses that extend beyond the temple and concert hall. Here, I propose a theory of "collision of genres" and discuss the role of participatory musical performance in generating what scholars of religion have termed a "theology of embodiment."

I hope that this book offers new perspectives on nationalism, reform, and devotional music in India. This study rethinks the written bias of nationalist theory and the limited vision of nationalism as a process of the "outside" that is carried out by politicians. Focusing on hereditary elites requires new theories for the relationship between nationalism and music that complicate the assumption of cosmopolitan reform. Studies of religion, nationalism, and music are increasingly relevant at the beginning of the twenty-first century, when religio-ethnic conflict is surging in South Asia and around the world. Music is a powerful component of these movements and provides a lens for examining how and why people gain allegiance to ideologies of exclusivity.

PART ONE

Marathi Kīrtan and Modernity Before 1947

2

Nāradīya Kīrtan for "Modern Educated Graduates"

"Had I not become a journalist, I would have been a kīrtankār." This statement of Bal Gangadhar Tilak is ubiquitous in publications promoting Marathi kīrtan, and it speaks not only to the nationalist leader's interest in Marathi devotional arts but also to his continuing importance as a signifier of cultural and political identities in Maharashtra (e.g., Pathak 1980: 1). In the early twentieth century, Tilak, "The Father of Indian Unrest" and a leader of the Indian National Congress, belonged to a group of Marathi intellectuals who organized kīrtan conferences to generate interest in kīrtan among "modern educated graduates." Tilak and his colleagues believed that kīrtan would be useful as nationalist art if it could appeal to cosmopolitan classes by reconciling Hindu tradition with modernist reform and progress. Though he went to great lengths to promote kīrtan, Tilak's kīrtan advocacy is today rarely acknowledged outside of kīrtan circles. I propose that this gap in collective memory is due in part to the essential failure of his attempts to bring Marathi kīrtan to a new audience through modernist reforms. In this chapter, I introduce his ephemeral attempts and position them against the very different trajectory of cultural nationalism as it played out in the realm of "classical" arts.

In his groundbreaking study of anti-colonial nationalism, Partha Chatterjee explored the complicated habitus of the Indian nationalist middle class—cosmopolitans with primarily high caste backgrounds steeped in post-Enlightenment ideas through British education and employment (Chatterjee 1993: 35–37). Chatterjee argues that these nationalist elites sought independence in the "inside"/spiritual sphere when divested of political power in the "outside"/material sphere (Chatterjee 1993: 5–13).[1] Similarly acknowledging the dual, cosmopolitan nature of nationalism, ethnomusicologist Thomas Turino suggests that modernist reform balances the twin paradoxes of nationalism. To state his argument briefly, nations are necessarily cosmopolitan because they understand themselves in relation to other nations, but they must articulate distinctiveness from other nations to create and maintain national boundaries. Likewise, nations require local practices to generate the affective bonds of national sentiment, but locally distinct groups may also threaten the nation by claiming their own national status. According to Turino, these paradoxes are resolved through modernist reform in which aspects of local practice are combined with "the best" of modern, cosmopolitan aesthetics and ethics. For music, this usually involves the objectification and recontextualization of indigenous forms within cosmopolitan social contexts (Turino 2000: 15–16).

Chapters 2 and 3 explore opposing sides of a set of interlocking dialectics: discussed in this chapter are the reformist, appropriating, modernizing, institutionalizing hands of the cosmopolitan elite, while in the next chapter I attend to the traditionalist, independent, mythologizing responses of kīrtankārs. In the current chapter, I discuss how relationships between nineteenth-century *saṅgīt nāṭak* (music drama) actors, Hindustani musicians, and kīrtankārs led Marathi kīrtankārs to begin publishing kīrtan texts as dramatists had done and to found modern institutions as Hindustani music promoters had done. Nurtured by cosmopolitan discourses of systematization, revival, and modernization, cultural nationalists' interest in Marathi kīrtan of the nineteenth century gained a more explicitly political, anti-colonial focus in the early twentieth century, when Lokmanya Tilak advocated changes in nāradīya kīrtan that would appeal to "modern, educated" people seeking national sovereignty. His call encouraged kīrtankārs to turn toward nationalist topics and brought a new prestige to those who were already politicizing kīrtan.

This chapter also uncovers an earlier layer of history to complicate the notion that Tilak abruptly introduced rāṣṭrīya kīrtan onto the cultural landscape through Dattopant Patwardhan, who is widely (though not universally) considered Maharashtra's first rāṣṭrīya kīrtankār. I trace how rāṣṭrīya kīrtan emerged from a convergence of historical storytelling and sung devotional literature that predated the nationalist era by at least 300 years. Marathi kīrtan is documented in oral literature of the thirteenth century, and since the seventeenth century it has developed a branch that emphasizes soloistic virtuosity over participation. By the eighteenth century, that branch began cultivating entertainment in addition to religious instruction and opened the door to a religious and musical eclecticism that brought secular genres into the devotional world of kīrtan. When this style became consolidated as nāradīya kīrtan in the nineteenth century, its Brahman performers were poised to incorporate nationalist song genres and ideas into their popular, virtuosic, learned, and polysemic performances.

THE EMERGENCE OF NĀRADĪYA KĪRTAN AS ART AND PROFESSION

Before embarking on a historical account of the emergence of rāṣṭrīya kīrtan, I need to briefly introduce the two primary types of kīrtan currently practiced in Maharashtra: nāradīya kīrtan—of which rāṣṭrīya kīrtan is a subtype—and vārkarī kīrtan. Vārkarī kīrtan is associated with the Maharashtrian vārkarī sect, which centers on devotion to the god Viṭṭhala of Pandharpur and his devotees, the Marathi poet-saints Jñāndev, Nāmdev, Janābāi, Eknāth, Tukārām, Bahiṇābāi, and others. Nāradīya kīrtankārs also worship Viṭṭhala and respect the poet-saints, but their stories and songs just as frequently praise pan-Hindu gods like Śiva, Gaṇeś, and Rāma. The presentational orientation of nāradīya kīrtan and the participatory orientation of vārkarī kīrtan account for most differences in sound and performance structure between the two styles.[2]

In a typical vārkarī kīrtan, the kīrtankār, who is almost always a man[3] but may belong to any caste, stands facing the deity of a temple with the audience sitting on the floor between him and the god, men on one side and women on the other (see Plate 2.1). He is accompanied by at least one cylindrical drum (*mṛdaṅg*) player and *ṭāḷkarīs*, a chorus of ten to fifty people who stand in a semi-circle behind the kīrtankār, singing and playing *ṭāḷ* (small, concave hand cymbals). A quiet drone is provided by a *vīṇā*, a lute that is ritually passed between the kīrtankār and an elected ṭāḷkarī. The music of vārkarī kīrtan consists primarily of well-known poems in specific meters by the Marathi poet-saints (*abhaṅgas*) and single-line songs in praise of God (*bhajan*). Audio example 1 is a bhajan excerpted from a vārkarī kīrtan performed by Dadamaharaj Manmadkar in his organization's temple in 2000 and audio example 2 is an abhaṇga from the same performance, performed first by Manmadkar with his ṭāḷkarīs, then by two ṭāḷkarīs as a duet, and finally intoned by Manmadkar before he begins the discourse with which the excerpt ends. These are songs that audience members and ṭāḷkarīs are likely to know and are sung in an unornamented style that is well suited to group singing. The chorus of ṭāḷkarīs often interrupts the kīrtankār's sermon with the singing of a topically relevant abhaṅga and may take over the performance of a song that a kīrtankār has begun. In fact, a vārkarī kīrtankār can easily deliver an entire kīrtan and sing only a few solo lines of song. When the ṭāḷkarīs sing, it is common for audience members to join in, as lines are often repeated several times in familiar melodies. Vārkarī kīrtan consists of the exposition (*nirūpaṇa*) of a primary abhaṅga through a spoken discourse—punctuated by collective singing—on the subtleties of the abhaṅga's meanings and its relationship to core vārkarī beliefs. A performance usually lasts between two and three hours.

A nāradīya kīrtankār, who is usually a Brahman man or woman, also performs kīrtan facing the deity of the temple in front of a sex-segregated audience (see Plate 2.2). Though women do not perform in all Indian storytelling traditions, they do perform Bengali, Marathi nāradīya, Telugu, and Tamil

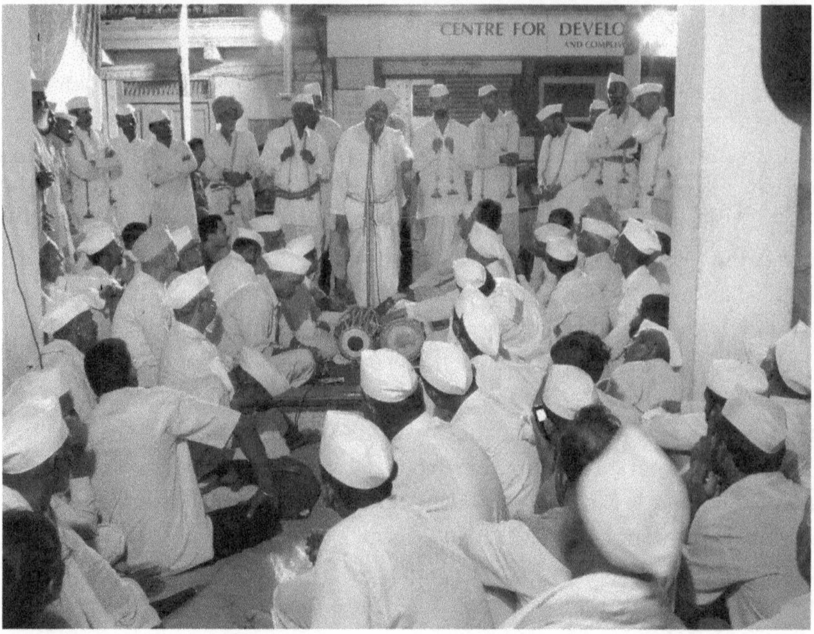

Plate 2.1.
Vārkarī Kīrtan performed by Ghule Maharaj, Pālkhī Viṭhobā Maṇdir. Pune, July 16, 2009. Photograph by Mark Nye.

harikathā kīrtan. Early twentieth-century references to women kīrtankārs in Maharashtra are very rare, but approximately 40 percent of the nāradīya kīrtankārs in Maharashtra today are women.[4] The performance ensemble of nāradīya kīrtan is much smaller than that of vārkarī kīrtan and generally consists of the kīrtankār, who accompanies herself on *jhāṅj* (small, flat hand cymbals) or *ciplīya* (an idiophone of wood clappers with small cymbals attached) and is joined by a harmonium player and a *tablā* player. One or two students or colleagues sometimes sit on the floor in front of her and provide additional jhāṅj accompaniment so that she may be free to use her hands for gesturing.

Nāradīya kīrtan is more oriented toward solo performance and smooth presentation than vārkarī kīrtan, though there are a few standard places at the beginning, intermission, and end of the kīrtan in which the audience sings along with the kīrtankār (see Chapter 6 for an expanded discussion of nāradīya kīrtan). The song types used in nāradīya kīrtan are more eclectic than those in vārkarī kīrtan, and the kīrtankār (or someone else) often composes or collects new songs for each kīrtan. Audience members rarely sing along with the kīrtankār, since the song texts may be unfamiliar or the melodies sung in a highly ornamented style that is difficult to follow in group song. Nāradīya kīrtans are divided into two sections of about an hour each, the pūrvaraṅga (or nirūpaṇa) and the uttararaṅga (or *ākhyān*), while vārkarī kīrtan has no such distinction. In the pūrvaraṅga, the kīrtankār sings a song by a well-known

Plate 2.2.
Shreeyash Badave performing nāradīya kīrtan. Pune, July 2009.

poet-saint and uses that poem as the basis of a discourse on some philosophical point. The uttararaṅga consists of a story from the life of a saint or an episode from the Hindu epics or *purāṇas* that illustrates the topic discussed in the pūrvaraṅga. Audio example 3 is excerpted from the beginning of a nāradīya kīrtan performed by Shreeyash Badave in the community room of a housing society in Pune in 2009; it includes the introductory songs up until the beginning of the pūrvaraṅga. Audio example 4 is the entire uttararaṅga of the same kīrtan.

The Marathi vārkarī saints are the first documented kīrtankārs in Maharashtra, and most of our information on kīrtan from the saints' era is gleaned from their songs,[5] which have been preserved and modified for hundreds of years through oral tradition. The descriptions of kīrtan in works by and about Jñāneśvar (d. 1290),[6] Nāmdev (1270–1350),[7] and Eknāth (1533?–1599)[8] reveal that their kīrtan philosophies and styles were similar in many ways. Some of these practices continue in Marathi kīrtan of today, while others have fallen out of practice with time. The kīrtans of pre-seventeenth-century saints (with the possible exception of Eknāth) were structured not as entertainment, but as venues for spiritual teaching and generating collective, ecstatic devotional experiences. The early saint literature describes loss of bodily consciousness and submersion in the divine resulting from singing, dancing, and reciting God's names in kīrtan, and it idealizes purity of emotion rather than musicianship and rhetorical skill (Machwe 1968: 53, Puri et al. 1977: 28). Tukārām,[9] who lived in the seventeenth century, likewise regarded kīrtan as a way to experience detachment from the mundane world, and his abhaṅgas describe the emotions of communal worship rather than the artistry of performance. Tukārām's abhaṅgas stress the importance of doing kīrtan as a means to salvation, positing kīrtan not simply as a vehicle for preaching *about* bhakti, but as bhakti itself. In one abhaṅga, Tukārām says, "the greatest merit is in kīrtan, through which a kīrtankār saves himself and others" (cf. Ranade 1988: 322).

> To perform a kirtan, i.e., to sing the name of God and praises unto Him is of the highest spiritual value. One forgets the consciousness of his tiny mind and body, and being one with Hari, the universal friend and the Lord, he dances and nods and sings with joy and love. My body itself is divinised, says Tuka, when I am doing a Kirtana, and what remains during that time is God alone. (Date 1976: 53)

Rāmdās, born into a Brahman family in the year 1608, employed kīrtan techniques and philosophies that stood in stark contrast to those of his contemporary, Tukārām (Bokil 1979: 18, 23). He broke with the vārkarī saṁpradāya to lay the musical and political foundations for rāṣṭrīya kīrtan in the seventeenth century. Though rāṣṭrīya kīrtankārs (like most Marathi kīrtankārs) are most likely to choose a Tukārām abhaṅga as the basis for their kīrtans, they recognize their intellectual, political, and artistic debt to Rāmdās and often refer to him as "the first rāṣṭrīya kīrtankār." Rāmdās rejected Viṭṭhala in favor of Rāma and upheld Brahmanical systems of knowledge rather than promoting the egalitarianism and personal devotion of the vārkarī tradition.[10] He also broke from vārkarī tradition by urging devotees to become involved in political action through their kīrtans and relationships with rulers.[11] His writings emphasized musical expertise and performance finesse, and his kīrtans combined didactics with entertainment and storytelling, all of which became features of the incipient nāradīya kīrtan tradition.

Rāmdās was the first Marathi saint to instruct his readers in matters of kīrtan performance. In the *Dās Bodh*, he explained that kīrtans can either consist of simple combinations of stories and songs about God, or they can include thorough examinations of the meanings behind the stories. He further expounded on how a kīrtankār should have good musical training and should employ a variety of song styles in various *rasas*[12] and meters (Tambwekar 1995: 61). He wrote, "You can make an effective presentation of the highest knowledge when you combine a knowledge of svara (notes), tāla (meter), and training in singing rāgas (classical modes)" (Bond 1998: 11). Nonetheless, he cautioned against the empty use of artistic skill, saying, "When one's mind gets trapped in artistic vocals, how can anyone think of the Lord?" (Bond 1998: 12). Earlier saints mentioned music, dancing, singing, and the use of instruments, but the *Dās Bodh* appears to offer the first indication that musical training should be part of the grooming of a kīrtankār (Tambwekar 1995: 60–61).

Rāmdās's interest in issues of kīrtan performance foreshadowed the nāradīya kīrtan *paraṁparā* (tradition). As Ashok Ranade states, Rāmdās's writings on kīrtan indicate that he "carried on the effort of the Eknāthi kirtan to be entertaining, interesting, and didactic" (Ranade 1984: 123). Bhaakare refers to Rāmdās's style of kīrtan as "harikathā nirūpaṇa," in which nirūpaṇa corresponds to the nāradīya pūrvaraṅga, and harikathā is equivalent to the uttararaṅga of nāradīya kīrtan (Bhaakare 2000: 65). In verse 4–2–23 from the *Dās Bodh*, Rāmdās wrote:

> Saguṇ harikathā is known as kīrtan
> Explain non-dualism in the nirūpaṇa.
> Protect the saguṇ but know
> How to explain the nirguṇ. (cf. Bhaakare 2000: 65)

From the inception of the vārkarī *paṅth* (way, order) in the thirteenth century until the Peshva reign of the eighteenth century, music in Maharashtra was allied either with the saint literature or with "secular" folk genres such as *daśāvatār*, *lalit*, *goṅdhaḷ*, and *bhārūḍ* (Vaidya 1997: 12). With the consolidation of Peshva power came new patronage for Hindu—particularly Brahman—artistic forms, and indeed, several new genres emerged during this era that blurred the boundaries between temple and court performance. Arts as entertainment had been associated with Muslim courts in the Deccan since the thirteenth century, but the use of Marathi music for the purpose of courtly entertainment was new. Nāradīya kīrtan, and in turn rāṣṭrīya kīrtan, was born in the new artistic space opened up by these changing political and artistic conditions.

The narrative genres of ākhyān poetry and povāḍā are first documented in the seventeenth century during the rule of Shivaji Bhonsle (1627–1680), a king belonging to the Maratha caste (Ranade 1961: 15). The performers and composers of these genres introduced the practice of Marathi music and poetry as courtly entertainment, a new concept in a musical landscape dominated by saints' songs and folk entertainment. Povāḍā is a sung epic storytelling genre that eulogizes the heroism of warriors. Traditionally performed by Brahman poets known as *śāhīr*, povāḍā was first incorporated into kīrtan in the early twentieth century and is now an essential element of almost any rāṣṭrīya kīrtan. Śāhīr is a term that originally referred to any courtly poets but now refers to Brahman poets of povāḍā and lāvanī, including those not associated with a court.[13] The earliest extant povāḍā, dated at approximately 1659, was written by Agnīdās to commemorate Shivaji's victory over Afzal Khan. At the end of this povāḍā Agnīdās mentions that he performed it in front of Shivaji and his mother, Jijabai (Deshpande 1988: 28). This povāḍā heralds the royal patronage of Marathi music but it was not until the next century that this system became truly paradigmatic.

The seventeenth century also ushered in ākhyān poetry written by Brahmans, beginning with Vāmanpaṅḍit (1608–1695), and ending with Shridhar (1658–1729) and Kṛṣṇadayārnav (Deshpande 1988: 33). Ākhyān poetry was intimately related to the world of Marathi kīrtan in the seventeenth century, and Vāmanpaṇḍit, who was also a kīrtankār, became extraordinarily popular during his lifetime in part because of his kīrtans (Pathak 1980: 71–72). The ākhyāns of this era—particularly the *svayaṁvar ākhyāns* (stories of self-arranged marriages) of Sītā, Rukminī, and Damāyaṅtī—influenced the structure of a branch of storytelling-oriented Marathi kīrtan that eventually became nāradīya kīrtan. The ākhyāns of seventeenth- and eighteenth-century poets continued to serve as the basis for many kīrtans of the nineteenth and twentieth centuries.

Shivaji was succeeded by his sons Sambhaji (1657–1689) and Rajaram (1670–1700) and his daughter-in-law Tarabai. These heirs maintained the Bhonsle dynasty but did not significantly expand upon Shivaji's landholdings or power (Gordon 1993: 101–113, Wolpert 1997: 165–167). The next major phase of Maratha history began when Sambhaji's son Shahu became *Chatrapatī* (king; literally, one entitled to a royal insignia) and appointed the Brahman Balaji Viswanath as his Peshva (prime minister) in Pune in 1714. For the next century, Balaji Viswanath and his successors served as the actual rulers of the Maratha kingdom, while the Bhonsles became mere figureheads. Shahu was technically a member of the Mughal aristocracy and was granted permission by Delhi to extract taxes and maintain an army. Through a brilliant scheme devised by Balaji Viswanath, the Marathas collected more taxes while giving less to the central Mughal government, and the Peshva regime gained in wealth and power, ultimately capturing most of central India and even Delhi (Wolpert 1997: 168–171).

The Peshva government was located in Pune, a city that became the nerve center for arts and learning in the Deccan. The Peshvas were avid patrons of the arts, and Brahman performance and literary genres—including kīrtan, povāḍā, and ākhyān poetry—fared particularly well in their courts. Peshva Bajirao II became the first ruler to employ a court kīrtankār, Anantji Manakeshwar, and the pant-kavīs Shridhar (1658–1729), Madhavmunishwar (1680–1734), and Moropant (1724–1794)—Brahmans who composed verses and ākhyāns in a mixture of Marathi and Sanskrit—also flourished in the Peshva era (Ranade 1984: 130). The new patronage in Pune led to an efflorescence of entertainment-oriented art genres such as *tamāśā* and lāvaṇī and to an increased emphasis on music intended for "rasika" audiences, that is, those who had the money and artistic education to enjoy and sponsor art for art's sake (Ranade 1984: 130, Vaidya 1997: 15).

As performers of both povāḍā and lāvaṇī, śāhīrs such as Anant Phandi (1744–1819), Ramjoshi (1758–1813), and Prabhakar eulogized and entertained the Peshvas Bajirao I and Madhavrao I (Deshpande 1988: 37). The śāhīrs chronicled the brave feats of Marathas and Peshvas through povāḍā, and entertained the courts with the finesse of their lāvaṇī singing that heralded a new interest in "aesthetically oriented" music. Lāvaṇī was performed by both śāhīrs and courtesans in a variety of contexts ranging from bawdy plays to sedate seated performances (Ranade 1984:130). The Peshvas were purportedly huge fans of tamāśā, a Marathi theater genre performed by women proficient in singing and dancing, and would pay thousands of rupees to hear performances of lāvaṇīs from tamāśā (Vaidya 1997: 23). Lāvaṇī singers developed an idiomatic method of singing tāns that was adopted by performers of nineteenth- and twentieth-century Marathi *saṅgīt nāṭak* (musical drama) as well as by some kīrtan singers.[14]

Kīrtan has been heavily influenced by lāvaṇī and povāḍā, in part because the well-known eighteenth-century śāhīrs, Ramjoshi, Anant Phandi, Prabhakar, Sangam Bhau, Parshuram, and Honaji Bala turned to kīrtan later in their lives (Pathak 1980: 76, Ranade 1984: 130, Vaidya 1997: 30). These śāhīrs-turned-kīrtankār brought a new musical virtuosity to the performance of kīrtan, and they may also have introduced povāḍā into kīrtan. The radically new kīrtan practices initiated by these śāhīrs led to the emergence of the nāradīya tradition of kīrtan. Like nāradīya kīrtankārs today, eighteenth-century śāhīrs were Brahmans with training in Hindustani music who told entertaining stories and impressed audiences with their knowledge of Sanskrit language and literature. According to Yashwant Pathak, kīrtan ākhyāns until the eighteenth century were based entirely on mythology, but in the eighteenth century some kīrtankārs began telling ākhyāns about Shivaji, Bajirao, and Madhavrao Peshva. By the early twentieth century, stories of kings and Peshvas made way for stories of nationalist heroes like Vasudeo Balwant Phadke and Jayaprakash Narayan, and this subtype of nāradīya kīrtan was known as rāṣṭrīya kīrtan (Pathak 1980: 9).

Many kīrtankārs of the eighteenth century, particularly those who had been śāhīrs, used the ākhyān poetry of Moropant, Shridhar, and Madhavmunishwar (Pathak 1980: 68, Ranade 1984: 130). These poets (usually called *paṅth-kavi* or *pandit-kavi*) employed a variety of verse structures, but Moropant composed almost exclusively in *āryā*, a recitation mold that is now a standard component of nāradīya kīrtan. Kīrtankārs used these poets' ākhyāns not only for their literary value, but also because the use of Sanskritized Marathi added to kīrtankārs' prestige (Pathak 1980: 68). Moropant, a *paurāṇik*[15] related to the Peshvas by marriage, was the most popular of the paṅth-kavis. One legend, as told by Yashwant Pathak, refers to a single incident as the source of both the incorporation of paṅth-kavi poetry into kīrtan and of Ramjoshi the śāhīr's turn to kīrtan. In this story, Ramjoshi invited Moropant to his tamāśā, but Moropant initially refused on the ground that it would be inappropriate for a paurāṇik to enjoy such lascivious entertainment. He eventually agreed to go on the condition that he would be permitted to watch the tamāśā from a somewhat removed balcony. Moropant was so impressed with Ramjoshi's voice that he advised the śāhīr to begin doing kīrtans. Ramjoshi liked the idea but said that he did not know which material he should use, to which Moropant replied, "what are my ākhyāns for?" Thus Ramjoshi began doing kīrtan, using Moropant's ākhyāns as his source material (Pathak 1980: 76).

For the greater part of the nineteenth century, Marathi nāradīya kīrtan continued to flourish as a court tradition for Indian nobles who retained varying degrees of power as landlords for the British. Nāradīya kīrtan became a lucrative profession, and several kīrtankārs were exceptional singers of Hindustani music and experts in vocal feats designed to please patrons and audiences (Ranade 1984). Perhaps the most innovative and renowned of these kīrtankārs was Govindbuva Hoshing (1814–1888), a nāradīya kīrtankār credited with formalizing the two-part pūrvaraṅga-uttararaṅga structure that is a defining characteristic of nāradīya kīrtan (Dhole 1925, Ranade 1984). Ramkrishnabuva Dhole, a kīrtankār and the son of a Hoshing *śiṣya* (disciple), writes that Govindbuva Hoshing's kīrtans were so enthralling that the Divan Govindrao Rode paid him 5,000 pearls, and Hinduraobaba of Lashkar placed a 50,000 rupee string of pearls around his neck (Dhole 1925: 5).

To my knowledge, Ramkrishnabuva Dhole's 1925 biography of Govindbuva Hoshing is the earliest account of the life and work of a professional kīrtankār. Though Hoshing was performing in the mid-nineteenth century, the book was written at a time when the nationalist movement had gained political momentum. The author of the preface, Govind Sakharam Sardesai, regards kīrtan as an institution that, in Hoshing's time, was un-"contaminated" by the West but had become a "memory" by the early twentieth century (Sardesai 1925). His pessimism is not consistent with newspaper, biographical, and oral accounts that attest to a flourishing early twentieth-century kīrtan practice supported by the middle class rather than a fading aristocracy. Rather, Sardesai's comments reflect an Indian nationalist discourse predicated on the notion of "protection," particularly of cows, women, and art forms. This strategy imagines an autonomous realm of "pure" Indian culture and marks difference from British colonizers, while providing moral justification for resistance to British colonialism.

> This biography of Govindmaharaj is not just an account of kīrtan; the reader will also be interested in anecdotes from that historical moment, and through them will understand how important kīrtan was for educating people. By observing

how useful this art form would be today, it will impress on your mind how much we need to take care of it. Though the western knowledge of today is contaminating our national life as it changes drastically, a biography like this is very useful for awakening in society the memory of old *dhārmik*[16] and moral traditions, and of an institution that was preserved. (Sardesai 1925: 1)

Hoshing was a transitional figure in the history of nāradīya kīrtan. He innovated the two-part structure of nāradīya kīrtan but continued to utilize the older ensemble of *taṁburā* (stringed lute used as a drone) and mṛdaṅg at a time when some kīrtankārs were replacing these instruments with tablā and harmonium. Hoshing's kīrtans lasted up to six hours over the course of several days, a format that was gradually replaced by the now standard two-hour kīrtan. Dhole writes that Hoshing had the ability to perform outstanding vocal and oratory feats, and reports that he spent four intensive months learning thousands of tunes from the well-known classical singer Sakharambuva Kashikar (Dhole 1925: 10). The Dhole account reads much like Mahipati's stories of miraculous Marathi saints, though no claims are made that Hoshing had supernatural powers; he is attributed only with the ability to sing better than the best classical singers even after a full night of kīrtan, and the ability to move even the most debauched person to tears with the intensity of his rasa:

Even when Shri Govindbuva did kīrtan for a long time he was able to sing in tune. Everyone could hear this. His singing voice was so excellent, on the harmoniums of today he could sing from the fifth note and double it without distorting his face. It is said that no one could sing in tune as low as he could; and though his high notes were like lightning striking, his throat did not become choked. He never had to cough because of phlegm. Because of this, great singers like Hahu Hassu Khan and Natthe Khan used to tell him, "Govindbuva, if you gave us the openness of your throat, then we would all be able to conquer the entire world." (Dhole 1925: 6)

Most of Hoshing's kīrtans were on paurāṇik stories such as Ahilyāuddhār,[17] Sitāsvayamvar,[18] Saubhadrā,[19] and Duhāśāsanvadhan,[20] but he also performed kīrtans on Tukārām, the *Bhagvad-gītā*, and the *Jñāneśvarī* upon request. His biography does not mention rāṣṭrīya kīrtan, nor do any of the songs listed in the book indicate nationalist themes. His life and work seem to have remained relatively independent of artistic, social, and political reforms gaining ground in nineteenth-century Maharashtra. In the last years of his life, he did come in contact with artistic innovators from the new genre of Marathi saṅgīt nāṭak when members of Annasaheb Kirloskar's Saṅgīt Nāṭak Maṅḍaḷī came to meet him in Benares. According to Dhole, the actors got goosebumps when Hoshing sang a song for them, and agreed that his reputation as an outstanding singer was well deserved. When Hoshing died in 1888, the members of the drama troupe attended his funeral (Dhole 1925: 46–56).

INSCRIBING KĪRTAN: EARLY PUBLISHED KĪRTANS, MARATHI MUSIC DRAMA, AND COLONIAL MODERNITY

The English East India Company and later the British Crown were the dominant economic and political forces in nineteenth-century India, and the British presence incited Indians to institute social reforms of both compliance and resistance. The Company was chartered by Queen Elizabeth I in 1600 and began administering India by the third quarter of the eighteenth century (Brown 1994: xxv, 39–45). By 1818 the Company had gained political and economic control over most of India, and the colonizers founded British-style schools and colleges to educate a new Indian middle class as mid-level clerks (Brown 1994: 46–47). This middle class—in between colonizer and the "masses"—is the social group upon which Chatterjee's discussion of the "inside" and "outside" is based. Following the Rebellion of 1857, the Crown disbanded the East India Company and shifted formal control of India to the British government, with Queen Victoria declaring herself Empress of India in 1877. Soon after this declaration, Indian political nationalism found expression in the 1885 founding of the Indian National Congress (Brown 1994: 85–96, 140).

Several Western-style institutes of higher learning were founded in the early to mid- nineteenth century in Pune and Bombay, including Poona College, Elphinstone Institute, and Grant Medical College (Rosse 1995: 64). This education taught Indians to believe that Europe was superior to India in scholarship and science, but it also provided them with the inspiration and intellectual tools for creating a movement to remove colonial obstruction to their national self-determination (Brown 1994: 123–167). Indian students were introduced to the post-Enlightenment notions of progress, rationalism, and self-determination that had resulted in nationalist movements in France and the Americas. Inspired by this spirit, they strove to combine the "rationalism" of the West with the "spirituality" of the East. These efforts began with Bengali and Marathi religious reforms directed toward "purifying" Hinduism and ridding it of its "superstitious" elements. New artistic practices also emerged from this hybridity, including Bengali and Marathi novels modeled on European counterparts, and theater forms that brought a European structure to indigenous stories (Chatterjee 1993: 35–75, Hay 1988: 36–72).

By reviving and reforming the arts and religion, the new Indian middle class sought to create a national identity that was both "modern" and Indian, systematic and indigenous. The reformism of India's nineteenth-century cosmopolitan elite is characteristic of cultural nationalism or what Chatterjee terms the "moment of departure," and comprises a first step toward nation building that prepares the ground for political nationalism. As Partha Chatterjee has discussed, colonized nations struggle to prove their essential difference and right to sovereignty from within a colonial discourse, and he outlines how this twin dilemma—the same but different—is negotiated through a series of strategies or "moments." The mid to late nineteenth century was India's "moment of departure," in which the intelligentsia began discovering, reforming, and nationalizing indigenous arts and religion (Chatterjee 1986: 54–84).

During this "moment of departure," kīrtan was used in service of religious reform, and members of the reformist Prarthana Samaj developed an interest in nāradīya kīrtan. Kīrtan came to be associated with a suitably ancient—even primordial—Hindu past, but as with many other arts it was considered insufficiently systematic, a problem addressed through the founding of kīrtan institutions and the publication of kīrtan texts. Religious reform of the nineteenth century has essentially disappeared from the kīrtan landscape, and reformist kīrtankārs have been largely forgotten. Institutional reforms, on the other hand, have had a more lasting—albeit partial—influence. Reform as a component of cultural nationalism is inseparable from revivalism, and this section also addresses how kīrtan and related genres were "discovered" and reformulated in the nineteenth century.

One inspiration for the modernization of nāradīya kīrtan in the nineteenth century can be found in Marathi saṅgīt nāṭak, a style of music drama first performed in Bombay in the mid-nineteenth-century (Patil 1993). Saṅgīt nāṭak, which was born from a fusion of Western narrative structures with Indian themes and Marathi performance traditions like kīrtan, paurāṇik nāṭak, and tamāśā, emerged at around the same time that Govindbuva Hoshing's innovations were ushering nāradīya kīrtan into its present form. Vishnudas Bhave and his troupe performed the first modern Marathi play for the Rājā (king) of Sangli in 1843 and the first ticketed Marathi play was staged in Bombay in 1853 (Ranade 1986: 4–15). Marathi drama had existed in the form of tamāśā for centuries, but tamāśā was peopled by low caste actors and contained lewd or erotic subject matter—that is, it was not fit to adopt the symbolic role of a national expression in the hands of the intelligentsia (Patil 1993: 60–61). As India sought to define its national character in these early days of cultural nationalism, elites and the middle class became interested not just in patronizing the arts, but also in shaping their style by becoming performers and creators. Though plays on nationalistic topics were not performed until later, saṅgīt nāṭak of the nineteenth century was a means to assert pride in indigenous cultural expression in the face of colonial disregard, while also responding to the cosmopolitan tastes of the new middle class.

Saṅgīt nāṭak both relied on the musical-rhetorical devices of kīrtan and influenced the performance practice of kīrtan. Kīrtankārs and actors had moved between the boundaries of the two genres since the early days of saṅgīt nāṭak, and saṅgīt nāṭak is similar to what kīrtan would be like if it were to be performed on stage by a troupe of actor-singers rather than by a solo kīrtankār. Like performers of kīrtan, saṅgīt nāṭak performers are usually Brahmans, the stories narrated/acted out in these dramas are primarily paurāṇik, and the written texts of saṅgīt nāṭak are referred to as ākhyāns. Saṅgīt nāṭak ākhyāns are surprisingly similar to kīrtan ākhyāns; both consist of texts for songs performed in different genres, such as *sākī, diṅḍī, āryā,*[21] and *aṅjanī gīt* (Ranade 1986: 50–53).

The similarities between nāradīya kīrtan and saṅgīt nāṭak were particularly striking in the early days of drama performance, when Vishnudas Bhave taught his scripts to actors by rote in a manner akin to the oral-aural method of kīrtan instruction. Indeed, Marathi plays were not written and published until 1861 (Ranade 1986: 4–15). In Bhave's plays, a *sūtradhār* (director) performed all of the songs and narration to the accompaniment of jhānj and mṛdaṅg while actors recited spoken texts and executed stage movements. The sūtradhār began the play by singing a *nāndī* consisting of *ślokas* (Sanskrit verses) and a *naman* (prayer of greeting). A similar set of invocatory prayers and songs is known as the *mangalācaraṇ*[22] in kīrtan. Later dramatists such as Annasaheb Kirloskar and Nanasaheb Joglekar were also familiar with the kīrtan idiom; Kirloskar used abhaṅgas and ovīs in his ākhyāns, and Joglekar began his career as a kīrtankār (Ranade 1986: 50–51, 62–63).

Just as saṅgīt nāṭak was influenced by kīrtan, drama music has helped shape the style and content of nāradīya and rāṣṭrīya kīrtan. Early twentieth-century kīrtankārs such as Vasudeo Kolhatkar, and contemporary kīrtankārs such as Dattadas Ghag and Charudatta Aphale, based their kīrtans on nāṭak tunes with new devotional texts. A major paṭhaḍī (performance lineage) of nāradīya kīrtan began with Haribhau Karhadkar, a śiṣya of the saṅgīt nāṭakkār, Bhaskarbuva Bakhle. Haribhau Karhadkar trained his son, Rambhau Karhadkar (now the Śankarācārya of Karveer Peeth), who in turn trained kīrtankārs such as Dattadas Ghag and Milinda Barve. Rāṣṭrīya kīrtankār Charudatta Aphale divides his time almost equally between acting in Marathi stage plays and performing kīrtan, a dual profession that he inherited from his father, rāṣṭrīya kīrtankār Govindswami Aphale.

Although Marathi kīrtan of the nineteenth century was only marginally popular among the middle class, the exchange between performers of kīrtan and saṅgīt nāṭak probably led a handful of kīrtankārs to adopt a primary technology of the middle class: mass-produced published texts. Within a couple of decades of the first published texts of Marathi plays, Marathi kīrtan ākhyāns were published with the goal of reviving "the old *saṁpradāya*" (tradition) and educating new kīrtankārs. These ākhyāns did not contain music notation but instead consisted of song texts with some general performance instructions. The first collection of kīrtan ākhyāns, *Kīrtanataraṅginī* by Raoji Shridhar

Gondhalekar (with Panduranga Abaji Moghe and Vaman Eknathshastri Kemkar), was written in 1867 and published in 1895. The author bemoaned the lack of knowledge and structure in many kīrtankārs' performances and wrote his book in an effort to correct some of these deficiencies:

> It seems that some people falsely think that in order to do a kīrtan one can pass the time by memorizing a few poems and putting together an unrelated pūrvaraṅga and uttararaṅga without even knowing the relationship between the two. Since the old saṁpradāya no longer exists, no one understands what kathā should be like. This is why we have prepared this book, *Kīrtanataraṅginī*. (Gondhalekar 1895: preface)

As this quote indicates, Gondhalekar envisioned his mission as reviving a tradition that "no longer exists." This discursive mode is characteristic of cultural nationalism and resonates with Sardesai's comments that kīrtan had become a "memory" in need of "awakening." Gondhalekar regarded systematic education as a means to revive the "old saṁpradāya," and since he intended the book as a pedagogical tool, provided performance instructions along with his kīrtan texts. For example, after listing ślokas to recite in the mangalācaraṇ he writes, "After doing [ślokas], lie prostrate in front of the deity" (Gondhalekar 1895: 1). The reforms (publishing, standardization) that *Kīrtanataraṅginī* suggests are intended to *prevent* kīrtan from changing in structure, content, and performance technique, and are meant to bring kīrtan closer to how it had been in the past, rather than transforming it into something new. The ākhyāns are based on ancient paurāṇik stories, including the story of Rāma's birth, the story of Kṛṣṇa's birth, the story of the Goddess, and others, and he used song genres that had been integral to kīrtan for at least a century.

Kīrtanataraṅginī established a model for published kīrtans that was imitated by subsequent authors of that era. This and other kīrtan texts from the late nineteenth and early twentieth centuries—such as Sadashiv Dhonde Tambeshastri's *Kīrtanamuktāhār* (1910)—consist entirely of song texts and scriptural excerpts, while most published books beginning in the 1920s and 1930s contain prose narratives along with song texts. Balasaheb Sathe's *Kīrtana-Kumudini* (1928) and Vasudeo Kolhatkar's *Tilak Janma-ākhyān* (1933) follow this newer model. Early kīrtan ākhyāns, like those of today, do not include musical notation, though performance instructions sometimes include rāga and tāla, the title of the tune to which the song is to be sung, or recitation mold (such as āryā or sākī). As is the case with most South Asian music, improvisation in kīrtan singing is highly valued, and there is wide variation in song style (classical style, saṅgīt nāṭak style, bhāvgīt[23] style) and tunes. Even members of the same paṭhaḍī might sing a naman to different rāgas depending on time of day or location. Books of abhaṅgas and religious songs are available in solfège notation, but none of the approximately one hundred published kīrtans that I have seen employ this system. Kīrtan texts cannot be used as complete guides to performance. Most commonly, only the genre of a song is given and the student is expected to independently learn tunes associated with that genre. Written kīrtans are used primarily as sources for song texts and for general story ideas, but each kīrtankār must make melodic and narrative choices. Kīrtans exist only in performance, and the cursory nature of kīrtan texts ensures the uniqueness of each performance.

REVIVALIST REFORM: INSTITUTIONALIZING NĀRADĪYA KĪRTAN

The institutionalization of kīrtan is intimately connected not only to saṅgīt nāṭak but also to Hindustani music. Many performers moved between kīrtan and Hindustani music, and institutions dedicated to the two performance traditions emerged at around the same time. Despite these mutual influences, the founders of Hindustani music institutions proposed much more sweeping reforms than did the founders of kīrtan institutions, and one implicit goal of music institutions was to transform Hindustani music from a profession dominated by Muslims into an amateur pursuit for middle-class Hindus (Qureshi 1991). Janaki Bakhle describes a complicated landscape in which music reformer V. D. Paluskar's motivations were both devotional and Hindu chauvinistic, while musicologist V. N. Bhatkhande sought to systematize and modernize Hindustani music. Bhatkhande only denounced traditional *gharānā* musicians inasmuch as they represented an obstacle to these plans (Bakhle 2005). Kīrtan institutions, by way of contrast, proposed no changes in performer demographics and only minor reforms in performance.

Following the first All-India Music Conference in Calcutta in 1869 and the founding of India's first music institution, the Gayan Uttejak Mandali (Singing Appreciation Group) in Bombay in 1870, the Poona Gayan Samaj (Poona Singing Society) was founded in 1874 (Rosse 1995: 96, 175). The membership of the Poona Gayan Samaj consisted of British officials, Maharashtrian Brahmans, minor royalty, and rich Hindu and Muslim businessmen. Unlike the Parsi-led Gayan Uttejak Mandali, there were very few Muslims in this institution (Rosse 1995: 96), and the Samaj's Hindu and elitist goals were clearly stated in their publications. One Gayan Samaj book articulated a primary Samaj objective as being "to revive a taste for our musical science amongst our brethren of the upper class, and to raise it up in their estimation" (Rosse 1995: 98). The activities they planned and executed included establishing music schools; organizing lectures, meetings, and concerts; developing a music notation system; and awarding prizes to outstanding musicians (Rosse 1995: 111). Most of the Samaj's teachers and performers were Brahmans, and there were five categories of performers: singers of the Gwalior gharānā, classically trained saṅgīt nāṭakkārs, scholar-musicians, Maharashtrian *dhrupad* (a genre of classical song) singers, and kīrtankārs. Michael Rosse quotes V. N. Bhatkhande as saying that classical musicians often looked down on kīrtankārs. Despite this low position in the musical hierarchy, Rosse asserts that kīrtankārs belonged to the Poona Gayan Samaj because their performance and teaching fees were low and because they were symbolically important as "Aryan" musicians (Rosse 1995: 116). Many kīrtankārs in Pune continue to obtain some musical training at the Poona Gayan Samaj, now known as the Bharat Gayan Samaj.

The efflorescence of music institutions continued into the early twentieth century. One of the most influential of these was the Gandharva Mahavidyalaya, founded in Lahore in 1901 by the Maharashtrian singer and son of a kīrtankār, Vishnu Digambar Paluskar (Rosse 1995: 152). Paluskar was born fourteen miles south of Miraj—a small Maharashtrian city famous for producing skilled musicians and instrument-makers—where he grew up accompanying his father's kīrtans as a singer and jhāṅj-player (Rosse 1995: 156–157). In addition to the types of activities carried out by the Poona Gayan Samaj, the Gandharva Mahavidyalaya produced nationalist songs and sponsored kīrtans and bhajans, and Paluskar was instrumental in the movement to create a national identity (Rosse 1995: 11).

With the loss of primary patronage by indigenous royalty during the nineteenth century, kīrtankārs began founding institutions based on Hindustani music models. For the most part, the founders of and educators at kīrtan institutions had been enculturated into traditional Brāhmaṇ practices of paurāṇik recitation, priesthood, and nāradīya kīrtan. Unlike Hindustani music reformers, these kīrtankārs did not attempt to "modernize" kīrtan by introducing cosmopolitan philosophies but instead hoped to revive an older style of performance, at times with the help of published texts. Because of its insularity, kīrtan presented possibilities for a nationalism of the "inside" that was autonomous and also incomprehensible to the British.

The first Hindu Marathi kīrtan institution, Harikīrtanottejak Sabhā, was founded in 1883 by Eknathshastri Kemkar (father to one of the authors of *Kīrtanataraṅginī*) to sponsor kīrtans, arrange kīrtan conferences and festivals, and convey titles to kīrtankārs.[24] The Sabhā, which is now housed on the premises of Nārad Maṅdir (temple) in the Sadashiv Peth neighborhood of Pune, is still one of the most influential kīrtan institutions in Maharashtra. The founder was Dharnidhar Shastri Gurjar and the second *adhyakṣa* (chairperson) was P. Bhilavdikarshastri, the teacher of the late rāṣṭrīya kīrtankār Gangadhar N. Koparkar. When the writers of *Caitanya*, a journal dedicated to kīrtan, reported on the Harikīrtanottejak Sabhā in 1936, the institution had recently started a kīrtan *pāṭhśālā* (school).[25]

Like the Poona Gayan Samaj and the Gandharva Mahavidyalaya, the Harikīrtanottejak Sabhā helped generate middle-class interest in Indian performance. As indigenous kings were increasingly divested of power and wealth, they were less able to support musicians and kīrtankārs, and institutions like the Poona Gayan Samaj and the Gayan Uttejak Mandali provided new patronage, relying on membership fees and/or collective resources to pay for the services of artists employed with them (Rosse 1995: 86–87, 111–116).[26] The early years of the Harikīrtanottejak Sabhā were similarly transitional. The Sabhā performed functions characteristic of the many Western-inspired societies of the latter part of the nineteenth century, such as topical meetings, performance festivals, exams, and teaching. Nonetheless, the instructional methods and social dynamics of the Harikīrtanottejak Sabhā were not significantly different from earlier practices. Some of the differences between Hindustani music institutions and kīrtan institutions are certainly related to differences in patronage—even as royal patronage decreased for concert performers and kīrtankārs, kīrtankārs still received some patronage from temples and templegoers.

Through my conversations with kīrtankārs G. N. Koparkar and Vaman Kolhatkar, I learned that kīrtan transmission in the early days of the Sabhā was structured around master-disciple relationships. Vaman Kolhatkar told me that his father, Vasudeo Kolhatkar, "took young Koparkar to the Harikīrtanottejak Sabhā, where he studied kīrtan with his guru Bhilavdikar for about 10 to 12 years."[27] Koparkar's tenure with his guru is characteristic of *gurukula* (guru's family) practice, in which a disciple lives with and serves a guru for an extended period of time, learning through direct instruction as well as by absorbing the guru's daily habits. Gurukula-style transmission was supplemented with European-style exams that students were required to pass before they could receive titles. Koparkar completed a "seven year course" at the Kīrtan Pāṭhśāḷā, which qualified him to earn the title "Kīrtanakalāniddhī" (treasure of kīrtan art) (Joshi 1982: 25).

In the introduction to his *Kīrtan Chiṁtāmaṇī, Part One*, B. R. Ghaisas describes his experiences as a student at the Harikīrtanottejak Sabhā in the first half of the twentieth century. Classes were held in the home of the school's gurus, Chintamanishastri and Dharnidharshastri Gurjar, rather than in the classroom that was later built on the second floor of the Nārad Maṁdir. Ghaisas writes that kīrtankārs skilled in singing would occasionally present *ādarśa* (ideal) kīrtans to the students, but that the Gurjar brothers conducted all of the classes (Ghaisas 1998: 4–5). In today's classes at the Harikīrtanottejak Sabhā, students learn subjects such as meter, singing, oratory, memorization, pūrvaraṅga, and uttararaṅga from five or six teachers employed by the Sabhā. Moreover, students no longer study kīrtan for extended periods of time at the Nārad Maṁdir, and all instruction is held in a month-long intensive kīrtan school in the spring.

While the decision to create a kīrtan institution may have been motivated by an underlying cultural nationalism, the founders of the Harikīrtanottejak Sabhā were not involved in overt political action or expression. The changes engendered by institutionalization were intended to preserve kīrtan as it was rather than to create new possibilities through ideological reform. Koparkar told me that he did not learn any rāṣṭrīya materials from his guru, and that it was only later, when he became involved in the Ram Rajya Parishad, that he began exploring rāṣṭrīya kīrtan. Ghaisas similarly said that he did not learn rāṣṭrīya kīrtan from his guru, but that he later learned to perform rāṣṭrīya kīrtan "on demand." It was not until the first half of the twentieth century that explicitly nationalist kīrtan institutions were founded. The Akhīl Bhāratīya Kīrtan Saṅsthā (All-India Kīrtan Organization) was founded in Dadar, Mumbai, in 1940 during the Quit India movement. The authors of a souvenir volume for the Saṅsthā's "diamond anniversary" in 2000 write, "the primary inspiration [for Saṅsthā's founding] was awakening society about independence."[28] This nationalist emphasis continues at the Akhīl Bhāratīya Kīrtan Saṅsthā through today, and an office-bearer told me that they continue to teach rāṣṭrīya kīrtan and avoid "mythological" material.[29]

VAMAN ABAJI MODAK: RELIGIOUS REFORM THROUGH KĪRTAN

A primary object of modernist reform in colonial India was religion, and it was through religious reform that a kīrtankār named Vaman Abaji Modak became active in the incipient nationalist movement. The first of the reformist religious sects was the Brahmo Samaj, a monotheistic Hindu society founded in 1828 by Rammohun Roy, who gathered inspiration from Islam, Buddhism, Christianity, and Hinduism, and regarded polytheism as the root of most Indian superstitions and harmful practices. His reform efforts also extended into social and political arenas: he founded schools, published newspapers in three languages, and fought British proposals to support *satī* (immolation of widows) (Hay 1988: 15–17). Serious efforts at religious reform began a bit later in Maharashtra than in Bengal with the founding of the Prarthana Samaj in 1867. Like the Brahmos, members of the Prarthana Samaj were monotheistic and opposed to ritualism, caste discrimination, child marriage, satī, and prohibitions against widow remarriage. A major difference between the two groups was that the Prarthana Samaj drew inspiration from the Hindu mainstream, while Brahmos regarded their religion as something entirely new (Brown 1994: 162). Prarthana Samaj literature had a strong Maharashtrian character that was based largely on the writings of Jñāndev and other Marathi saints (Manmadkar 1998: 319). Despite this interest in vārkarī literature, the Prarthana Samaj's insistence that the vāri and other vārkarī observances were unnecessary superstitions barred them from achieving mass appeal (Manmadkar 1998: 322), and the Prarthana Samaj remained a movement for the middle and upper classes.

Maharashtra's nationalist elite populated the Prarthana Samaj, and religious reform of the nineteenth century was intimately connected with sociopolitical reform and kīrtan. One of the Prarthana Samaj's most prominent members was the moderate leader, Justice M. G. Ranade. Though Ranade, as a judge, was prohibited from active involvement in politics, he worked to change colonial legal policies through the Indian National Social Conference, which met concurrently with the Indian National Congress. Ranade was an admirer of Vaman Abaji Modak, a nāradīya kīrtankār who became something like the official kīrtankār and spiritual advisor for the Prarthana Samaj, and an advocate of social reform and political change in his own right. Modak was considered an important nationalist leader during his lifetime but has been ignored by nationalist histories and is absent from the collective memory of rāṣṭrīya kīrtankārs. Historians of nationalism tend to look to the "outside," and even Partha Chatterjee, who posits arts and religion as arenas of nationalist mobilization, studies the "inside" world of cosmopolitan nationalists more than the "outside" activities of spiritual leaders.[30] Kīrtankārs of today, unlike most historians of nationalism, make room for both politicians and kīrtankārs in their histories of nationalist leadership. Although N. A. Modak can be considered a proto-rāṣṭrīya kīrtankār, rāṣṭrīya kīrtankārs do not include him in their genealogies because his politics and religious philosophies were moderate, while today's rāṣṭrīya kīrtankārs tend to be conservative and militaristic.

Reflecting his nonsectarian religious beliefs, Modak, the headmaster of Ratnagiri High School, performed kīrtans on stories from the purāṇas, the lives of Marathi saints, and Christian and Western topics. A collection of his kīrtans published in 1947 included titles such as "Nāmdev Caritra Nirūpaṇa" (A Discourse on Nāmdev's life), "Yājñavalkya and Maitreyī," "Yeśu Caritra" (The Story of Jesus), and "Socrates Caritra" (The Story of Socrates). Though none of the ākhyāns are on nationalist topics, the infusion of nāradīya kīrtan with new content and historical topics became characteristic of rāṣṭrīya kīrtan in the twentieth century. The ākhyāns are dated from the 1880s and '90s and are attributed to "Vaman Abaji Modak, Prarthana Samaj" (Modak 1947).

Nationalist-era Marathi writers acknowledged Modak's political significance, placing him on a par with more famous cosmopolitan elite nationalists. In his introduction to a collection of Modak's ākhyāns published posthumously in the year of India's independence (1947), Lakshmanshastri Joshi writes that Modak used his firm grounding in classical knowledge to elucidate concepts of "*svadeśi, svadharma, and svasaṅskṛtī*,"[31] and that he should be considered one of the great reformers (Joshi 1947:10–11).

> There are very few reformers. They are our great stars glimmering with beauty and patience among the ancient customs and the ignorance of darkness. Rammohan Roy, Ishwarchandra Vidyasagar, Jyotirao Phule, Nyayamurti

Ranade, Dr. Bhandarkar, and others are leaders among social reformers. The late Vaman Abaji Modak should be counted in this circle. (Joshi 1947: 10)

Other commentators regarded Modak as both a nationalist actor and a symbol of Marathi identity. In an English essay written soon after Modak's death in 1897, Justice M. G. Ranade wrote that although Modak's English was quite good, "he had no rival when he spoke in his own mother tongue," and he was respected for "the charm of his sweet voice and his sweeter modulation of the richest beauties of the Marathi tongue" (M. G. Ranade 1947: II). In today's context, it is taken for granted that a kīrtankār would express himself in Marathi, and most Marathi kīrtankārs that I met—including those with advanced degrees—often spoke only halting English. In the political climate of the late nineteenth century, when the ability to speak English was a marker of education and middle or upper social class status, Modak's skill in Marathi was a significant statement of indigenous pride. Ranade's gushing English description of Modak's abilities suggests a nationalist romanticization of indigenous art forms.

Later in Ranade's essay, it becomes clear that Modak's role in these early stages of nationalism went beyond a purely emblematic one, and that he was an active agent of both social and political reform. One of the most vital issues of reform was that of widow remarriage, an agenda that was taken up first by the Brahmo Samaj and later by the Prarthana Samaj. This was a key issue in a social climate in which widows were stripped of most rights and were considered impure. Ranade writes of Modak:

In the remarriage troubles of 30 years ago he was singlehandedly fighting in the good cause in every centre of Brahman orthodoxy. Pestered and troubled on all sides with petty annoyances he stood up manfully for the good cause but never an angry word escaped his lips and he never cherished any but the tenderest feelings for those who were giving him endless trouble. (Ranade 1947: III)

Moreover, Ranade writes that Modak promoted not only social change but political change as well. Ranade refutes the claim made by some that Modak was interested only in social and religious reform, but not political reform. Ranade's description of Modak as a moderate with an interest in gradual rather than "spasmodic" change mirrors his own political style.

[Modak] was one of the keenest political thinkers in our midst. Only his politics were not of the superficial character which with some people is mistaken for patriotism. As in all other matters the idea of growth—not spasmodic but graduated growth—regulated and controlled by the necessity that it must be the result of habits acquired by long continued discipline, was one to which he subscribed and no temptations swerved him from that ideal. (Ranade 1947: V–VI)

Maharashtrian leaders such as B. G. Tilak, who sought complete and immediate independence from the British, rejected the moderate approach. In part because of Tilak's lead, rāṣṭrīya kīrtankārs have tended to express conservative ideologies rather than those of Ranade or Modak. Modak engaged in debate with Hindu nationalists such as Vishnushastri Chiplunkar, the eighteenth-century leader who published a series of essays ("*Nibaṅdhamāḷā*") on topics of national concern. In these essays, Chiplunkar criticized Modak for his reformist stance on widow remarriage, to which Modak responded by reiterating his position and continued respect for Chiplunkar. In another letter, Modak wrote a lengthy response to Chiplunkar's essay on Indian oratory. According to Modak, Chiplunkar's descriptions of oratory in ancient texts ignore the modern-day svadeśi oratory of kīrtankārs. He also suggests that Chiplunkar's article would be more comprehensive if he were willing to consider writings on oratory by Greek, Roman, or French thinkers.[32]

B.G. TILAK, THE ALL-INDIA KĪRTAN CONFERENCES, AND RĀṢṬRĪYA KĪRTAN

By the late 1910s and early 1920s, some young kīrtankārs began performing kīrtans on nationalist topics—much to the chagrin of older nāradīya kīrtankārs—and became known as rāṣṭrīya kīrtankārs. Rāṣṭrīya kīrtankārs infused the medium with new topical material and vigor, but maintained the structure and songs of nāradīya kīrtan and supported conservative values. Rāṣṭrīya kīrtankārs replaced stories of saints with stories of nationalist leaders or other figures from secular history and sang a greater density of song genres considered "nationalist" or "historical," such as povāḍā, *kaṭhāv*, and *rājahans*. This new subgenre of kīrtan was wildly popular, with audiences regularly numbering in the thousands, but kīrtankārs' preoccupation with worldly matters and their break with aspects of kīrtan tradition have been the subject of debate and controversy since rāṣṭrīya kīrtan's inception. The Harikīrtanottejak Sabhā's annual festival included discussions of whether rāṣṭrīya kīrtan should exist, and in 1942 Bhilavdikarbuva[33] organized a much-publicized debate on this issue at Ghanekar Dattāmaṇdir (Barve 1963: 31). The debates subsided after about twenty or thirty years, because, as one kīrtankār told me, after freedom, "rāṣṭrīya kīrtan became accepted due to the fame of rāṣṭrīya kīrtankārs."[34] Scholar Yashvant Pathak refers to rāṣṭrīya kīrtan as the "new paṭhaḍī" that the "old kīrtankārs didn't like":

They used the povāḍā in kīrtan and, later on, new stories from Vasudeo Balwant Phadke to Jayprakash Narayan came to be known as rāṣṭrīya kīrtan. The old kīrtankārs didn't like this idea of rāṣṭrīya kīrtan and the modern kīrtankārs were for it. (Pathak 1980: 9)

In 1929, with the blessings of Dr. Kurtakoti, the Śaṇkarācārya of Karvīr Pith, a group of rāṣṭrīya kīrtankārs began publishing a series called the *Saṅgīt Aitihāsik Kīrtan-Ratnamāḷa* (The Bejeweled Garland of Musical Historical Kīrtans). In the first "gem" of this series, Dr. Kurtakoti defends the new type of kīrtan, arguing that it is the most effective way to teach knowledge of ancient religious ideas to the young generation:

In order to protect religion, presenting ākhyāns from recent history has a more favorable effect on society than paurāṇik ākhyāns. From this point of view, our *māḷa*[35] gives correct knowledge of *sanātan*[36] dharma, so feel confident that it produces appropriate change in the younger generation. (Kurtakoti 1929, my translation)

In the decades preceding independence, rāṣṭrīya kīrtankārs used music to combine religion and politics, a strategic move with multiple ramifications. The media were controlled and monitored by the British, but since the colonizers theoretically supported freedom of religion, kīrtan enjoyed an unusual autonomy. Moreover, religion is a powerful motivator and, as Tilak said, "One who is inspired by this spiritual force is not afraid of anything" (Tilak 1976: 827).[37] When *deśkārya* (work for the nation) becomes *īśkārya* (work for God), actions in the mundane world are imbued with transcendent significance and are thought to effect lasting spiritual benefits. Rāṣṭrīya kīrtankārs supported and politicized socioreligious issues like cow protection, the caste system, and Brahmanism. By detailing the scriptural basis for these customs, rāṣṭrīya kīrtankārs positioned themselves at the zenith of a caste and religious hierarchy, and they argued that the British, as outsiders, were unable to protect these systems.

Tilak sought to create mass nationalist sentiment through large public Ganesh and Shivaji festivals, but his approach to inciting nationalist change was not entirely "grass roots." His primary medium of communication was newspaper journalism, and he founded the Marathi newspaper *Kesarī* and the English newspaper, *Mahratta*, to create an autonomous realm for non-colonial and anti-colonial dissemination of information. Tilak envisioned the leadership of the nation as emerging from the cosmopolitan elite, but he recognized the limitations of newspapers, a medium of the educated few, to communicate with the unlettered majority. For this reason, he appointed volunteers to read *Kesarī* aloud in village squares (Pathak 1980: 191). Perhaps the limits of written communication also prompted Tilak to say, in his address to the Second Annual Kīrtan Sammelan (conference) in 1918: "Kīrtankārs must realize that they are even more important than teachers and editors of newspapers. One shouldn't underestimate their role in shaping the future of society" (Tilak 1976: 826–827).

Issues of literacy may have contributed to this statement, but just as important to Tilak was the dual role of kīrtankār as performer and preacher (Pathak 1980: 191). In the same address, he said that drama is inadequate as a medium for promoting social and religious change. People are more willing to accept the word of kīrtankārs since their comportment during and after kīrtans is consistent: they practice what they preach.

> If the element of religion is not there, kīrtan is only theater.... Just as sammelans (conferences) are organized to bring reforms in theater...it is very essential that independent sammelans be organized to bring changes in kīrtan. Today, efforts are made to preach religion through theater by writing and presenting dramas on the life of saints like Tukārām. But, according to me, the goal will be achieved through kīrtan better than through theater. I believe that the actor playing Tukārām is in some sense ridiculing the great saint. The majority of the audience knows very well about his activities behind the screen. So, even if in the play he presents a great religious analysis, people know that it is not real and is only a drama. So, regarding religion and morality, I give more importance to kīrtan.[38] (Tilak 1976: 822)

The increased middle-class interest in kīrtan became manifest in All-India Kīrtan Conferences (Akhil Bhāratiya Kīrtan Sammelan) held in Maharashtrian cities between 1917 and 1922 (Pathak 1980: 252). Tilak himself was adhyakṣa of the Second Annual Kīrtan Sammelan in Nagpur. The primary concern of Tilak's keynote speech was how kīrtan could be reformed to be more appealing to "modern educated graduates," and how those graduates could use kīrtan to institute social and political change. Ideally, kīrtan would rally together the traditional prestige of brahmanical knowledge, the popular appeal of devotional and historical storytelling, and a "modern" appeal to reason.

> This institution is sinking today because of neglect; its real value is not with the old kīrtankārs, but instead, our main goal is to bring it to the attention of the new educated people. Reforms in kīrtan would come more quickly if modern educated graduates turned toward the institution. (Tilak 1976: 827)

During the conference, he argued in favor of a resolution that kīrtankārs be encouraged to learn English or some other European language. By studying English, he argued that a kīrtankār could read religious texts in other languages and acquire the widened perspective of "comparative religion" from which to argue in favor of conservative Hinduism. V. A. Modak had earlier studied non-Hindu religious texts but used their insights as inspiration for Hindu reform. The motivation for Tilak's language advocacy was essentially conservative and he did not support reforms in Hindu beliefs or structures. Instead,

> one of the qualities of the present day kīrtankār is that he should apply the religious and moral knowledge gained through the study of English to re-establish Hindu dharma. I am very happy that after long discussions/arguments, my point is accepted in this sammelan. (Tilak 1976: 825)

Tilak regarded the educated elite as the appropriate leaders of the nationalist movement and argued that kīrtan should reach them by addressing their concerns.

> The western education given in the schools nowadays has created a suspicion about religion in the minds of educated people. So, if kīrtan is to be performed in front of such an audience, it is important that it should have the capacity to answer all the doubts and questions. (Tilak 1976: 821)

Tilak proposed that kīrtankārs could tell stories of historical personalities and current events as a way to appeal to the younger, Western-educated generation. "If the kīrtankār wants to reach the new western educated audience, he has to seek help from the new culture, using new and up-to-date examples, phrases, information, and also telling life stories of new historical heroes" (Tilak 1976: 824). Justification for these changes is found in history; Tilak cited a precedent during the Peshva Rule, when kīrtankārs began telling humorous Akbar-Birbal stories and using Kabir poetry to appeal to new tastes. At one point in his lecture, Tilak made an analogy between Westernization adding to Indian knowledge and the use of "modern heroes" in kīrtan:

> Any wise man will easily agree that there are so many good things in foreign countries or languages that add to our knowledge. The same applies to contemporary history and geography too. If Shivaji was inspired by the story of Pandavas, why can't Shivaji or any other modern hero's life inspire a future hero? (Tilak 1976: 825–826)

The "new historical" or "modern hero" he provided as an example was Shivaji, who had lived almost 300 years earlier. For Tilak, politics and rule are modern, even if they existed in the past, and spirituality is traditional or old, even if it exists today. The notion of modernity is further theorized in his commentary on the *Bhagvad-gītā* called *Gītā Rahasya*, in which he writes that *karma yoga*, or the path of action, is favored in the *kali yuga*.[39] During the kali yuga, bhakti and *jñān* (knowledge) are important, but less so than karma, and "serving the world, and thus serving His will, is the surest way to salvation" (Brown 1958: 199, Tilak 1918: 235). This emphasis on karma in favor of bhakti and jñān buttressed much of the advice Tilak gave to kīrtankārs.

The Kīrtan Sammelans operated differently from rāṣṭrīya kīrtan as it was performed in temples and on streets. In everyday practice, rāṣṭrīya kīrtankārs were agents in the wider nationalist movement—but through Kīrtan Sammelans, the nationalist elite attempted to transform kīrtans (even ones that weren't "political") into passive *symbols* of the nation. Nationalist elite leaders who participated in Kīrtan Sammelans sought to systematize and modernize kīrtan to better suit the national identity they were trying to create: one that was "modern," Hindu, and educated.

Respected kīrtankārs and politicians composed the organizing committee, and the Sammelans were a primary means of communication between the nationalist elite and kīrtankārs. The All-India Kīrtan Sammelans were structured like Congress meetings, with discussions on various aspects of kīrtan performance culminating in a set of resolutions passed by the *maṅḍaḷ* (committee). The maṅḍaḷ consisted of kīrtankārs (Ramchandrabuva Dandekar, Bhingarbuva Chitnis, Shankarshastri Bhilavdikar), scholars (Chintamanrao Vaidya), and nationalist leaders (B. G. Tilak, Dadasaheb Khaparde, Dr. Munje, S. M. Paranjpe).[40] With a maṅḍaḷ composed of both political and religious experts, it is not surprising that many of the Sammelans' discussions and resolutions were premised on the notion that kīrtankārs have nationalist and social responsibilities.

Writers for *Kesarī* covered the Kīrtan Sammelans in some detail, including synopses of speeches, a list of resolutions, names of maṅḍaḷ members, and kīrtan performance listings. I was able to locate only the lists of resolutions for 1918 and 1919.[41] The five resolutions were similar in both years: the first two items addressed texts and languages that kīrtankārs should use in kīrtan, the third item addressed ideal comportment of a kīrtankār, the fourth item was about kīrtan institutions, and the fifth resolution defined the relationship between kīrtankārs and "learned people." In both years, the first item addressed appropriate materials for the pūrvaraṅga and uttararaṅga, and it was agreed that kīrtankārs should do kīrtans not only on figures from the purāṇas and the Mahābhārata but also from history. Maṅḍaḷ members also agreed that it was essential for kīrtankārs to study Marathi and Sanskrit and learn religious texts in these languages. Additionally, the 1918 resolution included a provision that kīrtankārs should study Hindi if they plan to travel outside of Maharashtra, and that they should become familiar with texts from various religions (presumably in response to Tilak's pleas), as well as with current events by reading newspapers. This resolution is essentially the same in 1919, which includes an additional note that kīrtankārs should read newspapers and magazines in English.

The third resolution stands out from the others because it does not address kīrtan per se but rather advocates a stance on the heated sociopolitical issue of caste. As might be expected from a community of conservative Brahmans, they proposed that kīrtankārs should act according to *varṇāśramadharma*, that is, upholding one's caste duties and maintaining the caste system. In 1919, this resolution was passed partially in response to an impassioned speech by nāradīya kīrtankār Yashvantbuva Kavishvar. In 1918, the fourth resolution states that the kīrtankār "should be simple, shouldn't envy anyone, shouldn't be greedy, should act according to varṇāśramadharma, should be loving, and should behave in such a way that people will follow him."[42] Varṇāśramadharma is only one item in a list of behavioral ideals that a kīrtankār should follow. Given the Brahman demographics and conservative rather than explicitly reformist orientation of most kīrtankārs and maṅḍaḷ members, I surmise that participants were considered de facto supporters of the caste system.

The fourth resolution calls for kīrtankārs not only to observe the obligations of their caste, but to live in an exemplary fashion in other ways as well. While actors and musicians were expected to behave in an ordinary or even corrupt manner off-stage, the kīrtankār's role as keeper of traditional knowledge extended beyond "Nārad's mat." Kīrtankārs were and are expected to uphold much higher standards, and even today, kīrtankārs do not typically smoke, drink, or go to movies. Their special position is reflected in everyday attire. While most men of their social standing and caste wear Western-style pants and a shirt, male kīrtankārs usually wear a *kuḍtā* (tunic) and *dhotī* (long piece of cloth wrapped around legs and waist) or *paijāma* (pajama) pants even when they are not doing kīrtan.

CONCLUSIONS

The term "rāṣṭrīya kīrtan" dates to the beginning of the twentieth century, but the genre's political and performance groundwork was laid as far back as the seventeenth century, when Rāmdās urged bhaktas to become involved in politics and instructed kīrtankārs on matters of solo performance. These two elements of Rāmdās's teachings became paradigmatic in the eighteenth century, when the Peshvas of Pune began patronizing performers of Marathi art forms. The fact that vārkarī kīrtan did not develop a nationalist subtype suggests that nāradīya kīrtan's performance structure, religious orientation, context, and performer/listener identities were better suited to India's young nationalist movement. Peshva patronage encouraged the development of scholarly and virtuosic Brahman performing arts, and dialogue between paṅth-kavis who composed ākhyān poetry, śāhirs who performed povāḍā, and kīrtankārs led to movements of performers and song genres between temple and court contexts. In the process, a Brahman subtype of kīrtan crystallized in the nineteenth century that emphasized virtuosity and storytelling. Moving beyond the strictly vārkarī song genres of bhajan and abhaṅga, they incorporated song genres with associations that varied widely on a sacred-secular spectrum. The eclecticism of this new style of kīrtan was well suited to a changing political context, and the stories of nāradīya kīrtan needed only minor shifts to be read in a nationalist light. Moreover, associations with art music and brahmanical tradition made nāradīya kīrtan suitably "classical" for cultural nationalists of the nineteenth century who sought to consolidate an elite Indian, Hindu national identity.

During India's "moment of departure" in the nineteenth century, Indian elites resisted British denigration of Indian arts and religion by reforming music, kīrtan, theater, religion, and literature. As participants in this cultural revival, kīrtankārs published their ākhyāns for the first time and founded kīrtan schools with the goal of "awakening" a form of expression that was perceived as being in decline. Processes of elite appropriation and institutionalization affected art music and dance more profoundly than kīrtan, in large part because the Hindu intelligentsia regarded Muslim musicians trained in the oral tradition as flawed signifiers of the scientific, Hindu nation they sought to create, while they framed kīrtankārs as scholarly, Aryan musicians who could preach and sing for nationalism if only they would abandon their pre-modern ideas. Thus, while the founders of both kīrtan schools and music schools sought to imbue their art forms with the prestige of institutional rigor, music school founders additionally hoped to make music a respectable endeavor for amateurs and middle class Hindus. Kīrtan school founders did not seek to repopulate kīrtan with members of a different caste or religious community, or even to transform it in radical ways, and thus the early kīrtan institutions represented a conservative continuation of traditional modes of instruction and discipleship.

The nineteenth century was also an era of religious reform, when movements like the Brahmo Samaj and Prarthana Samaj emerged from intellectuals' attempts to identify the essence of Hinduism and to rid it of "superstitions." These movements captured the nationalist spirit of combining Western "reason" with Indian spirituality, and many early nationalists were involved with either the Brahmo Samaj or the Prarthana Samaj. In Maharashtra, Vaman Abaji Modak became a spiritual guide for the Prarthana Samaj, and his maverick kīrtans were often based on historical or non-"mythological" topics. This practice later became a standard feature of rāṣṭrīya kīrtan, though Modak has largely been forgotten, probably because his reformism and ecumenical stance ran counter to the conservatism typical of twentieth-century rāṣṭrīya kīrtan.

A space for communication between kīrtankārs and nationalist leaders was opened by the All-India Kīrtan Conferences, where Lokmanya Tilak, other nationalist elites, and kīrtankārs addressed assemblies with suggestions on how to render kīrtan relevant for modern life and the nationalist struggle. With the emergence of rāṣṭrīya kīrtan, the latent political implications of the newly semi-institutionalized kīrtan became foregrounded. Tilak was particularly interested in Dr. Dattopant Patwardhan, and he advised the rāṣṭrīya kīrtankār to strip his nationalist narratives of miracles in favor of stories of the practical struggles of the incipient nation's leaders. As we will see in the next chapter, these efforts to modernize kīrtan in content, context, and form were only partially successful; rāṣṭrīya kīrtankārs paid homage to the nationalist elite while setting their own agendas.

3

Rāṣṭrīya Kīrtan: Resisting Modernity, Devotionalizing Nationalism

In the first two decades of the twentieth century, Marathi rāṣṭrīya kīrtankārs rallied support for the anti-colonial struggle by singing about the brave deeds of nationalist leaders. Vasudeo Kolhatkar was among the first generation of rāṣṭrīya kīrtankārs, and by the 1930s he had collected a significant following, leading people to donate weapons to the nationalist movement and prompting them to abandon tea drinking in a defiant gesture against the colonial tea industry. Sometime in the late 1930s, Kolhatkar became concerned by the scope of Gandhi's religious and social reforms and wondered if he should stop performing kīrtans on Mahatma Gandhi's life. To put his mind at ease, he decided that he must meet Gandhi. I'll paraphrase his son Vaman Kolhatkar's telling of this event:

> One week, my father had gone to Wardha (a village in Maharashtra) to do kīrtans while Gandhi was in the same village at his ashram. Through a messenger, he told Gandhi that he would like to meet with him to better understand his ideas, so that he could tell about them in his kīrtans. Gandhi granted him ten minutes. In three or four minutes, my father was able to succinctly ask his question, which was: "You have said that you have not seen the light, so why do you want to reform an old religion devised by people who have seen the light?" Gandhi looked down and sat for the remaining seven minutes not saying anything. At the end of the time, my father told him that he would really like an answer because he wanted to use Gandhi's ideas in his kīrtans. Gandhi said that it is too vast a topic and cannot be properly discussed in such a short time. So, my father asked when he would have more time, because he really wanted to know Gandhi's thoughts. Gandhi just laughed and the time was up.[1]

This story illustrates the ambivalent relationship between regional religious leaders like Kolhatkar and cosmopolitan nationalists who reformed religion in the service of a national identity that was both progressive and rooted in the Hindu past. Vaman Kolhatkar tells this story as a critique of reform, in which his father has the upper hand in a conversation with India's most famous nationalist, who sits mutely, refusing to communicate.

Given that cosmopolitan elites introduced nationalism to India and were the primary architects of the Indian National Congress, it is not surprising that histories of Indian nationalism are narrated as a series of middle-class actions and writings. As discussed in the previous chapter, this is the same class that sought to reform religion and to classicize, stage, institutionalize, and systematize kīrtan and the classical musics of India. I have no argument with Turino's and Chatterjee's characterization of nationalist modernist reform (see Chapter 2) as it relates to the Hindu middle class, but my experience with rāṣṭrīya kīrtan suggests a nationalist world beyond middle-class reform that is vast, variegated, and shaped by local leaders who sang for the nation without worrying about whether it was homologous with other nations. They left that up to the cosmopolitan elite. The majority of early rāṣṭrīya kīrtankārs favored a conservative and brahmanical brand of Hinduism that has become virulently chauvinist at the onset of the twenty-first century, but others articulated inclusive counter-discourses in a language and idiom distinct from that of progressive elites.

Religious reform movements such as the Arya Samaj and Prarthana Samaj are given ample treatment in literature on Indian nationalism, but there is a gap in research on nonreformist religious movements and on religious leaders who were important to the anti-colonial movement beyond providing spiritual inspiration to the nationalist elite (e.g., Chatterjee 1993, Van der Veer 1999). Indeed, nationalist ideas adopted by rāṣṭrīya kīrtankārs via Western-educated Indians acquired qualitatively different associations and weight within the regional religious sphere. For cosmopolitan elites like Tilak, Hinduism provided a powerful set of symbols around which an anti-colonial (and also anti-minority) identity could be formulated, while for rāṣṭrīya kīrtankārs, nationalist ideology was concerned with inspiring the formation of local ethical communities. Tilak's directives for religious and performance reform illustrate a top-down political orientation and his call to bring kīrtan into the world of "modern educated people" reflects a cosmopolitan orientation that was partially and quietly resisted by the same rāṣṭrīya kīrtankārs who looked to him for guidance.

Having addressed the Kīrtan Sammelan when rāṣṭrīya kīrtan was young, Tilak's speech inspired young politically minded kīrtankārs in the 1910s and 1920s to tell stories of Maratha kings and nationalist heroes. Despite Tilak's attempts to fashion kīrtan that would appeal to the cosmopolitan middle class, rāṣṭrīya kīrtankārs of the early part of the twentieth century were by and large not "modern educated graduates," nor did they study English and comparative literature or lead dual lives straddling an "inside" and "outside" of their own creation. Instead, they conceived of politics as a matter of devotion, received extensive traditional education in Sanskrit and Marathi religious literature, and in most cases supported conservative, Brahman values. Rāṣṭrīya kīrtan was wildly popular in its early years, with audiences regularly numbering in the thousands.[2] The popularity and nationalist power of kīrtankārs was due in part to their skill as singers and storytellers, but also because of their ritual significance as representatives of the divine sage, Nārad.[3] Kīrtans are usually performed in temples, but even when they are performed in tents or concert halls, kīrtankārs sing from a sacred space called Nārad's mat (*Nāradāṅcī gādī*[4]).

Early rāṣṭrīya kīrtankārs preached and sang about the nation, and led their many followers in acts of resistance against the colonizers. Their prestige as leaders was derived from their skill as performers, their caste status, and their links with and extensive knowledge of a scriptural past. Their kīrtans framed the nationalist elite as saints and deities, paradoxically supporting them while rejecting their religious reforms, and they used the affective power of regional performance to generate nationalist sentiment. We will begin with the Chapekar Brothers, who harbored a disdain for the nationalist elite that sets them apart from most rāṣṭrīya kīrtankārs. Our next exemplars of early rāṣṭrīya kīrtan are Dattopant Patwardhan and Vasudeo Kolhatkar, rāṣṭrīya kīrtankārs who preached and sang about the nation, and who led their followers in acts of resistance against the colonizers. Dattopant Patwardhan was in direct contact with Tilak, but he evaded Tilak's call to use kīrtan as a vehicle for social reform and instead assigned Tilak the role of traditional saint. Kolhatkar similarly conflated musical-poetic signs of devotion and nationalism in his kīrtans, but was openly critical of the nationalist elite. While Chapekar, Patwardhan, and Kolhatkar were Brahmans, one of Maharashtra's most prominent rāṣṭrīya kīrtankārs, Gadge Maharaj, was an illiterate farmer-turned-kīrtankār of the washerman caste. In the following discussion, I hope to demonstrate the diversity of interpretations of nationalism among these early rāṣṭrīya kīrtankārs, each of whom related to the nationalist elite in distinct and complex ways.

REVOLUTION AT THE MARGINS OF THE COSMOPOLITAN NATION: THE CHAPEKAR BROTHERS

On June 22, 1897, Damodar and Balkrishna Chapekar, Citpāvan Brahman sons of a kīrtankār, shot and killed Charles Walter Rand, Pune's assistant collector and chairman of the Special Plague Committee, and Lieutenant C. E. Ayerst of the British police force (Echenberg 2006: 66, *New York Times* 1897b).

Rand and his forces had outraged Indians by violently forcing their way into homes in a campaign to curb the spread of a plague outbreak. In his autobiography, Damodar Chapekar wrote: "There were new tyrannies every day. Sacred places were destroyed everywhere. Everywhere women's honor was plundered. Idols were smashed" (Chapekar 1974: 82). Damodar Chapekar, who actually fired the shots, described the planning and execution in a cursory, matter-of-fact manner. He made no mention of nervousness or misgivings, and recounted his elation at completing the assassination: "At home we praised Īśvar with much reverence and couldn't sleep for joy that night" (Chapekar 1974: 92).

Standard histories of nationalism attribute the Chapekar brothers' assassination of Rand to the influence of Tilak and/or dismiss it as an anomaly within an overwhelmingly peaceful Citpāvan Brahman mind-set (e.g., Khan 1992: 101–104, Popplewell 1995: 32). Tilak was arrested a month after the shooting "on the charge of having incited the natives to violence" with his editorials in his *Kesarī* newspaper that called Rand a "tyrant," so the idea that the Chapekars were simply followers of Tilak has deep roots in colonial history (*New York Times*, 1897; Popplewell 1995: 32). Rāṣṭrīya kīrtankārs today, conversely, narrate a history in which the Chapekars are central figures in Indian nationalism and exemplars of religiously motivated action. Indeed, the Chapekar story is a frequent topic of rāṣṭrīya kīrtans, and Damodar Chapekar's name is commonly included in oral genealogies of Indian nationalists. Vaman Kolhatkar told me that "after [Phadke's] death, things really started with people like Kane, Savarkar, Chapekar, and Tilak."[5] In a nationalist kīrtan performed on August 25, 2000, Sudhatai Dhamankar narrated a nationalist genealogy that included Mainavati Peshva, Phadke, Chapekar, Savarkar, and Tilak.

There is not very much evidence for or against the notion that the Chapekars were compelled to pull the trigger because of Tilak's *Kesarī* articles (though the timing makes this likely), and Damodar's writings open the possibility that they were motivated in part by a different set of commitments. This chapter's investigation of early rāṣṭrīya kīrtankārs will reveal that the Chapekars are not as atypical as standard political histories might suggest. Their priorities aligned more with rāṣṭrīya kīrtankārs than they did with Tilak, but unlike kīrtankārs, they erupted dramatically into cosmopolitan nationalist narratives through Rand's assassination. Had they not done this, they would likely have remained in the oral history of kīrtankārs through their performances, poetry, and minor rebellions but would not have been considered significant in the political history found in court proceedings, Congress reports, and newspaper articles.

Though the Chapekar brothers were not rāṣṭrīya kīrtankārs, Damodar accompanied his father's kīrtans on harmonium while his brother played the *svarmaṅḍal* zither (Chapekar 1910: 963). V. G. Khobarekar, who wrote the introduction to Chapekar's autobiography, reports that Balkrishna and

Damodar Chapekar became disillusioned with the British as young teenagers while touring as a family kīrtan troupe. During that time, they were appalled at the conditions in which people were living and "started thinking of the English as staunch enemies" (Khobarekar 1974: 3). Their father, Hari, worked for a short time as a clerk in a British collector's office but "became bored of this" and rejected it to become a kīrtankār. Hari raised his children in a strict Brahman manner, requiring that they perform a daily regimen of *sūrya namaskār* (sun salutations), *saṅdhyā* (morning and evening prayers), and recitation of *ślokas* (Sanskrit verses). Damodar was taught that *dhārmik* (religious) education was more valuable than English education, and he wrote that "defending religion" was his life's calling (Chapekar 1974: 6, 70–76). When he and his brother told their father of their plan to shoot Rand, he did not attempt to dissuade them.

In the months leading up to Rand's assassination, Damodar Chapekar and the other members of his group harassed ordinary Europeans, attempted to set fire to the tent of an Indian reformist meeting, and attacked a reform-minded Indian schoolmaster named Bhave (Chapekar 1974: 27–74). The nationalist motivation for his attacks is expressed most vividly through songs and ślokas that he and Balkrishna wrote and performed at festivals. Damodar provides the text for some of these verses in his autobiography, including a śloka that they sang during the Gaṇeś festival. As is characteristic of Chapekar's writings and philosophy, the śloka advocates decisive action and violence:

Fools, what is the use of your being men?//
Of what use are your big moustaches?//
Alas, you are not ashamed to remain in servitude,
Try, then, to commit suicide//1//[6]

Alas, he who kills calves and cows//
Is an evil, wicked person like a butcher//
For their pain, die but kill the English//
Let us not be idle and burden this enchanted land//2//[7]

Come everyone, and be called the people of Hindustan//
It is a great shame that the English have created a *svarājya*[8] here//
Don't forget your name, be proud of your *deś* (country)//
Rise, rap your upper arms, encounter and slaughter the wicked//3//[9]

How valiant were our forefathers on the battlefield//
They died after winning glory protecting their country//
We who were born from them are like Saturn whom the Sun has produced//
We are not ashamed, though our kingdom has been wrested from us//4//[10]
(Khobarekar 1974: 53)

Chapekar wrote that when he and his brother performed these ślokas, people told him, "What you say is true, but there are spies in society. Be careful" (Chapekar 1974: 53). The Chapekars, who prodded their countrymen to "die but kill the English," were unabashedly direct in ways that Tilak could not have been, but the imagery of this poem resonates with the language of "extremist" Congress Party nationalists. The poem's justification for independence is in the past and nature—in ancestral roots and the "enchanted land." They also called upon Indians to protect cows from English slaughter, a nationalist sentiment that excluded Christians and Muslims and was shared by the conservative wing of the Congress Party (Chapekar 1910: 994).

Chapekar addressed the 1895 Indian National Congress on the topic of svadeśi, but despite his interest in national independence and his occasional involvement with the INC, he wrote disparagingly of all-India nationalist leaders. In his opinion, reformists such as Justice Ranade were betrayers of Hinduism, while he viewed Tilak as a hypocritical cosmopolitan who only *claimed* to support Hinduism but was more talk than action. In Chapekar's words, only someone like himself, who participated in kīrtan and was opposed to any religious or social reform, was a true "defender of religion." Chapekar considered Tilak's cosmopolitan worldview—in which he was "ashamed to eat biscuits, but not to drink tea"—to be disingenuous and hypocritical.

> I know most people have a good opinion of Tilak. But they are without reason. In my opinion . . . he is neither a true reformer nor a true defender of religion. For if he were to be known as a defender of religion, then [it should be remembered] that he supports the removal of obstacles for widow remarriage. The beef-eating Daji Abaji Khare is his close friend. . . . He's ashamed to eat biscuits, but not to drink tea. . . . Has anyone ever seen him listening to kīrtan or purāṇa, doing śravaṇ, or other dhārmik things? I don't think anyone has ever seen this. . . . That's why we don't have a good opinion of Tilak. But we believe that he is much better than the reformers. We want people to say that Chapekar was a true defender of religion. (Chapekar 1974: 55, my translation).

Political theorist Anthony Smith similarly (though without Chapekar's disparagement) characterized Tilak as a "neo-traditionalist" who "utilizes modern methods of mobilizing people but for traditionalist ends" (Smith 1994: 117). The best-known examples of this are Tilak's Gaṇeś and Shivaji Festivals, established to mobilize Hinduism for anti-colonial nationalism (Smith 1994: 117). Of the three categories of nationalist intellectuals that Smith describes—assimilationists, reformists, and neo-traditionalists—neo-traditionalists are the most conservative and inward looking. While Chapekar condemns Tilak's dual life as a cosmopolitan and a revivalist, Smith argues that all intellectuals engage in border crossings between "religious authority" and the "scientific state" (Smith 1994: 116). Compared to "moderate" nationalists such as

Gandhi, Ranade, and Gokhale, Tilak's invented traditions were backward looking and Hindu-biased. But to less cosmopolitan and more orthodox Hindu nationalists such as Chapekar, they appeared insufficiently grounded in ancient traditions.

DATTOPANT PATWARDHAN: MYTHOLOGIZING THE NATIONALIST ELITE

Dr. Dattopant Patwardhan was the most popular of the early rāṣṭrīya kīrtankārs, and his vigorous energy transformed kīrtan aesthetics without presenting ideological and political alternatives to mainstream Indian nationalism. By all accounts, he followed very closely the precepts of Tilak and Gandhi, and cosmopolitan nationalist leaders recognized his role in popularizing their movement. Patwardhan's performances became a standard component of Congress meetings, and he "had the sole privilege" of singing the national song, "Vande Mataram," at the beginning and end of Congress district meetings (Katgade 1969: 4–5). Known for his vigorous physical training, he was Tilak's bodyguard at the 1907 Congress in Surat,[11] and people who heard Patwardhan's kīrtans refer to the bravado of his performances. Like the Chapekar Brothers, Dattopant Patwardhan (b. 1878) was a Citpāvan Brahman who followed a rigorous regime of daily austerities.[12] He grew up doing *snān* (ritual bath), *sūrya namaskār*, *saṅdhyā*, and *rāmrakṣā* (a cyclical song in praise of Rāma) (Katgade 1969: 8).[13] After he became a rāṣṭrīya kīrtankār, these religious observances helped to define his character and added weight to his nationalist messages.

As a traditional Brahman, Patwardhanbuva was meticulous about the food he ate, and many of his dietary restrictions resonated with the concept of svadeśī.[14] Govindkrishna Kanhere, an elderly man from Wai, where Patwardhan had spent a good portion of his life, said of Patwardhan's dietary habits: "He actually acted as he preached."[15] Patwardhan ate honey instead of sugar, did not drink tea, and ate only unpolished rice. Kanhere told me that Patwardhan avoided tea because it led to psychic and material dependence on the British.[16] He drank only cow's milk, ghee, and buttermilk rather than the less expensive but more fatty buffalo milk. Not only did Patwardhan believe in the health benefits of cow milk,[17] but drinking cow milk was also a politically charged *sevā* (service) (Katgade 1969: 8). Sanctuaries to protect the sacred mother cow (*gau mātā*) had enjoyed a long history in India but gained fresh theological and political significance in the 1880s, to become one of the major concerns of incipient Hindu nationalism (Van der Veer 1994: 86–90). In 1881, Swami Dayananda, founder of the Arya Samaj, published a treatise on cow protection that named cow slaughter an anti-Hindu act and led to a rare alliance between this reformist group and "orthodox" Hindu leaders. When in 1888 the British high court declared that cows do not require protection because they are not sacred objects, cow protection was transformed into a leading (Hindu) nationalist cause supported by Tilak, and a profound rift developed between Hindus and those Muslims who sacrificed cows for Bakr-Id (Cashman 1975: 67–69; Van der Veer 1994: 91–92; Wolpert 1962: 65–66). On a walk through Wai, Kanhere showed me a shelter that Patwardhan had built to protect cows from slaughter. It continues to house cows today but functions as a dairy for imported Jersey cows rather than as a shelter for cows designated for slaughter.

Patwardhan supported several all-India nationalist leaders and made daily water offerings to deceased freedom fighters, but he composed and performed more kīrtans on Tilak than on any other single person or deity (Katgade 1969: 8, 86–92). Of the 114 kīrtans by Patwardhan listed in his biography, sixty-four are on historical or nationalist personalities, including two on Gandhi[18] and nineteen on Tilak. Yashvant Pathak, kīrtan scholar and son of one of Patwardhan's disciples, writes that Tilak used to give Patwardhan advice on the content of his kīrtans. For example, he told Patwardhan not to deify Rama:

> Don't tell such false philosophy. Rāma was not first among gods. He was a regular mortal human. But you should go and tell people without fail how it happened that only through hard work, sacrifice, and knowledge of duty—that is *karmayoga*—through these efforts and *Parameśvar*'s[19] justice, he became a god among humans. If not, people will just call him God and fall at his feet ten times without learning any lessons; they won't do any sacrifice or *karma* but will just rely on fate and become crippled and lazy. (Pathak 1980: 192)[20]

Patwardhan changed his kīrtans in response to Tilak's suggestion, saying, "From that time on, I copied Lokmanya to the best of my ability" (Pathak 1980: 192).

Although Patwardhan agreed to follow Tilak's orders to show the human struggles of Rāma, he not only continued treating gods as gods, but he was also just as inclined to depict nationalist leaders (Tilak included) as saints. I heard one such kīrtan composed by Patwardhan performed in 1998 by B. R. Ghaisas (Patwardhan 1950: 30–53). In this kīrtan, Patwardhan linked a discussion of the concept of saint with a story about Tilak, and Ghaisas Guruji foregrounded the emotion of devotion to Tilak through his skillful blending of speech and song. Ghaisas brought his own, late twentieth-century interpretation to Patwardhan's kīrtan, but the songs and the story were composed by Patwardhan. This kīrtan on Tilak was divided into the two standard sung-spoken sections of rāṣṭrīya kīrtan: the pūrvaraṅga and the uttararaṅga. The pūrvaraṅga-uttararaṅga form, and most sonic and contextual aspects of Patwardhan's rāṣṭrīya kīrtans are identical to the older, ostensibly apolitical style of nāradīya kīrtan.

Patwardhan's pūrvaraṅga described the need for keeping the company of the saints, who show limitless love and can lead the path to ultimate joy.[21] His uttararaṅga demonstrated how Tilak expressed the qualities of a saint through his kindness toward an elderly illiterate man from a low caste who fasted every Monday that Tilak was in prison. The climax of the uttararaṅga occurred when the man finally met Tilak, first touching his feet and then embracing him despite their difference in caste and station (see Musical Example 3.1).[22] Tilak was impressed with the purity of the man's emotions and the strength of his devotion and told him to transform his person-centered devotion into *deśbhakti*, that is, devotion to the nation. Patwardhan paradoxically interpreted Tilak's insistence that the devotee not worship him as evidence of the nationalist leader's saintliness.

Sung (āryā):
After doing namaskār, he rose and deeply embraced Lokmānya's neck/ (repeated once)

Musical Example 3.1.
Āryā, part 1.

[Interspersed with spoken narration of Tilak's reaction: Tilak also, forgetting that he was a great leader and this person in front of him was illiterate and wearing dirty clothes, embraced the old man.]
The people watched this unique occasion with surprise//

Musical Example 3.2.
Āryā, part 2.

Spoken: The boy was a little embarrassed and said, "What are you doing?! You shouldn't touch Lokmānya!" He said,

Sung (anjanī gīt):
"Baba, such a rich person/ Tell me why you touched him?"//
Tilak said, "Such a follower../ How could I discriminate?"//

Spoken: "It doesn't matter whether he is illiterate and poor or rich and educated." [Anjanī gīt repeated without accompaniment].

Sung (āryā):

The *Gaḍkarīs* (guards of the fort), *Molkarīs* [collect wood and sell], and *Kākarīs* [tribals] all gathered on the fort/
Lokmanya satisfied them by distributing the sweet *khavā* that was presented to him//

How is a sense of nationalist devotion communicated musically in Patwardhan/Ghaisas's kīrtan? Though it is impossible to know how Patwardhan performed the kīrtan because no recordings are available, Ghaisas built toward the climax by decreasing the amount of spoken narrative between songs, a strategy common to most nāradīya and rāṣṭrīya kīrtans. Ultimately, the songs—most of which expressed the characters' inner emotions—consumed the narrative to heighten the intensity of the action. While most rāṣṭrīya kīrtankārs today use genres with militaristic associations like povāḍa and kaṭhāv at a kīrtan's climax, Patwardhan's kīrtan instead employs āryā (see Musical Example 3.1 and 3.2) and anjanī gīt, both of which are associated with devotional themes. Because the songs in this kīrtan are primarily associated with devotional poetry, and because most genres are unmetered, this kīrtan conveys calm devotion rather than frenzied action.

Āryā was the main poetic form employed by Moropant, a Marathi religious poet of the eighteenth century, and the genre continues to index his oeuvre. It is an unmetered, two-phrase couplet genre in which the first phrase has twelve morae and the second has eighteen. The first line of an āryā is an unresolved antecedent while the second, consequent phrase descends to the tonic. This two-part, open-closed form helps to structure the affective aspects of storytelling. After singing the first phrase, Ghaisas leaves the image of the old man embracing Tilak to linger in the minds of listeners as he fills in details with spoken narration, finally rounding off the scene with a return to the song and resolution of the melody.

Anjanī gīt (songs of Anjanī) invoke Anjanī, an *apsarā* (spirit or nymph) cursed to become a monkey following some transgression. The curse is finally annulled when she gives birth to Lord Hanuman, son of Shiva, Vayu, or her husband Kesari (depending on the version) (Lutgendorf 2007: 177–185). The Anjanī gīt is in a quick quadruple meter, accompanied by tablā and jhāñj, and consists of four short, tuneful eight-beat phrases (AABC), with the A phrases circulating in the lower tetrachord, the B entering into the higher tetrachord, and the C returning to the tonic. The hummable, upbeat Anjanī gīt is allied with Tilak's inspirational statement, and comes just a few seconds after the third-person, narrative voice of the āryā. While Anjanī gīt is rarely heard in kīrtan, āryā has been standard kīrtan fare since at least the nineteenth century. Because unmetered genres like āryā do not require the entire musical ensemble, they are very commonly used to briefly color spoken narrative with song, but kīrtans require variety in tune, voice, and emotion through forays into other genres such as Anjanī gīt.

Supported by Tilak because of his ability to communicate nationalism through a regional idiom with strong emotional resonances for listeners, Patwardhan ultimately did not reform the devotional aspects of kīrtan in the ways Tilak intended. Indeed, he could not have and also maintained rāṣṭrīya kīrtan's position as a highly affective medium of communication; Patwardhan knew very well the limits of what listeners would accept as kīrtan, and positioning deities and secular leaders as regular people would have fallen outside of those limits.

GADGE MAHARAJ: HUMANIZING THE DIVINE

Gadge Maharaj (1876–1956; see Plate 3.1) was an illiterate farmer-turned-kīrtankār of the low washerman caste who preached and sang in an earthy, conversational, and rurally accented style (Kshirasagara 1994: 393). Before Gandhi became an important figure in Indian politics, Gadge Maharaj was traveling around Maharashtra preaching nonviolent resistance to the British, and educating audiences about anti-untouchability, hygiene, and education (Divekar 1990: 221). He later became a supporter of Gandhi, attended Congress meetings, and advocated his own type of nationalism. His kīrtans were participatory events in which he engaged the audience with a constant flow of questions and encouraged them to sing along with him. Like his kīrtans, Gadge Maharaj's political style was inclusive, and he challenged people to work together to make changes that were in the interest of both their local and national communities (Shirwadkar n.d.). Gadge Maharaj's personal narrative rather than cosmopolitan post-Enlightenment philosophies were the primary source of his desire for social change. His father Zingraji was a farmer and washerman who owned land and was quite successful during the first few years of his marriage. Zingraji soon became a severe alcoholic, abused his wife, and led his family into penury through drinking and wastefulness. One way in which he spent money and time was by sponsoring goat sacrifices to propitiate the gods, a practice that Gadge Maharaj came to view as a bloody, useless, and superstitious custom. This troubled background led him to advocate a social system in which people of all backgrounds have equal access to education and social models of empowerment (Maidamwar 1998: 1–14).

Gadge Maharaj was what Gramsci might have termed an "organic intellectual," that is, a thinker emerging from and directing the aspirations of a particular social group, rather than a "traditional intellectual" like a writer or a cleric who perceives himself as existing separately from the class system (Gramsci 1971: 3–23, 349). Gramsci theorized "intellectual communities" to conceptualize possibilities for transitioning from feudalism or capitalism toward socialism. Interpreters of Gramsci usually regard traditional intellectuals as obstacles to progressive change and organic intellectuals as

Plate 3.1.
Gadge Maharaj. Used with permission of the Gadge Maharaj Mission, Mumbai.

working-class leaders in the transition toward socialism, but—as Renate Holub has argued—Gramsci's usage is more nuanced than this (Holub 1992: 162–168). Gramsci's theories have been shown to have broad applicability, but they were formed in the context of early twentieth-century Italy and given empirical basis through his study of Italian history. Though he did not find organic intellectuals among the Italian peasantry, he also did not preclude the possibility that peasant organic intellectuals may exist elsewhere. Indeed, Gadge Maharaj's example and the work of Partha Chatterjee suggest that a classical Marxist understanding of peasant culture as anti-collective and oriented toward personal property may be less applicable in India (Chatterjee 1993: 221–239).

Gadge Maharaj is called a rāṣṭrīya kīrtankār because his kīrtans advocate political and social reform, but his kīrtans were stylistically different both from vārkarī kīrtan and nāradīya-style rāṣṭrīya kīrtan. Gadge Baba's style was so enmeshed with his own personality that even the close followers who constituted his *sevāmaṇḍaḷ* (company of worshippers) could not duplicate his style. The five kīrtankārs in his sevāmaṇḍaḷ—Vishwanath Wagh, Yeshwantrao Mani, Babanrao Kalaskar, Ramchandra Shelar (known as Shelar Mama)[23], and

Mirabai Shirkar—used the structure of vārkarī kīrtan and only a few elements of the Gadge Baba style.[24] Gadge Baba's other famous kīrtankār-disciples included Kaikadi Baba, Tanpure Maharaj, Gayabai Manmadkar, and Yashwantrao Gondavalekar (Divekar 1990: 222–223). Of the latter group, I have only heard a recording of Kaikadi Baba, who was quite true to Gadge Maharaj's kīrtan style. Through kīrtan, Gadge Baba enjoined listeners to stop making offerings to clay idols and to regard Gandhi as a God because of his service to the nation. He deified Gandhi, but redefined divinity as extraordinary service to humans. This contrasts with Patwardhan, who portrayed Tilak as a saint who achieved political goals through inherent spirituality and piety. In Patwardhan's kīrtan and other nāradīya-style rāṣṭrīya kīrtans, audience members are taught to submit to the combined political and spiritual authority of nationalist leaders, and to follow them as one would follow a *sadguru* (supreme guru), that is, with complete acceptance and trust in their enlightened decisions. In contrast, Gadge Baba expounded on Gandhi's extraordinary human efforts to empower listeners to make practical changes in their own lives.

Gadge Baba's last kīrtan was recorded in 1956 at the Bandra Railway Police Station in Bombay, where he had been invited by devout police officers to take part in their *satyanārāyaṇ pujā*, a ceremony performed before important events or in times of need.[25] (Refer to audio example 5, .) This was recorded after Independence, when deceased nationalist heroes continued to be invoked in the service of ongoing projects of nation building and development. In this excerpt, we hear Gadge Baba's technique for engaging the audience by inviting them to collectively chant answers to his rhetorical questions. He asked the audience if temple idols helped them to resist British rule, listing the deities of three temples in the Bombay neighborhoods of Dadar, Bandra, and Walkeshwar familiar to his Bombay listeners, and they responded "no" in a resounding unison. Gadge Baba exclaimed that none of those deities are effective and only Gandhi's actions in the world brought sovereignty to India and thus only he should be called a God. Like Patwardhan, Gadge Baba positioned a nationalist leader within the realm of the divine, here as a god rather than a saint. Patwardhan narrated Tilak's devotion, selflessness, and kindness as markers of an inherent saintliness, while Gadge Baba proclaimed that Gandhi should be called a deity because of what he had accomplished for the nationalist struggle. Who said "Quit India? Gandhiji! Then call Gandhiji a God!"

Gadge Baba proclaimed that the simplest and most effective method of devotion was to sing devotional songs called bhajan, and he intermittently engaged the audience in the repetition of his signature single-phrase bhajan, "Devakīnandana Gopāḷa." As soon as he proclaimed that Gandhiji should be called a God, he began singing this bhajan with one line of text that translates as "Gopāḷa [Kṛṣṇa], the joy of his mother, Devakī." The melody is similarly accessible, employing stepwise motion and the range of a fourth. Bhajans like

Musical Example 3.3.
Bhajan, "Devakīnandana Gopāḷa."

this are repeated indefinitely and can continue as long as the group or the song leader desires, and because of the accessibility of this text and melody, even those unfamiliar with the song could easily participate after just one cycle (see Musical Example 3.3). Singing bhajans not only provided a means for participants to express their devotion to Gopāḷa, but the participatory performance structure of bhajan also modeled the democratic political and social structures Gadge Maharaj promoted, and engaged listeners in an embodied experience of the nation. Though this particular bhajan is unique to Gadge Maharaj, the practice of singing bhajans is integral to Hindu collective devotional practices throughout India.

(In Marathi): The British government brought a great calamity on us. Then did the people carry on a *satyāgraha*[26] or not?

— Yes!

Did the god of any temple come to help? Did anyone see there the Rām of Bandra or the Viṭhobā of Dadar?

— No!

Did anyone see the Mahādev of Malkeshwar there?

— No!

Then who did satyāgraha there? Men! Who did it?

— Men!

Who did it?

— Men!

And who said "Quit India"? Gandhiji! Gandhiji! Who said "Quit India"?

— Gandhiji!

Then call Gandhiji a god. He said to those who ruled for hundreds of years, he said in a word, "Quit India." And did they go or not?

— They went!

Call Gandhiji a god.

— Bhajan: "Gopāḷa Gopāḷa Devakīnandana Gopāḷa."

(In Hindi): With a great shout, with great love, say, "Mahatma Gandhi kī jay,
Mahatma
Gandhi kī…"

— Jay![27]

As this example illustrates, Gadge Baba idiosyncratically located Gandhi's divinity in his political courage, and communicated his own philosophy of rural justice in a dialect and song style that was meaningful to his Maharashtrian audiences. According to his followers, Gadge Baba met Gandhi at the latter's Sevāgrām Ashram as well as at the Faizapur Congress meeting. Like Gandhi, Gadge Baba advocated greater equality between castes, religious tolerance, *ahiṁsa,*[28] cow protection, and a national community constructed of a federation of local governments; some rural Maharashtrians found Gadge Baba to be a more compelling advocate of these issues than Gandhi was. Debhoji, who had been among Gadge Baba's followers as a boy, said of the saint: "For many of us, Gadge Maharaj was Gandhi's equal or greater."[29] Gadge Baba's followers insist that he was sweeping the streets and halls of towns where he performed kīrtan long before Mahatma Gandhi began using the broom and spinning wheel as icons of self-sufficiency (Meshram 1998: 114). The well-known Marathi author P. K. Atre wrote of Gadge Baba:

> There is a belief among the educated people that Mahatma Gandhi introduced the "broom technique" in this country. But that is wholly incorrect. For fifty years, Gadge Baba is roving in the land with a broom in his hand and a piece of earthen pot on his head. Whichever village he might step in, the first thing pressed into service is the broom in his hand. Then the people are awakened and they come running with their brooms. In the morning he cleans the dirt in the village and in the evening the dirt in the heads of the people. That is the aim of his life and the technique of his service.[30]

Though Gadge Baba used kīrtan to spread ideas of social reform and nationalist sentiment, it was the broom that brought him briefly onto the national stage. His broom gained national significance through the 1936 Faizapur National Congress, the first Congress to be held in a small village rather than in a big city (Divekar 1990). According to one account, the organizers of the Congress struggled with logistical problems because there was insufficient labor in the village to accommodate so many people. Gadge Maharaj enlisted at least 400 "broom volunteers" to join him in sweeping the area and worked through the night to make the site presentable (Shirwadkar n.d.: 71). After Independence, Gadge Baba enlisted the help of his bhaktas to clean the toilet areas of the 1950 Nasik Congress. Vasant Shirwadkar, Gadge Baba's socialist biographer, writes: "Gadge Baba made the broom a symbol of cleanliness and self-help. He gave it a respectability which in turn meant dignity for manual labor" (Shirwadkar n.d.: 71).

VASUDEO KOLHATKAR: ORTHODOX PHILOSOPHY IN A NEW VOICE

Vasudeo Shivram Kolhatkar (1904–1977) was a rāṣṭrīya kīrtankār and a younger contemporary of Dr. Patwardhan (see Plate 3.2). Like Patwardhan,

Kolhatkar told historical kīrtans, was conservative, and used only svadeśi goods; but while Patwardhan's kīrtans were inspired primarily by Lokmanya Tilak, Kolhatkar engaged in *independent* political action and performed long, learned kīrtans based on his extensive knowledge of Sanskrit scriptures. Kolhatkar was born in 1904 into a very poor, rural Brahman home in Anjarle, a small village on the Konkan coast, but since the Anjarle school went only to fourth standard, he left home at a young age to continue his studies (Barve 1963: 1). After leaving home, his first four years were spent with his mother's wealthy brother in Malkapur, but family disputes led him to finish standards 8 through 11 at schools in Indore and Roha. Since Kolhatkar's school followed the British system, he left school after his eleventh year in response to Gandhi's noncooperation movement and Tilak's call to boycott British education.[31]

In 1921, Kolhatkar went to the Princely State of Sangli, now in southern Maharashtra, to study at a Vedic Academy (*Veda Pāṭhśālā*). While studying, he began a type of *tapascaryā* (austerity, penance) known as Gāyatrī Puraścaraṇ, which involved not cutting the hair or nails, sleeping on the floor for only a few hours each night, reciting god's names with a rosary, meditating, remain-

Plate 3.2.
Framed picture of Vasudeo S. Kolhatkar in the home of his son, Vaman V. Kolhatkar. Pune, July 2009. Photograph by Mark Nye.

ing socially detached, not touching other people, and so on (Barve 1963: 4–5). He and the other students lived at the school and supported themselves through *madhukarī*.[32] It was during his stay at this Vedic Academy that Kolhatkar decided to become a kīrtankār. The philosophical and scriptural knowledge he learned during this period formed the basis for his erudite kīrtans.[33]

After completing his studies in Sangli, Kolhatkar moved to Goa, where he and two colleagues founded a Marathi school called *Sattar Śikṣaṇ Prasārak Sansthā* (Society for the Diffusion of True Education) that provided religious, political, and general education (Barve 1963: 8). The energetic Kolhatkar wrote historical plays to instill nationalist sentiment in his students and performed *pravacan* (religious lectures) and kīrtan after school to "awaken" people. The Portuguese secret police followed Kolhatkar's activities carefully, and the state ultimately pulled the plug on funding for Kolhatkar's school because of his anti-colonial activities (Barve 1963: 9–10). After staying in Goa for about five years, Kolhatkar tried to settle in Pune, but he caught malaria at each attempt over the course of three years and was forced to leave. He was finally able to settle in Pune in 1929, not long after marrying the fourteen-year-old sister of Sitaram Krishna Barve, his former student from Goa.[34] The two friends (and brothers-in-law) traveled everywhere together and Barve became an integral part of Kolhatkar's kīrtans.

Beginning in 1929, Kolhatkar decided to make kīrtan his full-time profession, thenceforth maintaining a busy schedule of kīrtans on svadeśī, svarājya, and historical and paurāṇik personalities like Shivaji, Rāmdās, Tilak, Rana Pratap Singh, Subhashchandra Bose, and others (Divekar 1990: 226–230). In contrast with Patwardhanbuva and Gadge Baba, Kolhatkar was less likely to deify cosmopolitan nationalist leaders in his kīrtans, not because he was against creating hagiographies of living politicians, but because he recognized a contradiction in performing saintly narratives of leaders who challenged the Vedic Hinduism and Brahman ritual he professed. The vignette of Kolhatkar's meeting with Gandhi illustrates that tension, but he was equally skeptical of V. D. Savarkar, a Marathi Brahman who split from the Indian National Congress to espouse an ideology asserting that India is by natural law a place for Hindus. Many conservative Maharashtrians were less attracted to Gandhi's pan-Indian symbols of identity than they were to V. D. Savarkar's Hindu nationalism in Marathi idioms. The latter has been a favorite uttararaṅga subject for kīrtankārs from the first quarter of the twentieth century through today, but Kolhatkar was almost as dissatisfied with Savarkar as he was with Gandhi, again because of his reforms to Hindu tradition.

In an effort to unite Hindus against British colonizers and Muslim Indians, Savarkar attempted to make Hinduism appealing and open to Hindus of all castes. A gesture of this new inclusiveness was Savarkar's founding of a temple into which people of all castes and backgrounds were permitted to enter. This was a departure from traditional strictures against "untouchables" entering temples (Hay 1988: 290). Savarkar invited Vasudeo Kolhatkar to perform kīrtans at the temple soon after it opened, and after the kīrtans, Savarkar invited Kolhatkar to join the Hindu Mahasabha. Kolhatkar told him that he would join only if Savarkar could convince him of the validity of the reforms he proposed, so Savarkar invited him to participate in an eight-day debate in the temple. Even after the eight days of this debate, Kolhatkar remained unconvinced, so he never joined the Hindu Mahasabha.[35]

For Kolhatkarbuva, rāṣṭrīya kīrtan required a deep foundation in ancient (Brahman) scripture and an understanding of philosophy. Although he agreed that kīrtan can be assigned contemporary significance, he insisted that its philosophical core should remain impervious to the vicissitudes of social and political fashion. In his book *Kīrtankalā āṇi Śāstra* (The Art and Science of Kīrtan, 1963), Kolhatkarbuva expressed dissatisfaction with those kīrtankārs who turned to historical kīrtans only after witnessing the popularity of genuine rāṣṭrīya kīrtankārs struggling against foreign rule. He objected to the use of the title "rāṣṭrīya kīrtankār" for kīrtans that are "vulgar, uncontrolled, and without research or goals." Although these may be historical kīrtans, he argued, they are not nationalist (Kolhatkar 1963: 206–207). A rāṣṭrīya kīrtan, according to Kolhatkar, is one that is excellent (*uttam*) and ideal (*ādarś*), but he wrote that the use of the term rāṣṭrīya dates only to the colonial era, when Lokmanya Tilak worked to counteract English education by supporting national education and kīrtan (Kolhatkar 1963: 188). National identity, according to Tilak and Kolhatkar, is defined by its essential spiritual and philosophical difference from the colonial: "Philosophy is the life of our nation. And the experience of philosophy is our soul (*ātma*)" (Kolhatkar 1963: 189).

Accordingly, his kīrtans were philosophically dense, but this broadly "national" approach was often supplemented by a more explicitly political "national*ism*." He preached about *rājadharma* (kingly duty) as outlined in the *Manusmṛti* and other ethical (*nīti*) texts and as exemplified through the Hindu epics. Kolhatkarbuva's pre-1947 discourses on Yudhiṣṭhira and Dhṛtarāṣṭra —warring kings of the *Mahābhārata* —referenced India's political situation in a manner understood by the audience but veiled from the British. As conveyed to me via his son Vamanbuva, rāṣṭrīya kīrtan should express four realms of rājadharma: *ānvīkṣikī*, *trayī*, *vārtā*, and *daṇḍanīti*. Ānvīkṣikī is logical thought, which a king must possess in order to strategically analyze his nation's situation; trayī is education, which a king should cultivate in all its scientific and artistic dimensions; vārtā refers to economic policy and industry, a realm that should change with the times; and daṇḍanīti relates to law and justice, which should be upheld both within the nation and between nations.[36] This

Sanskritic theorization, in which Manu is "re-applied" to modern governance, was basically absent from the long history of kīrtan described in the previous chapter.[37]

In contrast to Patwardhanbuva's perfunctory pūrvaraṅgas, Kolhatkar's were long and detailed, guiding the listener through a labyrinth of philosophical intricacies from the Vedas and purāṇas.[38] These pūrvaraṅgas had dual ramifications: they educated listeners about specific scriptural matters and were performances of scholarly virtuosity that demonstrated the rigor of Brahmanical Hinduism. Here is an example of Kolhatkar's dense narrative, excerpted from the pūrvaraṅga of a kīrtan recorded about thirty years ago on Shivaji's soldier, Tanaji[39]:

> All these śāstras and Upanishads assume that there are 3 types of *śarīr* [bodies] used as a medium for *jīv* [life]. These types are *sthūla*, *sūkṣma*, and *kāraṇa*. There are four types of organisms: *jāraja* [humans, mammals], *andaja* [born from eggs—birds and reptiles], *svedaja* [microorganisms], and *ṛddhija* [those that break open earth]. *Parabrahma* exists in everything, so do we consider trees and stones living? Yes, when there are these three qualities (*sat*, *cit*, *ānand*). Sat means the very existence. That a stone exists means that it has caitanya [the quality of cit]. Cit is actually mind plus ānand (emotions). All of these things that we don't usually see as living are actually living, because they have these qualities, so God really does exist in everything. Even the trees have three qualities, *sattva*, *raja*, and *tama*. Trees like a banyan tree and lemon, and certain trees, herbs, and roots that have mainly *sattvaguṇa* [the quality of sattva] in them. Why? Because they're helpful to others. Like a banyan, which gives shade and whose fruit are eaten by birds.
>
> This division according to the three guṇas (sattva, raja, tama) is found in andaja and is also easy to find among human beings. It is now accepted worldwide that India has a long spiritual tradition, and so people living in India are in an advantageous position spiritually. This is accepted by other countries and continents like America, Europe, and Australia. Bhārat is a *karmabhūmi* (land of religious rites), whereas other countries can be called *bhogabhūmi* (land of suffering). Sāttvikatā is the basic accepted value in India for ages. Now, due to the encroachment of foreign lifestyles, our old traditional way of living is overshadowed by them. The original sāttvik form is changing to the rajas way of living. I am sure that it will once again come down to its original form, because we have always believed in satkarmas. In this period of enjoyment and worldly pleasures, we have forgotten about the mysteries of our own existence: why are we born, where are we going after this life? We have a treasure of traditional knowledge on these topics that we seem to have forgotten. But we are fortunate to have that treasure of traditional knowledge (*pārampārik jñān*). If we consciously pass on this knowledge to the younger generation, this will solve many of the present-day problems. Hundreds of young children from 9–12 years of

age came to us to learn the *dharmaśāstra*, and we are happy to see that they are now living a very peaceful, happy, and *maṅgala* (auspicious) life.

This pūrvaraṅga is free of songs or any other elements of "entertainment," and illustrates Kolhatkar's erudite discursive style. Kolhatkar described how all things can be organized according to a spiritual hierarchy of sattva, raja, and tama, and how people from within and outside of India acknowledge Indians' sāttvik nature. Through kīrtan, he instructs listeners on the categories and subtleties of Sanskritic ontology and teaches them that these ideas *belong* to them as Indians, which in turn allows him to make the political point that this inheritance is threatened by rājasik influences from outside. This kīrtan was performed at least thirty years after Independence, but Kolhatkar's discussion of Hindus' need to curb the "encroachment of foreign lifestyles" reflects continuity with a central topic of pre-Independence kīrtan. Kolhatkar's pūrvaraṅgas were always dense and thorough, but became increasingly so after Independence. Most kīrtankārs today complete a topic within one to five days, but Kolhatkar would spend several months performing a series of kīrtans on a single text. For example, he took about five or six months to perform kīrtans on the *Bhagavad-gītā*, discussing one śloka per day until the text was completed. He also taught the entire Śānti Parva section of the *Mahābhārata* through kīrtan and wrote a Marathi translation of the Śānti Parva in abhangas called *Abhanga Bhārata.*[40]

Kolhatkaruva was a captivating storyteller who introduced new song genres to his rāṣṭrīya kīrtan uttararaṅgas. He was one of the first kīrtankārs to use *bhāvgīt* (emotional songs) and nāṭya gīt in his kīrtans, straying from the more standard recitation molds such as āryā, sākī, and diṅḍī. Kolhatkar's sonic innovations, combined with his use of new rāṣṭrīya ākhyāns, made for a radically new uttararaṅga style that stood in stark contrast to his orthodox and learned pūrvaraṅga style.[41] This apparent contradiction highlights an important distinction between socioreligious reform and performance reform. Nāṭya gīt and nationalist storytelling provided new ways for Kolhatkar to illustrate what he considered the timeless underlying philosophies expressed in his pūrvaraṅgas. Kolhatkar resisted any reforms of Hinduism, including those by nationalist elite leaders who were considered conservative. Not all kīrtankārs shared Kolhatkar's willingness to accept new garb for old ideas, and several public meetings were held at the Nārad Mandir to debate this issue. Kolhatkar was an active participant in these debates, but he was unable to convince many older kīrtankārs of the acceptability of permitting nationalist storytelling in kīrtan.[42]

Nāradīya kīrtankārs generally sing familiar melodies, but Vasudeo Kolhatkar's kīrtans included many newly composed songs for which he wrote the texts and his brother-in-law, S. K. Barve, composed the music. Barve was a skilled musician with an excellent aural memory who served as Kolhatkar's harmonium player, backup singer, and composer.[43] Since Barve knew the tunes better than Kolhatkar did, he would often sing along with Kolhatkar or would complete songs that the latter introduced in the course of his storytelling. The innovation of Kolhatkar and Barve's musical style within nāradīya and rāṣṭrīya kīrtan contexts cannot be over-emphasized. Because their style was so unique, Vaman Kolhatkar told me that it is difficult to find harmonium players who can accompany him properly when he performs his father's kīrtans. This was, of course, not an issue for Vasudeo Kolhatkar since he always performed with the same harmonium accompanist. Indeed, Barve routinely anticipated songs with the harmonium before Kolhatkar sang them, and he supported Kolhatkar with his own voice. Like nāṭya sangīt songs, many of their tunes were catchy and pithy, with a good deal of isorhythm enhanced by some surprising melodic leaps.[44] They are most often accompanied by lilting *ṭhekās*[45] that expand beyond the limited scope of nāradīya kīrtan, which employs *bhajanī* ṭhekā (8 beats), *kīrtanī dhumāḷī* (8 beats), and the occasional *jhaptāl* (10 beats) and *dādrā* (6 beats). Kolhatkar/Barve's use of unmetered genres like āryā is minimal compared to Patwardhan as well as to most kīrtankārs performing today.

I only have a recording of the first few minutes of the uttararaṅga of the Tanaji kīrtan excerpted above, but within this short section it is clear that Kolhatkar makes a dramatic shift in patterns of speech and song as he moves away from the pedagogical mode. The storytelling section is cued with songs that introduce the uttararaṅga's highly figurative and evocative spoken language.

Song:

How to learn from history
The past is like an ocean
You have to collect knowledge from that ocean
And store it in your mind like a pearl.

Spoken: The garden of history has blossomed. In this garden of the past, what you see is the blooming flowers, fresh green trees, waterfalls. It's a vast, wide-open wilderness, where you can find mountains as well as some scary, dark pathways. A new lotus flower has blossomed in the garden of Maharashtra. All of these years the black bee has been collecting honey from this garden, but now there's a new lotus.

Song: (words and tune unintelligible).

Spoken (explaining song): History repeats itself. On top of Sahyādri (a peak), there sits a Rajput woman. Just like Sītā sat in the Aśoka garden surrounded by women, the Rajput woman was surrounded by elephants and was crying. She was very beautiful and was imprisoned there, which is why she was crying. She's praying to Lord Kṛṣṇa for her freedom, saying, "Oh Lord Kṛṣṇa, since you liberated your own mother from prison, you should also help me and free me from this imprisonment."[46]

The Maharashtrian past is described first as an ocean and then as a garden with a pesky bee (colonizers) and a freshly blooming lotus (post-colonial promise). This metaphorical garden then becomes the actual garden imprisoning the distressed heroine, who is mythologized through a comparison with Sitā in the Aśoka garden. Mythologization is a recurring strategy of Indian nationalism and provides a persuasive religious imperative to national protection while excluding those who do not participate in the myth. Nature is one of the most compelling metaphors of nationalism;[47] in Kolhatkar's iconic description of the garden as nation, he succinctly claims India's essential and inextricable right to the land.

Kolhatkar regarded kīrtan as an autonomous realm not shaped by colonial discourse—an autonomy that functioned as a signifier of India's independence. When viewed in this way, even those kīrtans that did not address political issues overtly were imbued with nationalist significance. While the nationalist elite looked to spirituality as a retreat from their beleaguered position in the "outside" material world, Kolhatkar argued that Indians were experts in *both* the "inside" and the "outside" realms, and in fact shifted the significance of both in a way that resonates with the use of these terms in Marathi devotional literature dating back to the thirteenth century. In an article entitled "Śriharikīrtan" in his kīrtan journal *Caitanya*, Kolhatkar wrote:

> Our Indian nation is an ancient place of extreme purity that can show the path of happiness to the whole world. Until now, no one else has thought as much as India about mankind and the condition of its inner and outer realm, its great desire, and its final peace.... In such a great country, great practices of this type were going on for a long time—that is what we can consider India's real independence. (Kolhatkar 1936b: 2, translation mine)

For Kolhatkar, the inner realm referred to personal thoughts of devotion and spirituality, while the outer realm referred to the fulfillment of worldly obligations, and managing the interplay between the two realms was itself a religious exercise. Rather than accepting the Orientalist and mainstream nationalist assumption that India has a heightened understanding of the spiritual, "inner" realm while the West is superior in the "outer" realm, Kolhatkar stated that India can effectively negotiate both realms. The unspecified time period in which Indians had the freedom to realize their excellence in both realms was "India's real independence." Indian tradition, for Kolhatkar, was more than simply a sign around which identity could be mobilized, but was a guide for life and freedom in the contemporary inner and outer realms.

TEMPLE AND PILGRIMAGE: DEVOTIONAL CONTEXTS FOR NATIONALIST ACTION

Vasudeo Kolhatkar's nationalism was not restricted to the arena of performance and discourse, and his kīrtans often became events of resistance. He collected bombs for the freedom struggle and money for political prisoners at his kīrtans.[48] Kolhatkar also encouraged kīrtan audiences to abstain from drinking tea as an act of protest against the British monopoly of India's tea plantations. An article in *Kesarī* from 1930 states:

> Seeing the drift of the times, rāṣṭrīya kīrtankārs and contemporary intellectuals of the country need to advance audiences by teaching them about the situation, so that people will be powerful once they are awakened. It is said that an example, H. Bh. P. V. S. Kolhatkar, a young rāṣṭrīya kīrtankār of Pune, in the Keskar Viṭhobā Mandir impressed on people the need to abandon the drinking of tea in his kīrtan. At that time, 50 people vowed to abandon the vice. Is it possible for other kīrtankārs to motivate people in the same way?[49]

I asked Vaman Kolhatkar about this incident and he confirmed that it was true and that people around Maharashtra had taken vows to stop drinking tea at his father's kīrtans. Once when Vamanbuva went to Jesuri to perform a kīrtan in the 1980s or 1990s, a few people approached him after the kīrtan and told him that they still abstained from drinking tea because of a vow they had taken at his father's kīrtan before Independence. Vaman Kolhatkar does not drink tea, but said that this is "just for fun" because British control of tea plantations is no longer an issue.

Kolhatkar formed a society to support the efforts of freedom fighters and through this society, collected clothes, wheat, and rice for the families of people in prison, often collecting these items at his kīrtans. His society also made bombs and hand grenades for freedom fighters, which were stored at his home in Pune.[50] Vaman Kolhatkar told me that his father used kīrtan to convey messages between freedom fighters in ways that raised little suspicion from the police. Though his father was never jailed, the undercover police usually attended his kīrtans, so he had to be careful not to utter any of the words that had been banned by the British government. Vasudeo Kolhatkar was an avid supporter of and participant in the anti-colonial movement, but as a religious teacher, he felt that the movement needed to be infused with new ethics and morality. To paraphrase Vaman Kolhatkar's memories of this era in his father's life:

> My father was engaged with people who fought with bombs and weapons. When some of those people were caught, they would tell on the other members of their

movement. My father thought that this must have been because of a deviation from religion and morality. Because of this, he began to be interested in rebuilding morality, so he founded the Dharma Caitanya Saṅsthā. He felt that politicians were after success, not morality.[51]

At Dharma Caitanya, the temple built on the compound of Kolhatkar's home in the Sadashiv Peth area of Pune, Vasudeo Kolhatkar taught religion to children in the morning, and in the evening he gave kīrtans attended by crowds of thousands. Vaman Kolhatkar describes it as a lively cultural center that people visited all day long to ask for his father's guidance.[52] After the founding of Dharma Caitanya, Vasudeo Kolhatkar published books on kīrtan and Marathi translations of Sanskrit texts, often funding them by taking out a mortgage on his home.[53] The Dharma Caitanya compound still stands, though it is no longer a center for religious activity. The temple (to the Vaman incarnation of Vishnu) is very rarely used, and piles of Vasudeo Kolhatkar's books are stored to the side of the temple. The compound is now home to one of Vasudeo Kolhatkar's elder sons, and is also the site of his daughter's Ayurvedic medical clinic as well as the offices of the Kolhatkar family company that manufactures and distributes Kailas Jeevan, an Ayurvedic cream invented by Vasudeo Kolhatkar.[54]

Kolhatkar expanded into written media in his quest to invigorate the nationalist movement through serious considerations of spirituality. He wrote several books and edited a kīrtan journal, extending the written presence of kīrtan beyond the published akhyans discussed in the previous chapter. He began publishing the journal *Caitanya* in 1934 but had to halt publication in 1940 because of the wartime rationing of paper (Barve 1963: 29–30). Each issue included two or three kīrtan ākhyāns written by Kolhatkar or some other well-known kīrtankār. It also included articles—most of them written by Kolhatkar—on nationalist or religious matters, as well as quotes by nationalist leaders on the importance of kīrtan, and each volume begins with the famous "nationalist" quote by Rāmdās:

Mukhya harikathā-nirupaṇa/	Most important is harikathā-nirupaṇa/
Dusre te rājkāraṇa//	Second is politics//
Tisre te sāvadhāpaṇa/	Third is alertness/
Sarvaviṣeyi//	To all topics//

While Kolhatkar appealed to his audiences through both writings and kīrtans, Gadge Maharaj communicated with his mostly illiterate rural audiences through nationalist reinterpretations of kīrtan, rural pilgrimage, and devotional practice. Mirabai Shirkar, a disciple of Gadge Baba, organized a *diṅḍī* from Pandharpur to Nagpur performing kīrtan and promoting nationalist messages. A diṅḍī is (among other things) a group of people who share resources and chores as they make the pilgrimage to Pandharpur together. Large diṅḍīs are devoted to a particular sant-kavi like Jñāneśvar or Tukārām, while smaller diṅḍīs are composed of devotees of living or recently deceased saints. The "Mirabai Shirkar Gadge Maharaj Diṅḍī," also known as the "Rāṣṭrīya Diṅḍī," belonged to the second category.[55] Mirabai Shirkar was deceased when I began fieldwork, but the now late V. K. Wagh, who was eighty-five when I interviewed him in 2000, had taken part in her diṅḍī along with Yashwantrao Gondavalekar, Jijaba Patil, Ramchandra Shelar, and Babanrao Kalaskar. The diṅḍī was formed at the height of the Quit India movement, and Wagh recalled how Gadge Maharaj used kīrtan to educate people about anti-British opposition while on the diṅḍī. When I asked what the reaction was like, he said,

> It was very good. At that time, the government spread the word in all the towns not to give anything to the diṅḍī. But people worked together to give things. People gave proper food to 700 people. At that time there were bullock carts, and they would use them to bring food to all the people.[56]

In fact, he said, the British government actively tried to stop the diṅḍī from proceeding, and many people in the diṅḍī did not make it as far as Nagpur. Ramchandra Shelar was arrested in Pavnar and jailed for thirteen months for his underground nationalist activities, and Kalaskar was arrested in Nagpur and served a jail sentence (Divekar 1990: 223–224). Both a pilgrimage providing otherworldly merit and a protest march asserting collective power by claiming public space, this diṅḍī was premised on the notion of personal sacrifice for the nation that drew on a parallel discourse of devotional sacrifice. The Shirkar Gadge Maharaj diṅḍī entered small towns where there was limited access to newspapers and radio, and where Gadge Baba's reputation as a saint attracted people who might or might not have been interested in a political event. According to Gadge Baba's philosophy, devotional and nationalist work were not fused but were in fact the same—service to the nation is a spiritual practice, God is found in people rather than idols, and devotion needs no more expression than doing bhajan as a group.

Though not a Dalit, Gadge Baba was from a low caste and was outspoken in the fight to abolish caste and casteism. In 1925, he finished constructing the Cokhāmeḷā Dharmśāḷa in Pandharpur, the first *dharmśāḷa* (resting-place) for Dalit pilgrims (Shirwadkar n.d. 69). An almost life-sized painting depicting Gadge Baba with Babasaheb Ambedkar, the Dalit leader who drafted the Indian constitution and who fought for untouchable rights, is prominently displayed at the Chokhamela Dharmashala. After 1947, Gadge Baba's social programs came to be sponsored in part by the newly independent government. B. G. Kher, the first chief minister of Bombay State, provided Gadge Baba with a government car to facilitate his work against untouchability and alcoholism. One biographer writes, "whenever Gadge Baba made a suggestion that a certain work be carried out for the welfare of the people, Kher most promptly acted on it."[57] In 1952, Gadge Baba founded the Shree Gadge Maharaj Mission with the purpose of abolishing animal sacrifice and educating backward classes and tribals. The ashram schools now service some 40,000 students across Maharashtra. Ninety percent of the funding for the Gadge Maharaj ashram schools is from government grants, and the remaining 10 percent is from individual donors.[58]

CONCLUSIONS

Most histories of Indian nationalism are based on the work of the nationalist elites who communicated through written media. For many Maharashtrians, however, particularly those with minimal British education, kīrtan was a primary source of religious, social, and political information during the anticolonial national struggle. Kolhatkar and Patwardhan were purveyors of caste-based, "traditional" knowledge, and many of their most devoted followers belonged to the social class of people with similar pedigrees. Gadge Baba, on the other hand, drew followers from all castes, including both Brahmans and Dalits (former untouchables), and he garnered support through his compelling rhetoric of practicality as well as through his challenging disregard for convention. By opening the field of nationalist leadership to include those who do not belong to the middle class, we are forced to consider that nationalist action might not always be a schizophrenic dance between the "inside" and the "outside." Through their skillful negotiations of music and speech, these kīrtankārs transformed cosmopolitan nationalists into saints and nationalism into a matter of Hindu history and devotion.

Bourgeois political leaders such as Tilak created alliances with rāṣṭrīya kīrtankārs through Kīrtan Sammelans and other activities, but it would be inaccurate to characterize these kīrtankārs solely as "mouthpieces" for all-India politicians. The translational gaps between more cosmopolitan and less cosmopolitan worlds, between written and oral communication, between speech and song, and between the national and the nationalist rendered the Tilak of kīrtans very different from the Tilak who advocated for kīrtan. In kīrtan, Tilak was saint-like, an ideal devotee rather than an architect of legislation and courts. By embedding nationalist leaders like Tilak and Gandhi into those segments of kīrtan reserved for oral hagiographies, kīrtankārs not only created influential public mythologies that bolstered the popularity of those all-India leaders, but they also enhanced their own authority as performers and religio-nationalist leaders. Indeed, a kīrtankār's power comes from a combination of the privileged position of standing on Nārad's mat, performance prowess, and embodying the divine by singing songs of saints. Without being transformed into saintly personages, cosmopolitan nationalists would have no place in kīrtan and would thus be unavailable as sources for kīrtankārs' identification. A key to this story, which will be discussed in greater detail in later chapters, is music's role in activating this series of identifications and translations.

PART II

Nationalist Kīrtan Within and Beyond the Post-Colonial State

4

"From 'Self Rule' to 'Good Rule'"

Nationalism and Kīrtan after Independence

In 1947, India gained independence from British colonial rule and the subcontinent was divided into the two nation-states of India and Pakistan. As kīrtankār Sudhatai Dhamankar told me, the post-Independence period marked a shift in the purposes of rāṣṭrīya kīrtan: "we attained svarāj (self rule) and now it is time for *surāj* (good rule)."[1] India was formed as a secular state—though, as Partha Chatterjee (1998) argues, secularism has a particular meaning in the South Asian context—and Pakistan was formed as an Islamic republic. The elation of achieving the long-awaited Independence was mixed with trauma as the partition of the subcontinent led to a bloody divide between religious communities. Maharashtra, like most parts of India, continues to feel the simmering effects of partition and has contributed some of the most vociferous Hindu nationalist parties and organizations. Maharashtrians were active in the Indian National Congress from its inception in 1885, but their politics of relative moderation were eclipsed in 1948 by the assassination of Mahatma Gandhi by a Maharashtrian Brahman named Nathuram Godse. This national tragedy signaled the year-long banning of the RSS (Rashtriya Swayamsevak Sangh), a Hindu nationalist organization founded in 1925 (also by a Maharashtrian Brahman) to which Godse belonged. The assassination was met with a wave of anti-Brahman sentiment throughout Maharashtra, particularly in rural areas, and led many Brahmans to migrate to cities (Bhave 2009: 82–83). This urbanization of the Brahman community has made nāradīya kīrtan, which is performed by Brahmans, primarily an urban phenomenon.[2] Following Gandhi's assassination, only the most conservative Brahmans stayed with the RSS in Maharashtra, which led it to develop into what Thomas Hansen has called an insular "alternative civil society" (Hansen 1999: 123). Although kīrtankārs in the 1940s and 1950s were not engaged with the RSS, there was an overlap between some rāṣṭrīya kīrtankārs and RSS discourses and activities. Many Brahman rāṣṭrīya kīrtankārs were dissatisfied with the Nehruvian post-colonial state and responded to the post-assassination attacks by retreating to an even more insular "alternative civil society" than that of the RSS. This changing ethos found institutional expression in a short-lived wave of new kīrtan schools. Only toward the end of the twentieth century were alliances forged between the RSS and the main Marathi kīrtan organization, the Akhil Bhāratīya Kīrtan Kula, which will be addressed in the next chapter.

While the repercussions of partition and Gandhi's assassination contributed to the increased isolation of Brahman rāṣṭrīya kīrtankārs, the formation of the Indian state generated new opportunities for low caste, rural, and reform-minded kīrtankārs. Jawaharlal Nehru, India's first prime minister, aggressively pursued policies of rural development through agricultural and educational reform. When the state of Maharashtra was formed in 1960, regional concerns mirrored national ones, and local activists were employed to popularize governmental policies. The kīrtankārs Gadge Maharaj and Kaikadi Maharaj, whose listeners were primarily rural or urban working class, were sometimes referred to as a "government kīrtankārs" because they mirrored governmental initiatives and received support from the state. Nehru's secularist, development agenda resonated with Gadge Baba, who had encountered hardship related to under-education and limited resources in village India. However—as during the anti-colonial movement—regional variants of nationalism were subject to cultural translation and were molded to reflect the individual concerns of kīrtankārs. In contrast with colonial era rāṣṭrīya kīrtans, early post-colonial rāṣṭrīya kīrtans no longer deified contemporary all-India nationalist leaders. Indeed, Nehruvian reform was antithetical to the goals of Brahman rāṣṭrīya kīrtankārs, and lower caste rāṣṭrīya kīrtankārs had never really performed hagiographies of nationalist leaders.

In this chapter, I briefly describe the landscape of rāṣṭrīya kīrtan during the first three decades after Independence. The popularity of many of the kīrtankārs discussed in the previous chapter declined in the post-colonial era and the emphasis of their kīrtans changed. Vasudeo Kolhatkar lived from 1904 to 1977[3] and continued performing kīrtan until the last years of his life, but his kīrtans became increasingly philosophical and decreasingly "historical." Vaman Kolhatkar told me that his father remained a rāṣṭrīya kīrtankār until the end of his life, but that he distanced himself from political action after Independence. His legacy continued only through Vamanbuva, who performs kīrtans in the style of his father. Adheesh Sathaye notes that Vaman Kolhatkar's kīrtans diverge significantly from his father's: Vasudeo Kolhatkar's kīrtans were quiet, measured, and portrayed an idyllic nation, while Vaman Kolhatkar's juxtapose the grandeur of ancient texts with the noise and chaos of India today.[4]

Dr. Patwardhan continued performing kīrtans until 1960[5] and passed away at the age of eighty-nine in 1967,[6] but his influence waned after Independence[7] since his kīrtans were designed to support the freedom movement. Several of Patwardhan's disciples continued performing after his death. Rāṣṭrīya kīrtankār Narayanshastri Godbole (b. 1931) was a dedicated disciple who stayed with Patwardhanbuva and currently lives in Karnataka but often travels to Goa (Shevde et al. 2000: 74),[8] and the late Gautambuva Pathak had been one of Patwardhanbuva's accompanists and later became a popular rāṣṭrīya kīrtankār in the Nashik area (Pathak 1980: 126). Though Patwardhanbuva lived in Pune and Wai, his widely dispersed disciples have not been as influential in Pune as have the śiṣyas of other pre-Independence kīrtankārs. Only his disciple Govindswami Aphale lived in Pune, attracting huge crowds with his rāṣṭrīya kīrtans (Divekar 1990: 26).

Gadge Maharaj was quite elderly by the time of Independence and only lived until 1956 (Dandekar 1998: 223). While nāradīya-style rāṣṭrīya kīrtan has seen a recent upsurge in popularity as Hindu nationalism becomes mainstream, Gadge Maharaj's style has gradually waned in popularity as his era of pragmatic ecumenicism becomes a moment in an increasingly distant history. Because of Gadge Baba's disdain for hierarchies, he did not formally take any disciples, but several of his followers and companions continued performing kīrtans after his death. Most of them were inspired by Gadge Baba's philosophy but did not attempt to imitate his very idiosyncratic kīrtan style (though they did adopt elements of it). Some of his better-known followers include Kaikadi Maharaj, Tanpure Maharaj, Gayabai Manmadkar, and Shelar Mama.

NEHRUVIAN SOCIALISM AND "GOVERNMENT KĪRTAN": GADGE MAHARAJ, KAIKADI MAHARAJ, AND NĀRADĪYA KĪRTANKĀRS

While many nāradīya style rāṣṭrīya kīrtankārs withdrew from contemporary political agitations after Independence, rural kīrtankārs in the vārkarī orbit lent support to policies of the new Nehruvian socialist state. As Srirupa Roy articulated eloquently in *Beyond Belief* (2007), just as nations are imagined as communities (Anderson 1991), post-colonial states achieve a foothold in the imagination of individuals through repeated experiences of institutional effects (i.e., waiting in line at a post office) and through state performances like National Day parades (Roy 2007: 8–19). In this vein, several ethnomusicologists have addressed state-sponsored cultural performances that help citizens to imagine the state, such as the Bulgarian *narodna muzika* ensembles that performed with socialist precision and regional diversity during the socialist era (Buchanan 2006). Less of this research has been conducted in India, but there is rich material in the performances of Gadge Baba and Kaikadi Baba, who helped construct an imagination of the state while hiding the governmental hand. It is only during Indira Gandhi's rule in the 1960s and 1970s that the hand was tipped and kīrtan performers receiving state stipends became known as "government kīrtankārs." As with anti-colonial rāṣṭrīya kīrtan, post-colonial kīrtankārs used the affective power of regional narratives and genres to generate nationalist emotion in a state no longer ruled by Europeans. Those kīrtankārs who supported Nehruvian policies had to negotiate a relationship to a post-colonial state, while those who did not support a secular state continued to perform kīrtans on unresolved issues of national identity.

Governmental policy during the Nehruvian years was directed toward ideologies of citizenship and social change, and in 1951 the Indian state initiated a series of five-year plans designed to end feudalism, illiteracy, and caste discrimination. The first two five-year plans focused on agrarian modernization, with most of the funding directed toward massive dam and irrigation projects, and other funds pledged to transportation, industry, communications, and social services (Guha 2007: 214). Also among the plans for new India was a commitment to educating people of all classes and castes. Immediately after Independence, a policy of universal, free education for four years was instituted, becoming fully realized in Maharashtra in 1959 when all elementary education became free (Kamat 1968: 15). These massive economic, social, and educational reforms were met with varying degrees of understanding and acceptance in rural and working-class communities, and kīrtankārs assisted in making these ideas available and attractive to people who were becoming gradually incorporated into the institutions of the nation-state.

The early post-colonial Congress Party in Maharashtra became quickly Maratha-ized[9] and bolstered by rural support, ending the era of urban, Brahman nationalist political hegemony that had peaked in the years leading up to Tilak's 1920 death. This dramatic change was ushered in by universal franchise, which coincided with the wave of anti-Brahman sentiment accompanying Gandhi's assassination that led the Maratha plurality to vote for political leaders of their own caste (Sirsikar 1995: 64). An additional factor in Maharashtrian politics and voting relates to agriculture: Maharashtra is India's second largest producer of sugarcane and Maharashtrian state politics has been profoundly affected by the sugar industry (Sirsikar 1995: 72). Sugar was efficiently commercialized through a cooperative agricultural economic structure, and the enormous power and resources of sugar cooperatives meant that their support of a given candidate would usually result in that candidate's success. Until an alliance of the Shiv Sena and the Bharatiya Janata Party secured a majority in the 1995 state elections, candidates supported by the sugar lobby were overwhelmingly of the Congress Party. The Congress Party was so tightly linked to rural governance, schools, and other insitutions in Maharashtra that the system became a model of rural success (Hansen 2001: 34–35).

Yashwantrao Chavan, a rural leader of the Maratha caste, was the first chief minister of Maharashtra following the formation of the unilingual state, having already served as chief minister of the bilingual Bombay State. Chavan had been active in the Quit India movement since 1942 and was an early conduit for Nehruvian policies of agricultural and educational reform before he left state politics to become Nehru's defense home minister in 1962 (Sirsikar 1995: 140–141). When Chavan left Maharashtra for Delhi, a new system of local governance called Panchayat Raj was put into effect along with programs to generate public support for the development and planning process. The Maharashtrian version of Panchayat Raj encouraged a particularly decentralized system of governance, with much of the state power residing at the district (*zilla*) level (Joshi 1968: 209–210). This has led to an active local and regional political scene in Maharashtra and has contributed to the fluency in matters of rural reform that is exhibited by rural Maharashtrian kīrtankārs.

Another factor in the post-colonial discourse of rural development that influenced Gadge Maharaj is the legacy of Mahatma Gandhi's *sarvodāya* ("uplift of all") movement. The sarvodāya movement emerged from Gandhi's paraphrased Gujarati translation of John Ruskin's tome on social justice, *Unto the Last*. Through his ashrams, Gandhi hoped to spread sarvodāya principles of the dignity of labor and equitable distribution of wealth, and after his death in 1948, sarvodāya became a widespread movement led by a Maharashtrian Brahman named Vinoba Bhave (Chatterjee 1986: 99–100; Jayapalan 2003: 219–235; Mishra 1999: 37–42). Having been active in the Quit India movement, Gadge Maharaj continued to spread his own version of Gandhian thought after Independence, even as state-centric Nehruvian India was moving away from the Gandhian discourses that had fueled the nationalist movement (Chatterjee 1986: 131–166). Dadamaharaj Manmadkar, the son of Gadge Maharaj's follower Gayabai Manmadkar, writes that Vinoba Bhave spread sarvodāya by invoking the authority of vārkarī saints, and that Gadge Maharaj's kīrtans and the bhajans of the *rāṣṭrasant* (national saint) Tukdoji Maharaj further closed the gap between remote Maharashtrian villagers and Gandhi's ideals (Manmadkar 1998: 324–329). Gadge Maharaj and Tukdoji Maharaj were from poor families in the Vidarbha region, and they used metaphors and idioms that were especially familiar and stirring for rural Maharashtrians.

After Independence, Gadge Maharaj continued preaching the ideals of self-sufficiency, education, and cleanliness. He had become canonized within the rural imagination because of his inspiring kīrtans, anti-colonial actions, and selfless dedication to improving rural life. Acknowledging the power of Gadge Baba to inspire change in Marathi-speaking India, the first chief minister of Bombay Presidency, B. G. Kher, provided Gadge Baba with a car in 1948 that helped him to perform in a different town each night (Maidamwar 1998: 36–37, Meshram 1998: 75).[10] Gadge Maharaj wanted to create immediate, material change in the places he performed, so he established resting houses (*dharmaśāḷas*) and schools for orphans, *ādivāsīs* (aboriginal people or "tribals"), *dalits* (former "untouchables," lit. "oppressed"), and other disadvantaged people throughout Maharashtra. On February 8, 1952, he passed the administration of these institutions on to the Gadge Maharaj Mission in Bombay, which currently receives about 700,000 of its 1 million rupee per year operating budget from the government of Maharashtra.[11] Several of his kīrtankār followers have taken over leadership in these institutions. V. K. Wagh, until his recent passing, ran a school for ādivāsī children in Bhiwali, and Yashwantrao Mane was past president of the Gadge Maharaj Mission (Maidamwar 1998: 55).

Born in 1905[12] in Mandavgaon, Ahmednagar district, as Rajaram Bhagoji Jadhav,[13] Kaikadi Maharaj was from the scheduled *kaikāḍī* quarry-working caste (Divekar 1990: 222–223). Like Gadge Baba, he communicated with audiences in a rural vernacular and generated enthusiastic audience participation using a range of rhetorical and musical devices. He imitated Gadge Baba's participatory kīrtan style with some small variations in themes, rhetoric, and song repertoire. Within the spoken portions of his kīrtans, Gadge Maharaj encouraged audience participation by posing rhetorical questions, while Kaikadi Maharaj asked questions but also provided their answers. In this excerpt from one of Kaikadi Maharaj's kīrtans,[14] he emphasizes key thoughts by first saying a phrase and then repeating it, leaving off one word for the audience to finish. This ensures vigorous participation since the audience members don't have to guess which answer the kīrtankār is seeking.

KM: Dwarka . . . Rameshwar, Jaggannath, I took my dindi and went to these pilgrimage sites. I took my dindi and went by myself. Alone I traveled. Alone I—

People: traveled.

KM: Kīrtans, I did. Kīrtans, I—

People: did.

KM: I stayed there two or three years and always took a day to learn things in their language. Language—

People: I learned

KM: A little bit in various languages, I know. A little bit in various languages—

People: I know

KM: I couldn't say things that were too difficult, so I would get a translation. That is, I spoke in Marathi, and whoever was there would tell others in Telugu, someone in Kannade, someone in Oriya language, someone in Tamil, someone told in their Marmar language. This was done in the kīrtan. Now all the men raise your hands, women don't raise your hands.

BHAJAN: *Rāghav rājārām raghupati, rāghav rājārām.*

This excerpt ends with the Ram Dhun, Gandhi's favorite bhajan and a staple of the anti-colonial nonviolent resistance movement. Gandhi's version includes six lines of text and a melody by the famous singer and music reformer V. D. Paluskar,[15] while Kaikadi Baba used a different tune and only the refrain, thereby invoking Gandhi while transforming his song into a cyclical, participatory bhajan idiomatic of vārkarī kīrtan.

Although Kaikadi Baba's rhetorical style was modeled after Gadge Maharaj, his philosophical themes and bhajans also resonated with the vārkarī tradition. His recorded kīrtan includes abhangas by vārkarī saints performed in a participatory vārkarī style, as well as songs attributed to or invoking Gadge Baba, such as Gadge Baba's bhajan, "Devakīnandana Gopālā," and the *jayjaykār* (exclamation of praise), "Gadge Maharaj kī jay!"[16] Kaikadi Baba preached a Gadge Baba-inspired message of dedication to humanity rather than ritual, and the theme of this recorded kīrtan was "Don't become ascetics, become human beings." A second theme resonated more with vārkarī philosophy: "If you make God yours, or if you become one with God, then you will be happy." He sang "Jayjay Viṭhobā Rakhumābāi" more than Gadge Maharaj's "Devakīnandana Gopāḷa," and his discourses invoked bhakti tropes of devotional communion.

Kaikadi Maharaj's oeuvre seems profoundly influenced by specific government initiatives and Congress ideals. This contrasts with Gadge Maharaj's kīrtans, which appealed to government officials on a more general ideological level. After preaching about happiness through devotion and service to humanity, Kaikadi Maharaj brought his kīrtan to a close with a call for listeners to have fewer children and to shape those children in the image of Mahatma Gandhi, Jawaharlal Nehru, and Shivaji Maharaj. And finally, he proclaimed that the only way to prosper is to "be united" (*ekī karā*), regardless of caste, before returning to the main song, "don't be ascetics, be human beings," performed as a call-and-response with the audience (see Musical Example 4.1).

> Don't give birth to too many children. You should have only two children. Tell your wife about it. If you have too many children, it becomes very difficult to take care of them. Population problems have become a great hurdle in the development of our country. We want children but they should be like Subhashbabu. We should have children like Shivaji Maharaj, Pandit Nehru or Mahatma Gandhi.
>
> *Ekī karā ekī karā*—be united. If there are differences in a village, then it will be destroyed in no time. All villagers should be united. And all castes should come together. There should not be differences between different castes.
>
> *Bhajan: Mānavāno māṇuskīla jāgā, māṇuskīla jāgā. Jara mānāsat miloni wāgā.*
> [Don't become ascetics, become human beings].

This short excerpt illustrates Kaikadi Baba's endorsement of three government initiatives of the 1950s through 1990s: slowing population

Musical Example 4.1.
Bhajan, "Mānavāno māṇuskīla jāgā."

growth, generating nationalist sentiment, and reducing caste prejudice. While the denouement of Kaikadi Maharaj's kīrtan aligns with Nehruvian policies, the chapter titles of his posthumously published book, *Sukhācī Wāṭ* (*Path to Happiness*, 1992), mirror the independent Indian government's concern with population control, isolationist economics, citizenship, and social reform to an even greater extent, perhaps suggesting the involvement of the editor, his nephew Ramdas Maharaj. Chapter titles include the following:

> "Throwing money in the river is a waste of national currency,"
> "Family planning will make society happy,"
> "Forgetting patriotic people means that nationalism is dead,"
> "Encouraging people to buy svadeśī means making a *surājya* (good rule),"
> "Banning caste-ism means that everyone will get the opportunity to work in the government,"
> "If the people in the country are aware, it is a sign of good government."

Kaikadi Maharaj did not achieve the widespread popularity of Gadge Maharaj, but his teachings have been enshrined in the Kaikadi Maharaj Maṭh, a popular destination for pilgrims in Pandharpur, Maharashtra's busiest pilgrimage town. Although it is unclear if Kaikadi Maharaj received government support, his messages and those of his family members suggest a close attachment to early post-colonial Nehruvian socialism. His *maṭh* (hermitage, retreat, or ashram) is currently maintained by Ramdas Maharaj Jadhav, also a kīrtankār.[17] The Kaikadi Maharaj Maṭh is a brightly painted cement structure in which visitors are led through a series of passages that take them into the mouths of fish, birds, and a train. The first passageway is lined with statues of saints and deities in recesses along the wall, their painted toes and knees worn through to the cement where people have touched them in *namaskār* (gesture of greeting and respect). In later passageways, dioramas with scenes from Hindu mythology and modern Indian history position Marathi saints resolutely at the table of Indian and international politics and policy change. Gadge Maharaj and other Indian saints and deities, for example, are depicted in dioramas sitting next to all-Indian leaders like Gandhi, Patel, and Nehru.

Nuclear nonproliferation was a major trope in the maṭh exhibits, which Ramdas Maharaj Jadhav said represents his father's interest rather than that of Kaikadi Maharaj. His father, Kondiram Kaka, built the maṭh for his brother and was involved in the movement to ban nuclear weapons. Ramdas Maharaj speaks against nuclear weapons in his kīrtans, and the maṭh was the site of a large function on United Nations Day to promote world peace.[18] During a visit to the maṭh in 1999, I found one diorama to be particularly striking. Divided into two halves, one side depicts a Neanderthal clubbing another Neanderthal to death, while on the other side the *Enola Gay* drops a nuclear bomb on Hiroshima. A little farther down the passageway was the maṭh's largest diorama, depicting a meeting in the United Nations on nuclear weapons, with an idol of Kaikadi Maharaj watching from a recess in the wall. On the outside of the diorama were placards that read, "Stop nuclear weapons" and "Support UNO."

The depictions of Congress Party nationalist leaders and nonproliferation policies reflect the support of the Congress Party by Kaikadi Maharaj's family members when the maṭh was built. After the Bharatiya Janata Party replaced Congress as India's ruling party in 1998, one of its first initiatives was to conduct nuclear testing. The Congress Party had secretly conducted nuclear weapons research for decades, but the BJP's position was new in that it openly declared India's nuclear capabilities. A faction of Gandhian Congress politicians had opposed nuclear proliferation,[19] and it was with these politicians that Ramdas Maharaj and his father felt a kinship. Ramdas Maharaj continued his anti-proliferation work and association with the Congress Party even while the BJP was in power, but his political affiliations have shifted in the twenty-first century as new parties and affiliated cultural organizations have emerged in Maharashtra. He now goes by the name Shivraj Maharaj and is the president of the Sant Namdeo-Tukaram Warkari Parishad, a wing of the Maratha Seva Sangh.[20]

Following the success of Kaikadi Maharaj and Gadge Maharaj in buttressing government initiatives through the vārkarī (or vārkarī-like) kīrtan idiom, nāradīya kīrtankārs based in Pune were enlisted as state propagandists in the 1970s and 1980s. The person most often cited in this regard is the late *śāskīya kīrtankār* (government kīrtankār)[21] Govinda Khare, but Manjushree Khadilkar actually began performing government kīrtan about a decade before Khare. While rāṣṭrīya kīrtankārs usually attempt to distance themselves rhetorically and symbolically from politics and the state, both Khadilkarbai and Kharebuva expressed pride in their social work, in earning a government stipend, and in meeting with famous politicians, and both cited Indira Gandhi as the source of their beginnings in śāskīya kīrtan. The photo on the cover of Dr. Khare's book, *Ārogya Dhanasampadā* [Health Is Wealth] (1985), depicts a garlanded and happy Dr. Khare greeting Indira Gandhi, who sits smiling behind a long table.

Manjushree Khadilkar continues to perform kīrtan regularly and teaches bhajan to a group of women in her flat in the Kothrud neighborhood on the outskirts of Pune. When her husband Shrikant Khadilkar was still living, I knew him to be an enthusiastic supporter and manager of his wife's performances. He traveled with her throughout India and internationally for kīrtan performances. As she told me in an interview in 2009, her father, a high court judge, nurtured her talent as a singer when she was a child.[22] He found her a teacher and introduced her to classical music, kīrtan, and nāṭya saṅgīt, and he arranged her first solo performance when she was ready. After marriage, Khadilkarbai continued studying classical music with her mother-in-law, honed her skills performing nāṭya saṅgīt, and incorporated elements of both into her kīrtans. With this solid musical foundation, she began performing on the radio, where she attracted the attention of the government. Other kīrtankārs appreciate her as a singer of Hindustani music.[23] In her words:

> I am an A class artist for *Ākāśwāni*, the national Radio Station. The kīrtans performed on radio had an extremely wide reach. The program is called *Māzha ghar, māzha śet* (my home, my farm/land). I have been performing kīrtans for them for a very long time now. I started in the year 1970, and through those kīrtans I was brought into the eyes of the government. They thought my kīrtans were really good and that I was able to express a point of view and talk about it with the people through my kīrtan. And at that time Indira Gandhi was the Prime Minister. I got a letter directly from her addressed to me. The letter said that the government was planning on working on some themes and projects for the development agenda and needed my help with it. I was asked to perform kīrtans on the topics and subjects they selected. "We will arrange for everything else that's required."
>
> So in the year 1972, I received my first government kīrtan. The topic of discussion was Mahatma Gandhi's biography and I was required to go to various villages and perform this kīrtan. We went around to a lot of villages performing this kīrtan about Mahatmaji's life for almost six months. We performed a total of about 100 such kīrtans in small villages.[24]

Other topics requested by the government included Sant Nāmdev Mahārāj, a thirteenth- and fourteenth-century Marathi saint who settled in Punjab later in life and is worshipped by both Sikhs and Hindus. Khadilkar's Nāmdev was an icon of religious and regional unity, and she performed kīrtans on his life in Hindi in Sikh *gurdwārās* throughout Punjab. The third assignment she received was Family Planning, and her kīrtans on this topic expounded on the relationship between poverty and population density. Following this, her other assignments included Ayurveda and health, with advice for lifestyle changes to help prevent diabetes, high blood pressure, and other conditions; five-year plans; and most recently, hygiene and environmental stewardship.[25]

Both Manjushree Khadilkar and Govinda Khare attracted government attention when performing kīrtan in a nonritual context. For Khadilkar this was the radio, and for Khare it was a kīrtan (his first) performed at a tuberculosis hospital. According to Dr. Khare's widow, whom I interviewed at her flat in the old city in 2000, her husband was a *vaidya* (Āyurvedic doctor) who came from a long line of vaidyas.[26] She had meticulously maintained scrapbooks, recordings, and photos related to her late husband's kīrtans, including a cassette of a kīrtan on Tilak on the sixty-eighth anniversary of the Lokmanya's death. I was surprised to learn from her that Tilak was her grandfather, which Khare also mentioned in his kīrtan on Tilak.

Dr. Khare was working at a tuberculosis (TB) hospital in Pune when the director of the hospital organized a gathering in which each doctor was to present a lecture on some TB-related topic. Dr. Khare, then in his forties, decided that he would do a kīrtan instead of a lecture, which proved to be a wise decision as it led to a wildly successful side career as a kīrtankār.[27] A good but not exceptional singer, Dr. Khare's strength as a kīrtankār was his knowledge of medical issues, his humorous delivery, and his training in Sanskrit. For example, in his kīrtan on Bal Gangadhar Tilak, he led the audience in singing a bhajan with the antecedent phrase of "Hari Ram, Hari Ram, Ram Ram Hari Hari," and a tongue-in-cheek consequent phrase of "Hari Krishna Hari Krishna, Krishna Govinda Khare Khare" that referenced his own name. Although Khare performed in the nāradīya style, he composed all his songs, including the muḷpad.[28] Like Vasudeo Kolhatkar, he used tunes from nāṭya sangīt in his kīrtans, but even Kolhatkar did not discard the tradition of using an abhanga by a poet-saint as the muḷpad. Composing his own muḷpad was characteristic of Dr. Khare's iconoclastic and less esoteric approach to kīrtan.

According to Mrs. Khare, doing medical kīrtans was Khare's own idea, but he quickly captured the attention of the government. During Indira Gandhi's second term in office in the 1980s, Govinda Khare received a government contract to perform kīrtans on medical topics in twenty-six districts, with five kīrtans per district, to be performed over the course of five years.[29] While Khadilkarbai performed kīrtans on various topics of interest to the government, Dr. Khare limited his kīrtans primarily to medical issues, such as mental health, diet, family planning, and tuberculosis. On June 15, 1981, he attracted much media attention through his performance at the inaugural event of the Seventh Joint Conference of Central Councils of Health and Family Planning in New Delhi. Indira Gandhi was in the audience, as were many other ministers and politicians at both the state and national levels. The gathering was covered by at least seven Pune-based newspapers—six in Marathi and one in Hindi. Clearly, the most significant aspect of the performance was that he performed it in front of Indira Gandhi, and five of the six Marathi papers had a title that was a variant of "A Nāradīya Kīrtan in Front of Srimati Indira Gandhi."[30] The articles also noted with pride that he wore a "Puneri" *pagaḍī* (red hat worn by kīrtankārs) and *dhotar* (long white cloth wrapped as pants), and that he performed in English and Hindi in front of high-level politicians. By performing in English and Hindi, he made kīrtan nationally intelligible, but his Maharashtrian outfit was a source of regional pride for people in his home city of Pune. Dr. Khare asked attendees to sign an autograph book with responses to his performance, and the first signature was from Indira Gandhi herself. Others noted that his "folk performance" is a very useful tool of communication.

Before 1947, rāṣṭrīya kīrtankārs had positioned themselves in opposition to the colonial state, but after Independence some performers vocalized a new support for state initiatives. The nationalist sentiment that had fueled the anti-colonial movement made way in the post-colonial era for more specific state-sponsored projects of national unity and development. In the 1950s and 1960s, Indian governmental priorities included education, rural development, and industrialization, all of which were reflected in the kīrtans of Gadge Baba and Kaikadi Baba. Because they spoke and sang in rural idioms, they were especially effective mediators between state policy and rural audiences, and although the resonances between their performances and state projects are palpable, the nature of their government connections is more inferred than documented.[31]

Manjushree Khadilkar and the family of Govinda Khare, on the other hand, attest to their sponsorship by the central government and to Indira Gandhi's interest in their work. In the wake of Partition, and through the conflict-ridden linguistic reorganization of states and the threat of a secessionist movement in Punjab, both Jawaharlal Nehru and his daughter Indira Gandhi desperately sought to increase national unity by quelling incipient separatist desires and (in Indira Gandhi's case) deflecting attention away from draconian measures against separatist groups. During the 1970s and early 1980s that were bookended by Indira Gandhi's regime, her propaganda machine was tightly controlled, and nāradīya kīrtankārs figured into her broad-based efforts to gain grassroots support. We can identify this regime's interest in Sikh assimilation through Khadilkarbai's assignment to perform kīrtans on Nāmdev, and Mrs. Gandhi's advocacy for family planning as reflected in the kīrtans of both Khadilkar and Khare.[32]

From speaking with Mrs. Khadilkar and Dr. Khare's family, I learned that they were grateful for the prestige and travel opportunities that accompanied government contracts. As kīrtankārs, they represented the artistry and literary depth of Maharashtrian tradition to other parts of India and were a source of pride for Puneri people seeking to connect to the past without appearing parochial or irrelevant. Although government kīrtankārs found support with career politicians, they regarded their kīrtans as the fulfillment of social and civic duty rather than as contributions to political party agendas. Indeed, they belonged to the ranks of government employees in the ministries of education or human resource development, and their political affiliations and sympathies were often different from those of their state sponsors. For them, śāskīya kīrtan is a prestigious and important occupation, and they are committed to its social programs even if their nationalist sentiments reside elsewhere.

NEW HINDU NATIONALIST KĪRTAN: APHALEBUVA AND KOPARKARBUVA

Following Gandhi's assassination, very few conservative Brahman kīrtankārs aligned themselves with the Congress government and their political campaigns. Instead, they either withdrew from the nationalist and/or political sphere altogether or they performed extreme Hindu nationalist kīrtans. A new generation of conservative, urban Brahman rāṣṭrīya kīrtankārs performing in the nāradīya kīrtan idiom aligned themselves with fringe Hindutva groups and experimented with institutional models designed for a "qualifications"-hungry, modernizing India. These kīrtankārs were severely dissatisfied with the socialist, secular orientation of post-colonial Indian government and voiced their resistance through kīrtan within a very small "alternative civil society."

In Pune, the most influential rāṣṭrīya kīrtankārs in the early postwar years were Govindswami Aphale (1917–?)[33] and Gangadharbuva Koparkar (1920[34]–2001). Koparkar is claimed as a guru by many Hindu nationalist kīrtankārs performing today and was regarded by other kīrtankārs as an erudite religious expert who scoured scripture in defense of conservative social mores. Aphale, on the other hand, was an actor and śāhir as well as a popular kīrtankār who was known for performing witty and inspiring kīrtans but not for erudite philosophy. Aphale's son Charudatta, also a kīrtankār, said:

> [Govindswami Aphale's] kīrtans and Koparkar's were different because Koparkar's were on the Vedas and Śāstras, they were in Sanskrit, and they appealed to educated people. He used stories from the *Rāmāyana* and *Mahābhārata*, as well as some less-known stories. After a while, he began his historical ākhyāns and ones on social problems like dowry.[35]

In the context of explaining how a kīrtankār should explain the eight fundamental aspects of Vedic dharma and how they can lead to *mukti* (release from the cycle of death and rebirth), one of Koparkar's śiṣyas said, "Other kīrtankārs don't know these things, only Koparkar because he is very learned. Even I don't know these things because I do not study."[36] This sentiment was echoed by other kīrtankārs and by students of Vedic Hinduism who attended Koparkar's religious instruction programs. Koparkar's politics fell on the extreme far right of the political spectrum, but supporters and detractors alike considered him to be a true expert in Sanskrit and Vedic literature.

Govindswami Aphale was a performer who donned many hats. Having received a master of arts degree (MA) and a degree in law (LLB),[37] he dedicated his life to performing kīrtan, to acting, and to singing nationalist songs. Aphale introduced Hindu nationalist populism to rāṣṭrīya kīrtan; his kīrtans were meant to generate mass religio-ethnic sentiment—Hindu and primarily upper caste—rather than to create a community of educated leaders as Tilak had advocated.[38] Aphale began his career as an actor and performer of povāḍā, switching to kīrtan in approximately 1941 after studying at Nārad Mandir and acquiring a nationalist approach through studies with Dr. Patwardhan.[39] When I told middle-class Indians that I was doing research on rāṣṭrīya kīrtan, those older than thirty often mention Govindswami Aphale and many said that they had attended his kīrtans. By all accounts, he was an imposing man with a strong personality and a keen sense for how to entertain a crowd. When Aphale performed kīrtans in the streets of Pune, traffic was rerouted to accommodate the teeming crowds. According to a Mr. Sapade, a middle-aged man who helped me operate the tape recorder at the All India Radio archives, "Govindswami Aphale's kīrtans were attended by thousands of people and were very effective and full of jokes. He was a great communicator about things like politics and family planning." Many people, especially cosmopolitans, did not attend kīrtans in temples but would attend Aphale's kīrtans on fields and streets. Govindswami's son Charudatta describes his father's kīrtans as both controversial and spellbinding:

> His kīrtans were full of a wide variety of poems, tunes from popular film songs, popular songs on cassettes and in society, plus the standard āryā, sākī, and diṅḍī. Some of the other kīrtankārs didn't like that he used film and popular songs, but he would respond by saying that he did kīrtan on the street, so he would use the things that people on the street are familiar with. He wouldn't use such songs in temples. The Shankaracharya from Kashi told people that they should fire Aphale because he used tunes from film songs. My father told him that he should come to his kīrtan and then say this. Shankaracarya came to his kīrtan, enjoyed himself, and never gave him any trouble after that. He used the good worship songs from films, not love songs.
>
> He was a good actor and would perform the death of a freedom fighter outside in such a way that 10,000 people would cry. There was pin drop silence at his kīrtans, and he would get 10–20 volunteers to keep dogs and cows out. He would also call the electricity board and tell them not to cut off the power during his kīrtan or an angry mob would come to kill them.[40]

As a kīrtankār for the masses, Aphale was drawn to any and all types of popular music—not just mythological drama songs like those used by Vasudeo

Kolhatkar. The use of theater and film songs was and continues to be a contentious issue for today's kīrtankārs, but these repertoires raise fewer eyebrows today than they did during the time of Vasudeo Kolhatkar and Govindswami Aphale. Charudatta Aphale is continuing the family rāṣṭrīya kīrtan and dramatic tradition, and like his father, he performs politically charged, entertaining kīrtans with the dramatic sensitivity of an actor. Charudatta is a less forceful personality but a more accomplished Hindustani singer than his father, and his musical prowess is an attraction for kīrtan and theater audiences. He is currently one of the most commercially successful nāradīya/rāṣṭrīya kīrtankārs in Maharashtra, having produced several cassettes, CDs, and videocassettes, and with performance credits in Marathi cultural organizations throughout North America.

According to Charudatta, Govindswami Aphale became involved in the 1940s with the revolutionaries V. D. Savarkar and Subhash Chandra Bose. His father worked with Savarkar's group to gain freedom from the Portuguese in Goa and to incorporate the Nizam of Hyderabad's independent kingdom into the Indian nation-state. Given his father's commitment to nationalist issues, I asked Charudatta Aphale if his father's kīrtans were ever shown on TV. He responded that the government-controlled TV stations did not show his kīrtans because he criticized Gandhi and Nehru.[41] He continued:

> He didn't like [Gandhi and Nehru] because they begged for freedom rather than fighting for it, as Vallabhai Patel and Subhash Chandra Bose had done. In his kīrtans, he used to say that Gandhi was partial to Muslims and bad for Hindus and the country. He actually proved this in his kīrtans. For these reasons, the government, police, and TV didn't support him.
>
> There was actually a court case against him for saying that Gandhi was partial to the Muslims. In court, he told about how a Hindu named Gopinath had killed a Britisher and was going to be hanged. People came to [Gandhi] for help, to come to court and urge the courts to imprison [Gopinath] rather than kill him. Gandhi refused because he said that he did not support such violent action. The next month, the same thing happened, though a Muslim had done the murder rather than a Hindu, and Gandhi went to the court and spoke on his behalf. My father did not like Gandhi's nonviolence.[42]

Govindswami Aphale was critical of government policies in his kīrtans, particularly those that he regarded as beneficial to Muslims rather than Hindus. A straightforward Hindu nationalist populist who thrilled audiences with his kīrtans on Savarkar and other Hindu nationalist revolutionaries, Aphale had little patience for stories of saintly miracles and instead tried to incite mass political action. According to Charudatta,

> Many people came to his kīrtans for information on politics. He used to warn people of things, like the rise in sugar prices. If the government was preparing to cut down trees, he would warn people so that they could organize protests. Many people in the government respected him and would tip him off about these things because they were powerless to stop what they didn't like.[43]

Unlike Koparkar, who appealed to listeners as a Sanskrit scholar and an authority on conservative Hinduism, Aphale was a voice for Hindu nationalism, an entertainer, and a political activist. He represented a new Hindu elite populism, generating nationalist sentiment more through accessible songs and metaphors than with Brahmanical scholarship. A middle-aged Marathi man who had lived in the United States for at least twenty years told me that as a boy and young man, he only went to those kīrtans "that were nationalist" and said that he was particularly fond of Aphale's kīrtans.[44] This sentiment was echoed by many people of his generation in Pune, which attests not only to his ability as a performer but also to the popularity of Hindutva rhetoric among a certain class of Pune residents.

G. N. Koparkar (see Plate 4.1) studied at the Nārad Mańdir after being brought to live with one of his gurus, Bhilavdikarbuva, at the Harikīrtanottejak Sabhā as a young boy.[45] Koparkar told me he began performing kīrtan as a child and transitioned to rāṣṭrīya kīrtan only after becoming involved in Ram Rajya Parisad, a party founded in 1948 by Swami Karpatriji, a religious figurehead who staged massive demonstrations against the Hindu Code Bill (Jaffrelot 1999: 103).[46] Proposed to the Constituent Assembly in 1948 and brought before the Lok Sabha in 1952–1957, the bill was divided into three parts. The Hindu Marriage Law outlawed polygamy and permitted inter-caste marriage and divorce; the Hindu Adoption and Maintenance Bill legalized the adoption of girls; and the Hindu Succession Bill allowed for girls to have the same inheritance rights as wives and sons. The Hindu Code Bill was intended as a secular code to replace Hindu personal law, but Koparkar told me that he protested the Hindu Code Bill because it was unconstitutional and took away the right to freely profess religion[47] (Jaffrelot 1999: 102–103).

I had occasion to hear only one of Koparkar's kīrtans, which was performed in celebration of Rāma's birth during the 1998 retreat to Pandharpur discussed in Chapter 7. His singing voice had become a bit shaky with age, but he had good pitch, rhythmic sense, and raga knowledge, and his eyes were full of energy and conviction. He needed to sit for the kīrtan because of his frailty, but this enabled him to accompany himself on the harmonium as he sang āryā, sākī, pad, and bhajan. Though these genres are standard fare in nāradīya kīrtan, he broke with convention by singing one of the āryās in English (perhaps for my benefit?). I later learned that this had been excerpted from an English kīrtan that Koparkar had composed on "protection of religion," dharma, and the Sage Viśvāmitra (Koparkar 1982a: 1–9). At the climax of his

Plate 4.1.
The late G. N. Koparkarbuva with his disciple, Sudhatai Dhamankar. Tapodham Warje, 2000.

uttararanga in Pandharpur, most songs were diegetic and included women's lullabies and swinging songs performed collectively in extra-kīrtan contexts to celebrate the birth of a child. Indeed, on Koparkar's instruction, a small swing symbolizing Rāma was set in motion, and audience members became participating members in the child's welcoming party.[48] This kīrtan was thematically similar to others Koparkar had published for teaching purposes—it was replete with Sanskrit quotes and it conveyed ideas of Rāma's supremacy, women's place in the home, the Otherness of non-Hindus, and the need to uphold dharma (religion/duty) (Koparkar et al. 1978, Koparkar 1979, 1982a).

Though elderly and ill when I knew him in 1998–2000, Koparkar was one of the most politically active rāṣṭrīya kīrtankārs I met in Pune. He sent monthly booklets on right-wing topics to thousands of Hindu homes in Maharashtra, regularly lectured on the "morally corrupt" ways of the West, had been active with the Ram Rajya Parisad, and—when he was well enough—performed inflammatory rāṣṭrīya kīrtans. He sang kīrtan less often when he was in his late seventies but continued to give lectures and to write booklets, brochures, and pamphlets. Many times when I went to see him and his disciple Sudhatai at their ashram in Warje on the outskirts of Pune, he was sitting at his Marathi typewriter, surrounded on all sides by books. He continued sending monthly booklets called *Tapodhām Pratiṣṭhān Prakāśan Bhāratīya Vāngmaya Māḷa Māsik* (Tapodham Pratishthan Publishing Indian Literary Monthly) until the very end of his life. The explicit aim of this publication was "*dharmapracār*" (popularization of religion), and each issue addressed a different topic related to orthodox Hindu ethics and/or social issues, such as "Are menstruating women untouchable?" "What does 'character' mean?" and "Beware of attack" (on "foreignness" of Muslims in India). As a younger man, Koparkarbuva had published many pedagogical books and booklets on kīrtan under the auspices of the Kīrtan University he founded with Aphale, and his later non-kīrtan publications address the same spectrum of Hindutva-related issues on which he had been preaching and publishing for decades.

Because of Koparkar's hearing loss and my imperfect Marathi, I realized toward the end of my dissertation research that he might have misunderstood what I was doing and why I was doing it. Afraid that he had interpreted my curiosity as support for his extreme convictions, I asked him very directly what he thought about my research, to which he responded with a thoughtful pause and then a surprising answer. He said I was "too interested in politics," an unexpected response from someone who seemed to have devoted his life to Hindu nationalist causes.[49] Indeed, when I first met him, he answered my question about his favorite political leaders with, "None, they're all *guṇḍas* (crooks)." Barraged by news stories of political bribery and tax money funneled toward lavish marriage ceremonies for children of politicians, Koparkar regarded himself not as a political person with selfish interests but as a "protector of religion" (a phrase often heard among conservative kīrtankārs) with altruistic motivations. At times, this protection entailed involvement with political parties such as the Ram Rajya Parishad, but more often than not, it meant working alone or with other nonaffiliated Hindu nationalists. Though he called himself a nationalist kīrtankār, he regarded nationalism as apolitical—much as the RSS claims to be a "cultural" organization.[50] This bifurcation of political discourse into two distinct regimes is, as Thomas Hansen has argued, a general characteristic of the Indian post-colonial secular state:

> What was pursued by the secular state was, in other words, a separation of two strategic and discursive realms in the public: one was a political realm wherein the interest of national unity, nonpreference, and the rationalities and naked imperatives of the state compelled political actors to speak and act in certain ways, while at the same time praising the cultural depth and diversity in India; the other was a cultural realm wherein any community could celebrate itself and its own myths and exclude others. (Hansen 1999: 54)

The secular state never effectively created a secular citizenship, so elite, modernizing forces instead essentialized and reified communities, which in turn generated a vibrant sphere of "anti-political" cultural/ist formations (Hansen 1999: 54–56). Indeed, the social politics of creating a Brahman social order was invisible to Koparkar, and he did not claim awareness of the similarities between his Hindu nationalism and that of Hindu nationalist political parties.

EXPERIMENTS IN RE-PROFESSIONALIZATION: TWO KĪRTAN UNIVERSITIES

Rāṣṭrīya and nāradīya kīrtan declined in popularity in the 1970s and early 1980s but experienced a renaissance when Hindu nationalist organizations gained political ground in the 1980s. Founded in 1951 as the political arm of the Rashtriya Swayamsevak Sangh (RSS), the Bharatiya Jana Sangh (BJS, predecessor to the BJP) distanced itself from the RSS in the 1970s. During that time, the BJS reemerged as a secular, populist party allied with the Janata Party in opposition to Indira Gandhi's 1966–1977 and 1980–1984 Congress rule, but a few events in the 1980s led to the communalist reformation of the BJS as the BJP. First, the Janata Party won in 1977 mainly through its opposition to Indira Gandhi's 1975–1977 state of emergency, but that coalition quickly broke down as ideological differences surfaced. Another factor in the transition of the 1980s was that traditionalists in the Congress Party had weakened the legitimacy of secularism in an attempt to co-opt the strategy of their opposition, but this had the opposite effect of strengthening the strategies of Hindu nationalist organizations. Additionally, the RSS and Vishwa Hindu Parishad (VHP) recruited many important Hindu spiritual leaders and launched the *rāmjanmabhumi* campaign, both factors rallying large numbers of Hindus who had previously not been involved with politicized Hinduism. Since the BJP had all but severed their ties with the RSS in the 1970s, the VHP and RSS looked to Congress as their new political arm, but when this alliance was thwarted they turned to the now-receptive BJP. This relationship with the RSS proved to be extremely effective for the BJP beginning in the late 1980s. They gained many seats in the Lok Sabha elections in 1989, won the majority briefly in 1996, and captured it more solidly in 1998 (Jaffrelot 1999: 314–410). In Maharashtra, the success of the BJP was bolstered through an alliance with the Bombay-based Hindu nationalist party, Shiv Sena, with this coalition winning the state assembly in 1996–1998 and 1999–2009. During the 1980s in Maharashtra, the Maharashtrian-born RSS was becoming realigned with the BJP while the Congress Party was remaking itself in the wake of Indira Gandhi's regime.

In this context, as Hindu nationalist discourse became mainstreamed by both the Congress and the BJP, Marathi kīrtan was touted as a means to "improve" the nation by teaching "eternal values." To support this reinvigorated kīrtan, two kīrtan *mahāvidyalāya* (universities) were founded in Pune: Koparkar and Aphale's Kīrtan Mahāvidyālaya, begun in 1987, and the Bhāratīya Vidya Bhavan's Sant Jñāneśvar Harikātha and Kīrtan Mahāvidyālaya, founded in 1984. The Harikīrtanottejak Sabhā at Nārad Mandir in Pune and the Akhil Bhāratīya Kīrtan Saṅsthā in Dadar, Bombay, had been teaching kīrtan classes since the late nineteenth century and the 1940s, respectively, but by the 1980s their main pupils were children, housewives, and retirees, that is, not people who were learning kīrtan as a profession. The founders of the new Mahāvidyālayas were responding to what they perceived as a declining interest in kīrtan as a profession and a dearth of learned, scholarly kīrtankārs. The idea was that they would provide full-time instruction for students who had already completed high school or college and were seeking instruction in kīrtan and higher education credentials possessed by their middle-class peers.

The kīrtan approaches and backgrounds of Govindswami Aphale and Gangadharbuva Koparkar were different, but the two men joined forces to run a Kīrtan Mahāvidyālaya (Kīrtan University) from 1977 through 1993.[51] As a result of his work as an educator, in 1996 Koparkar became the first recipient of a prestigious award given by the Maharashtrian government, an honor that included a 25,000-rupee prize and marked a decided governmental turn toward Hindu nationalism.[52] Aphale had been deceased for many years while I was conducting fieldwork in Pune, but Koparkar was available for interviews and I saw him on a semi-regular basis (he has since passed away). In these conversations, Koparkar stressed the need for "higher education" in kīrtan, and said that he and Aphale created the university to teach kīrtan to high school graduates in a systematic way. Koparkar had extensive education in both the British system (he had a bachelor of science degree) and in traditional Brahman knowledge. He learned scripture from the Harikīrtanottejak Sabhā's Gurjar Śāstri, who Koparkar described as a *śāstri* (scholar of the scriptures) rather than a kīrtankār. Koparkar wrote several textbooks for the Mahāvidyālaya, and his students continue to praise the program's rigorous exam schedule (Koparkar n.d., Koparkar 1979, 1982a, 1982b, Koparkar et al. 1978). The inside cover of *Kathā Haridāsācī*, published just a year after the founding of the kīrtan Mahāvidyālaya, explains that the Mahāvidyālaya was a five-year course that accepted seven serious students at a time. The goal of the university was to create "*vidvān*" (learned) kīrtankārs with in-depth knowledge of Sanskrit, Vedanta, music, and dharma, and the ability to perform kīrtans in Marathi, Sanskrit, and English (Koparkar et al. 1978). The Kīrtan Mahāvidyālaya educated thirteen kīrtankārs during its years of operation.[53]

Koparkar told me that although he and Aphale were both rāṣṭrīya kīrtankārs, their Mahāvidyālaya had nothing to do with rāṣṭrīya kīrtan, and was instead designed "to teach higher education and to supply good knowledge."[54] Most of the kīrtankārs who graduated from the Mahāvidyālaya consider themselves nāradīya or Rāmdāsī rather than rāṣṭrīya kīrtankārs. Nonetheless, many of today's rāṣṭrīya kīrtankārs, including Narahari Apamarjane, Narendrabuva Hate, Shrikrishna Sinnarkar, and Sudhatai Dhamankar, received some training from Koparkar on an individual basis, and topics addressed in Koparkar's Mahāvidyālaya textbooks are characteristic of Hindu nationalist rāṣṭrīya kīrtan.

Only a few years after Aphale and Koparkar began accepting students in the Kīrtan Mahāvidyālaya, a similar institution of higher kīrtan education was founded in Alandi by an educational trust called the Bharatiya Vidya Bhavan. Dr. K. M. Munshi, who founded the Bharatiya Vidya Bhavan in 1938, was a Congress politician embraced by Hindu Mahasabha members because of his anti-Muslim attitudes and gestures at nationalizing Hindu culture. Munshi created the Bharatiya Vidya Bhavan to promote "the reintegration of Indian culture in the light of modern knowledge and to suit our present day needs and the resuscitation of its fundamental value in their pristine vigour" (cf. Jaffrelot 84). For Munshi, "Indian culture" was equivalent to Brahmanical Hinduism, and the Bharatiya Vidya Bhavan was a venue for Hinduism's systematization, modernization, and nationalization. Munshi also worked to create a Hindu citizenry outside of the educational arena; as Union Minister of Supply, he supported the movement to rebuild the Somnath temple in Gujarat that had been partially destroyed by Mahmud of Ghazni in the eleventh century (Jaffrelot 1999: 84–85).

The Pune *Kendra* (Branch) of the Bharatiya Vidya Bhavan has since its founding in 1984 established the Sant Jñāneśvar Harikathā and Kīrtan Mahāvidyālaya, as well as four Western-style schools and colleges. The Bhavan also conducts classes on *saṅskār* (Hindu customs and manners), Sanskrit, music, dance, and the *Bhagavad-gītā*. Unlike Kolhatkar and Chapekar, who translated nationalism into a movement of the "inside," the Bharatiya Vidya Bhavan's approach is characterized by an underlying reformism in which ancient "Indian values" are rendered applicable for "modern" citizens. A brochure for the Pune Kendra states that the Bharatiya Vidya Bhavan's

> avowed aim is to revitalise India's ancient values and reintegrate them to suit the changing needs of modern times. [The Bhavan] has started more than 60 Centres in India and a few International Centres too with the avowed object of building up a commonwealth of faith, hope and human values.[55]

The Sant Jñāneśvar Harikathā and Kīrtan Mahāvidyālaya, which operated for twelve years, was a two-year residential course for college graduates located in the small pilgrimage town of Alandi. The course experimented in reviving nāradīya kīrtan as an art form that combined conservative and "modern" values, and the school was created not because of a great demand for kīrtan education but from a desire to generate such a demand. The Bhavan, with funding from the Birla foundation, provided full financial support for students, covering the cost of their tuition and board, as well as a small stipend. According to the scholar and kīrtan expert V. L. Manjul, Birla spent 300,000 or 400,000 rupees per year on the Bhavan.[56] A thirteen-page Kīrtan Mahāvidyālaya syllabus listed Marathi, Sanskrit, and English texts to study in preparation for exams in individual subject areas. Topics included the Epics and Purāṇas, Indian Philosophy, Sanskrit Language and Literature, Sects and Sampradāya, Cultural History, Bhagavad-gītā and Jñāneśvarī, Philosophy of Arts, and Kīrtan Theory and Practice. Mr. Rairkar, the general secretary of Pune's Bhāratīya Vidya Bhavan, said that the Mahāvidyālaya folded after twelve years because the students and the instructors lacked true interest and dedication. He felt that students were only interested in getting something for free, and that instructors did not always show up to lecture because they were busy with their full-time jobs.[57]

The English prospectus of the Harikatha and Kīrtan Mahāvidyālaya states that the goal of the Mahāvidyālaya is to train "preachers" to popularize "our culture" by rendering it relevant in the current era. Though the Mahāvidyālaya was not specifically designed to provide education in rāṣṭrīya kīrtan, the Prospectus lays bare the institution's nationalist aims.

> The aim of this institution will be to train a band of preachers, who will inculcate in the minds of the public the eternal values of our culture and at the same time dissuade them [from] those practices which have become absolute or anachronistic with the march of science or passage of time. A citizen is the custodian and torchbearer of his culture.
>
> The aim is not to emphasize the other worldly ideal of moksa or liberation, to the exclusion of the other ideals, namely morality, wealth and enjoyment. Again *equal stress is laid on National Integration and democratic values: Liberty, Equality and Fraternity*. Role of the eminent builders of modern India is also explained. (emphasis mine)

Kīrtan is posited not as a means to inculcate philosophical and moral lessons from the purāṇas and bhakti literature but as a path toward "National Integration" and as a way to teach citizens about the liberal principles of "Liberty, Equality, and Fraternity." In other words, kīrtan is a vessel that can be filled with new content rather than a genre with an associated body of literature. The Prospectus presents an official version of the aims of the Mahāvidyālaya and may emphasize the democratic qualities of kīrtan in order to appeal for government support. The syllabus demonstrates more interest in "other worldly ideals" than in National Integration, and lecturers may have decided to either follow or disregard both the syllabus and the prospectus.

CONCLUSIONS

The 1950s and 1960s represented a period of transition for rāṣṭrīya kīrtankārs in Maharashtra. With the elation of Indian independence came the pain of partition and its many aftershocks. Nathuram Godse expressed the RSS and Hindu Mahasabha sentiment that Gandhi was responsible for partition, and when he killed Gandhi he contributed to a widening of the divide between Brahmans and non-Brahmans and a loss of popular support for Hindu nationalist organizations. Because there was a trend away from Brahman leadership in post-Independence Maharashtra—particularly in rural areas—kīrtankārs like Kolhatkar did not find the same degree of mass support that they had before 1948. Moreover, after the goal of Independence from colonial rule was achieved, he and some other rāṣṭrīya kīrtankārs moved away from nationalist material to focus on spiritual issues.

The fate of Gadge Maharaj, Kaikadi Maharaj, and other low caste kīrtankārs from rural areas was different. They continued to capture the admiration of audiences and helped to shape new imaginations of both nation and state. By buttressing state policies through their colorful, participatory kīrtans, these kīrtankārs also earned state support. This modest government support for kīrtankārs was so successful that by the 1980s, some kīrtankārs—including Brahman nāradīya kīrtankārs—were awarded government titles and monthly stipends to generate enthusiasm for state initiatives. Govinda Khare and Manjushree Khadilkar, both nāradīya kīrtankārs from Pune, were among the most popular of these kīrtankārs.

During the 1970s and 1980s, Congress hegemony in Maharashtra and India was weakened in part by the abuses of Indira Gandhi's two-year state of emergency, which contributed to the gradual mainstreaming of Hindu nationalist discourse and political organizations. In this political climate, Govindswami Aphale found enthusiastic audiences for his stirring, entertaining rāṣṭrīya kīrtans, and G. N. Koparkar appealed to activists seeking scriptural support for Hindutva views. When Aphale, Koparkar, and the Bharatiya Vidya Bhavan opened kīrtan universities, the conservative branch of Congress lent support. Their collective goals, however, were so out of sync with prevailing ideas regarding university education that these Mahāvidyālayas collapsed after roughly a decade. The urban audiences for Marathi nāradīya and rāṣṭrīya kīrtan were small enough that it was difficult to recruit middle-class people to become full-time kīrtankārs without also offering them an ongoing government stipend. The cohort of rāṣṭrīya kīrtankārs was small during this time, but a resurgence of Hindu nationalism that would breathe new life into the genre waited just around the corner.

5

The Re-Institutionalization of Marathi Kīrtan

Hindutva Networks and Gender

The Akhil Bhāratīya Kīrtan Sammelan (All India Kīrtan Conference) was held in Nagpur,[1] January 21–23, 2000, in a conference center at the site of K. B. Hedgewar's passing (referred to as his *samādhi*[2] by RSS volunteers). He was the founder of the Rashtriya Swayamsevak Sangh. The Akhil Bhāratīya Kīrtan Kula (All India Kīrtan Family) organized the event with assistance from the local chapter of the RSS, and indeed many of the Kīrtan Kula officeholders were also RSS and/or Vishwa Hindu Parishad volunteers. Before traveling to Nagpur, I had only barely glimpsed the hand of the RSS in Kula-sponsored kīrtans in Pune, but my lingering doubts were removed by the presence of RSS head Rajendra Singh as chief guest, the conversations I had with kīrtankārs about their dual affiliations, and the proud invocation of Hedgewar in speeches. Almost as soon as the relationship between the two organizations crystallized before me, however, did I find that some kīrtankārs within the Kula actively resisted connections with the RSS and others declined participation in the Kula because of its Hindutva-ization.

The Akhil Bhāratīya Kīrtan Kula was founded in 1992 with a mission of "binding together kīrtankārs and pravacankārs from the entire country,"[3] a task that met with remarkable success in the eight years leading up to the Nagpur Sammelan. It seems no coincidence that the founding of the Kīrtan Sammelan coincided with the year that the Babri Mosque in Ayodhya was torn down by Hindu *kārsevaks* (volunteers) of the Bharatiya Janata Party, RSS, and VHP who claimed that the mosque was built on the spot of Rāma's birth. An elderly kīrtankār and RSS volunteer told me at the Sammelan that the Sangh and the Kula actually "have the same purpose," which is the "upliftment of the Hindu people" who are becoming disturbed by television and Western influence.[4] While the traditionalist orientation of Marathi kīrtan produces a particularly neat fit with the RSS, this kīrtankār told me that the RSS "uses any medium to do its work." Indeed, the RSS lends support not only to regional performance genres like kīrtan, but also to Hindustani music, Indipop, or any other genre through which it can spread its ideology.[5]

This turn-of-the-millennium Hindu national populist orientation marks a significant change from the last major wave of rāṣṭrīya kīrtan during the anti-colonial movement. Several of the Sammelan's inaugural speeches referenced the sammelan that Tilak had chaired eighty-two years prior, positioning their newly strengthened Kīrtan Kula and kīrtan sammelans in relation to this august past. For example, in their "Two Words" of introduction to the souvenir volume distributed at the 2000 Sammelan, the editors wrote:

> In the year 1918, with the guidance and chairmanship of Lokmanya Tilak, the second conference was held on the 15th and 16th of January, but this was for all intents and purposes the first All India Kīrtan Sammelan. In his speech, Lokmanya Tilak provided kīrtankārs with an accurate compass for contemporary times, and they received right and proper guidance. [In the interim sammelans,] . . . It was decided that kīrtan pāṭhshāḷās, kīrtan *vidyālayas*, kīrtan mahāvidyālayas, and kīrtan *vidyāpīths* [different words for schools and universities] should be founded. There have been intermittent discussions at sammelans about the form of kīrtan—and specifically, the purpose of ākhyāns—in contemporary times. Those topics are relevant even today.[6] (Shevalkar 2000: 3)

This past is invoked to illustrate continuity with the present, but the invitation to comparison also exposes differences in meaning and context. During Tilak's time, nāradīya kīrtan was more integrated into Maharashtrian Hindu experience, but it later became a marginal pursuit for those who are elderly or traditionalist. Since the 1990s, however, audiences for rāṣṭrīya kīrtan are growing. Kīrtan's Hindu themes, ritual contexts, Brahman singer/preachers, and historical depth render it an easy fit for sanghatana discourse, and early twentieth-century rāṣṭrīya kīrtan nationalist repertoires have been adopted and re-signified by 1990s Hindutva activists. Although kīrtan is discursively ripe for new Hindu nationalist appropriation, it is still performed mainly in old neighborhoods and employs literary forms and musical styles that are opaque to young people who live in ever-expanding suburbs with mass media soundscapes. I told more than one young cosmopolitan in Pune that I was researching Marathi kīrtan, only to learn that she either hadn't heard of Marathi kīrtan or didn't know that kīrtans are performed daily in temples throughout the city.

How does this old temple genre of devotional songs and stories not only continue to attract audiences but also expand? Much of this can be attributed to the organizational efforts of the Akhil Bhāratīya Kīrtan Kula, who have taken cues from the smoothly organized RSS and VHP. Kīrtans sponsored by the Kula attract large audiences—often in the hundreds or even thousands—through keen publicity that articulates the relevance of kīrtan for late twentieth, early twenty-first century life. By way of contrast, the most dependable place to hear nāradīya kīrtan in Pune is the Nārad Maṅdir in the old neighborhood of Sadashiv Peth, where the Harikīrtanottejak Sabhā presents kīrtans every day of the year to a small audience that rarely exceeds thirty listeners. The foregrounding of Hindu nationalist agendas and expansion of the dramatic and musical aspects of kīrtan performance render it more entertaining for those who sympathize with its messages but may have little knowledge of old song genres or paurāṇik texts. That said, Hindu nationalist rāṣṭrīya kīrtan is more appealing to traditionalist and Brahman-centric members of Hindu nationalist organizations than it is to those organizations' jeans-wearing, Indipop-loving constituents.

In this chapter, I discuss how the Akhil Bhāratīya Kīrtan Kula and other Pune/Mumbai kīrtan organizations are reshaping kīrtan aesthetics, goals, and contexts in late twentieth and early twenty-first century Maharashtra. This assessment of contemporary rāṣṭrīya kīrtan performance contexts and pedagogy will lead to an analytical discussion in Chapters 6 through 8 of kīrtan's affective power to generate nationalist devotion. One of the most significant changes in late twentieth-century nāradīya kīrtan is the increase of women performers, who are in turn re-gendering kīrtan aesthetics. The Harikīrtanottejak Sabhā in Pune and the Akhil Bhāratīya Kīrtan Saṅsthā in Mumbai have initiated kīrtan pedagogies that facilitate women's participation. Kīrtan's respectability and the value placed on women's education in Maharashtrian cities has eased the entry of women into the nāradīya kīrtan world, but female rāṣṭrīya kīrtankārs have a more difficult time negotiating the masculine-coded *vīr* (brave) rasa without challenging traditional modes of femininity.

KĪRTAN COMMUNITIES AND KĪRTAN PEDAGOGY IN CONTEMPORARY PUNE AND MUMBAI

To appreciate the impact of the Akhil Bhāratīya Kīrtan Kula on nāradīya and rāṣṭrīya kīrtan performance in Pune and beyond, I begin with a broad overview of the communities that currently support kīrtan performance and instruction. In Pune, the main nāradīya kīrtan communities include the Nārad Maṅdir (Harikīrtanottejak Sabhā), the community of people associated with the late G. N. Koparkar and his śiṣya Sudhatai Dhamankar,[7] and the Akhil

Bhāratīya Kīrtan Kula. In Mumbai, the main kīrtan organization is the Akhil Bhāratīya Kīrtan Saṅsthā, which is housed in a Viṭṭhala temple in the bustling Marathi neighborhood of Dadar. While the Akhil Bhāratīya Kīrtan Saṅsthā and the Nārad Maṅdir engage in many of the same activities as the Kīrtan Kula, the Kula is distinct in its aspirations to incorporate all kīrtankārs in Maharashtra and throughout India, as well as in its insistence on foregrounding nationalist discourses. Of course, not all kīrtankārs are affiliated with one of these organizations; many others were disciples to a parent or other guru and perform kīrtans independently.

I studied kīrtan according to the guru-śiṣya method from Vaman Kolhatkar, the only child of Vasudeo Kolhatkar to continue the elder Kolhatkar's kīrtan tradition (see Plate 5.1). When I first arrived in Pune, I considered learning kīrtan to enhance my understanding of how kīrtan is taught, to acquire more specific information about song genres and narrative style, and to develop relationships with kīrtankārs, but I didn't want to be associated with American/European spiritual converts to Hinduism who romanticize India while remaining naive to the social and political contexts of Indian religious belief. Kolhatkarbuva understood my concerns but encouraged me to learn kīrtan "for the experience" (as he would tell his friends). Having made the decision to teach me, he insisted that we should meet at least two or three times per week, which we did from October 1999 through December 2000. He refused to accept any money from me for lessons, saying that it was his duty to pass on his knowledge.

Vamanbuva's kīrtans are witty, cynical, erudite, and lively, and he sings with a rhythmic certainty born of the many years spent accompanying his father's kīrtans on the tablā. Like his father, he emphasizes the subtle shades of meaning in weighty philosophical texts, but he explains complex ideas with ample use of familiar examples so that I never feel bored or confused during his kīrtans. Indeed, Kolhatkar's Sanskritic knowledge and engaging delivery make his purvarangas among the best I have heard, and though his singing is very nice, he has only recently begun taking classical singing lessons. Vaman Kolhatkar's father had sent him to study the Vedas with a guru in lieu of Western style education, but after his eleventh year of study, the young Vaman decided that he did not want to finish. He had become fascinated with Vedic math and sciences and decided to study at the university. In one year, he was able to catch up with other students who were graduating from high school, took his exams, graduated, and studied math and physics at Poona University. He now runs a busy physics laboratory at his home, where students come to prepare for their college practical exams. Kolhatkarbuva, his wife, his son, and his four daughters (when they were still at home) help students with the experiments and explain physical concepts to them when they need assistance. His laboratory is called "Gaṇit Maṅdir," or mathematics temple, reflecting his dual interest in religion and mathematics.

Plate 5.1.
Vaman Kolhatkar at his home, 2009. Photograph by Mark Nye.

When his students leave at 6:00, Kolhatkarbuva conducts a daily purāṇa in his home in which he reads from, recites, and expounds upon a selected paurāṇik text to a small audience. In recent years, the pace of the Gaṇit Maṅdir has slowed and he is able to accept more invitations to perform kīrtan. During my last trip to Pune in 2009, he was performing kīrtans on the final portion of the Mahabharata at the Khunya Murlidhar temple in the Sadashiv Peth neighborhood (see Plate 5.2). Vaman Kolhatkar is a very traditional, even orthodox Brahman who will not eat "outside" (i.e., outside of the home) at all. From daybreak to sundown, he performs daily rituals in accordance with the Vedic tradition of his guru. Following strict guidelines, when his wife cooks, she purifies herself and will not touch anyone until the meal is finished. Despite this orthodoxy, Vaman Kolhatkar remains aloof from contemporary political appropriations of these practices. He is relatively detached from the kīrtan community, and though he sometimes teaches at the Nārad Maṅdir, he generally does not attend functions organized by the Nārad Maṅdir, Akhil Bhāratīya Kīrtan Kula, or other kīrtan groups.

Kolhatkarbuva spent the bulk of my lesson time expounding on classical Hindu philosophical concepts such as the three *guṇas* (qualities) of *sattva* (truth, essential core), *rajas* (activity, excitation), and *tamas* (inertia, ignorance). Because he values Sanskritic knowledge and philosophy, he taught me these

Plate 5.2.
Vaman Kolhatkar performing kīrtan at Khunya Murlidhar Temple. Pune 2009.

concepts divorced from any particular kīrtan with an eye toward a future in which I could recall these ideas extemporaneously in a kīrtan. Kolhatkarbuva taught me only one kīrtan over the course of about fifteen months; the ākhyān was by his father and we created the purvaranga together. He encouraged me to put my own unique flavor into the ākhyān and to paraphrase as long as I did not leave out key elements of the story. Songs were the only fixed, pre-composed elements of the kīrtan that Kolhatkarbuva taught me, but he spent less time with them because he prioritizes philosophy over music. Most of the songs featured tunes composed by his uncle with lyrics by his father. A few songs were in newly composed tunes, but many of the songs used standard melodies and poetic meters, including sāki, āryā, abhaṅga, and povāḍā. Kolhatkarbuva was insistent that I learn the tunes and rhythms properly, but (with a few exceptions) he did not encourage me to sing in classical rāgas with classical improvisation. As is typical of transmission in the guru śiṣya paradigm, Vaman Kolhatkar taught me his unique perspective on kīrtan performance, which had in turn been shaped by his experiences learning from his father. This relaxed instructional structure allowed me to gradually imbibe concepts that I could later remember and reorder as needed. Classroom-based kīrtan institutions, on the other hand, emphasize memorization of kīrtans in which discourse, story, and songs are all pre-composed.

The Harikīrtanottejak Sabhā at Nārad Maṅdir, founded in 1883, has been a hub for kīrtan instruction in Pune since the 1930s and has presented daily kīrtans for the last forty years.[8] Instruction at Nārad Maṅdir contrasts significantly from the individualized, flexible approach to transmission I experienced with Kolhatkarbuva. In May 2000, I became a student in the Harikīrtanottejak Sabhā's Vāsantik Kīrtan Śibīr (Spring Kīrtan School), a month-long intensive program. Before participating in the śibīr, I went to kīrtans alone and spoke with kīrtankārs and musicians, but did not know many listeners by name. After participating in the kīrtan śibīr, I felt much more incorporated into the community of listeners and became friendly with a few women and a group of teenage girls. Like other students, my interest in performing kīrtan grew from my interest in attending kīrtan and it enhanced my participation in kīrtan as a listener. Students at Nārad Maṅdir recognized that they were doing something unusual and often asked each other why they were taking the course. Through these student-initiated conversations, I learned that students' primary motivations could be grouped into either an artistic or a religious category. Two middle-aged women in the class said they were learning because they wanted to make use of their backgrounds in other performance genres—one had studied classical music and the other had been a stage actor. A younger woman brought her two young sons to the class and decided it would be more interesting to participate rather than just wait for her sons to finish. The students who participated with the greatest zeal were children, many of them aspiring to be professional kīrtankārs when they reach adulthood. Several students were children of kīrtankārs and many of them had been learning kīrtan independently from a parent. These students joined the class to supplement the knowledge they received at home and to become part of a community of kīrtan students. An older student asked a teenage girl why she joined the class and she responded by saying, "Because I love God!" as if there were no other answer.

Students at the Nārad Maṅdir spring śibīr memorize "ready-made" kīrtans (as one kīrtankār told me with tongue-in-cheek) and are introduced to the musical/rhetorical skills necessary for kīrtan performance. The instructors teach each group to perform a kīrtan from one of two kīrtan books written by Nārad Maṅdir's late adhyakṣa, Bhaskar Ramchandra Ghaisas, or Ghaisas Guruji as his students respectfully addressed him. The full course is spread out over five years of one-month spring śibīrs, and each student becomes eligible to pass on to the next "year" if he or she passes the exams at the end of the month-long course. The curriculum consists of Memorization, Music, Tāla, Pūrvaraṅga, and Uttararaṅga—each subject taught by a different teacher—and the exam is in two parts. The written portion tests memorization of songs, Sanskrit verses, and musical concepts, and the practical portion consists of a solo performance of the given year's kīrtan. Passing the course was far from given, and one girl in my class was in "year one" for the third time. Over the course of the five-year śibīr, students learn the basic performance requirements of kīrtan and are equipped with five memorized kīrtans.

Before retirement, Ghaisas Guruji had been a Sanskrit teacher at a Pune high school, where he had, coincidentally, been Vaman Kolhatkar's teacher during the one year that Kolhatkar was in Western-style school.[9] Like Koparkar and Aphale, he had learned kīrtan at the Nārad Maṅdir when the instruction method was more akin to the guru-śiṣya tradition. When I studied at the vāsantik śibīr, Ghaisas Guruji not only oversaw the curriculum but also taught the pūrvaraṅga. Since the pūrvaraṅga was given in his textbook, Ghaisas Guruji spent most of the class providing details about the etymology of Sanskrit terms we were using. In the latter half of the course, he called students up to the front of the class so they could practice performing the pūrvaraṅga. The uttararaṅga was taught in a similar way, though less time was spent explaining the uttararaṅga since the import of the story was more readily grasped.

At the beginning of each day, the various "years" came together to sing the *mangaḷācaraṇ* (series of invocatory songs and prayers) in unison as it is performed in the Nārad Maṅdir paṭhaḍī. There was very little explanation or instruction for this portion of the class, and it was assumed that daily repetition would serve to solidify our singing of the pieces. Following the mangaḷācaraṇ, classes were split up according to years and each group went to a different area in the temple compound. The class was open to people of all ages, and students ranged in age from about eight to about seventy. There were approximately thirty students in my class and, as in temples, men and boys sat on one side of the room while women and girls sat on the other side. Most of the students were Brahmans from the old, conservative Brahman neighborhood of Sadashiv Peth that surrounded Nārad Maṅdir.

Like Pune, Mumbai boasts an active kīrtan scene and is home to a thriving kīrtan institution called the Akhil Bhāratīya Kīrtan Saṅsthā. This organization was founded in Dadar, Mumbai, in 1940 by a kīrtankār named Govind Ganesh Bhosekar and a singer/scholar named Shankarrao Balwant Kulkarni at the height of the Quit India movement. The founders created the Saṅsthā to consolidate the efforts of kīrtankārs working to "awaken society" regarding matters nationalist, social, and religious. According to the Saṅsthā's former director, Dinanath Joshi, its "backbone" was the Kīrtan Vidyālaya (school) founded in 1948 (Joshi 2000: 12–13). The founders created a five-year course (it is now three years) that culminates in the awarding of the title of *kīrtanalankār*. When I last visited the Akhil Bhāratīya Kīrtan Saṅsthā, which occupies two floors of the Viṭṭhala Maṅdir in Dadar, the kīrtan vidyālaya was in session and a group of mostly female students were seated on the floor learning songs relevant for kīrtan (see Plate 5.3). Nowadays, the vidyālaya employs three teachers: a *prācārya* (professor) who is a kīrtankār, a singing teacher, and a tāla and tablā teacher.[10] There are also annual themed kīrtan festivals, such as the Children's Kīrtan Festival (Balkīrtan Mahotsav)[11] and the Women's Kīrtan Festival.

Both the Akhil Bhāratīya Kīrtan Saṅsthā and the Harikīrtanottejak Sabhā were founded to systematize the training of kīrtankārs, but their current students are primarily amateurs devoting only a couple of hours per week to kīrtan. Given that both of these schools have been operating successfully for over half a century, it seems that they have realistically judged how the curriculum should adjust to a changing post-colonial economy. The now defunct kīrtan universities discussed in the previous chapter, by contrast, fell under the weight of much grander plans for modern professionalization. According to former administrators and teachers in those universities, students were not committed enough to keep up with the demanding curriculum. Given the modest financial rewards of kīrtan, very few kīrtankārs can maintain a middle-class lifestyle as a full-time kīrtankār, making it unsurprising that students' commitments were divided. Indeed, the few kīrtankārs who can support themselves through kīrtan have generally received training and prestige from a parent/guru rather than from a kīrtan school. The more modest commitment required of students at the Akhil Bhāratīya Kīrtan Saṅsthā and Harikīrtanottejak Sabhā are appropriate for those who become part-time kīrtankārs or pursue kīrtan as a hobby.

Plate 5.3.
The author visiting the Kīrtan Vidyālaya of the Akhil Bhāratīya Kīrtan Saṅsthā, Mumbai, 2009. Photograph by Mark Nye.

MARATHI IDIOMS AND NATIONAL IDENTITY AT KĪRTAN KULA EVENTS

As a multifaceted institution, the Akhil Bhāratīya Kīrtan Kula has much grander designs than the Akhil Bhāratīya Kīrtan Saṅsthā and the Harikīrtanottejak Sabhā. The Kīrtan Kula sponsors śibīrs along the lines of those older kīrtan institutions, but devotes most of its efforts toward staging individual kīrtans, kīrtan mahotsavs (festivals), and huge kīrtan sammelans. The main priority of the Kīrtan Kula, as told to me by officeholders in the organization and as detailed in many of their publications, is to unite all kīrtankārs and pravancankārs, not just in Maharashtra but throughout India and even the world (Shevde et al., 2000: back cover). The Kula has made impressive inroads toward its goal of gaining the membership of all Marathi kīrtankārs, having enlisted 537 members and founding twenty-six *shākhā* (branches) by 2001.[12]

The Akhil Bhāratīya Kīrtan Kula has been instrumental in creating a public perception of kīrtan as a nationalist activity by presenting kīrtans on proscenium stages where they become available for nationalist framing through Hindutva speeches. Many officeholders in the Kīrtan Kula are also active in the VHP and the RSS, and most of the Kula events I attended were peppered with speeches on how kīrtan should be protected from the onslaught of Westernization or on how Hinduism can unite the nation. The Kula's nationalist discourse is distilled in the phrase "*dev, deś, dharma*" (God, country, religion), which appears in songs, publications, and speeches of the Kula. There has also been an increase in the performance of Hindu nationalist rāṣṭrīya kīrtan at Kula events, and the Akhil Bhāratīya Kīrtan Kula sponsored two rāṣṭrīya kīrtan festivals in the Pune area in 2000, one of them attracting a huge crowd. Though this has been the prevailing trend of the Kula, many members and even some officeholders are opposed to the convergence of kīrtan and Hindu nationalist groups. A former director of one of the Kula branches is strongly against Hindu nationalism and has threatened to leave the Kula many times because of their associations with the RSS and VHP. Other kīrtankārs belong to the RSS but oppose moves by the Kula to forge connections with the Sangh Parivār, but I heard no kīrtans and only one speech that denounced Hindu nationalism.[13]

Kīrtan Kula events are sometimes held in temples but are more often performed on stage in permanent or temporary concert halls. In kīrtan performances not sponsored by the Kīrtan Kula, the kīrtankār enters the temple, does namaskār to the deity, and immediately begins the kīrtan. The host saves his or her announcements and words of thanks for the intermission between the pūrvaraṅga and uttararaṅga. In kīrtans sponsored by the Kula, on the other hand, it is common for the kīrtankār to begin performing only after a series of talks introducing the event, its significance, and the background of the kīrtankār. In such performances, an honored guest lights an oil lamp in front of images of a deity, a saint, or a deceased kīrtankār, and then Kula officials and invited guests give speeches on the cultural and national importance of kīrtan. The hosts and guests are seated in a row of chairs on the stage, most often behind a long table. After the speeches, the Kula host felicitates each guest by presenting him or her with flowers, a shawl, a coconut, and a commemorative plaque, or any combination of these. Finally, the kīrtankār enters the stage and begins the performance.

This style of public ritual is not unique to Kula events but is common to "functions" throughout South Asia. At Kula events, the devotional ritual of kīrtan is framed within a larger Kīrtan Kula institutional ritual that objectifies kīrtan in a manner characteristic of many national/ist performing arts. Similarly, when Hindustani music was moved from the court to the concert hall, it became "Indian" music available for nationalist identification. It was an ideal choice as a nationalist art because it resonated across regions, was historically and sonically distinct from European music, and was a high art appreciated by elites that required years of practice. In order for this potential to become realized, however, Hindustani music needed to become available to the Hindu middle-class nationalist elite. As discussed in Chapter 2, this began happening around the turn of the century through the efforts of musicologists and educators like V. D. Paluskar and V. N. Bhatkhande, who founded schools and organizations that created a middle-class Hindu public of amateur musicians and aficionados (Bakhle 2005). The concert stage was an arena in which middle-class Hindu musicians could perform, and "respectable" students could study at institutions rather than with Muslim hereditary musicians (Qureshi 1991).

As is the case with Hindustani classical music, kīrtan becomes significant as an *emblem* of nationalist identity only when objectified on the concert stage, though rāṣṭrīya kīrtankārs *actively* use Nārad's mat for nationalist purposes in temples and on the street. The stage serves as a "display case" for kīrtan, distancing the kīrtankār from listeners and exhibiting kīrtan as an object needing explication by experts. This distance represents a palpable difference between staged and temple kīrtans; audiences at staged kīrtans traverse a middle ground between the participation of temple kīrtans and the quiet listening of audiences at concerts. In temples and on streets, audience members sit on the floor, sing with the kīrtankār at appropriate moments, and assemble at the front of the performance space to touch the kīrtankār's feet and make an offering before leaving the temple or tent. Listeners at staged kīrtans, in contrast, sit in chairs, sometimes clap after songs as they would at a concert, and rarely touch the kīrtankār's feet following a performance. Kīrtankārs at staged kīrtans do sometimes generate audience involvement in songs, but they are less able to respond to the voices of individual listeners and rarely reach the heightened emotional states that they do in temple kīrtans, when audience and kīrtankār merge at key points during the event.

THE 2000 ALL INDIA KĪRTAN SAMMELAN AND THE RSS

Following the kīrtan sammelans chaired by Tilak and Munje in the 1910s, there were semi-regular kīrtan sammelans throughout the twentieth century, and the Akhil Bhāratīya Kīrtan Kula began organizing sammelans after its founding in 1992. The 2000 Akhil Bhāratīya Kīrtan Sammelan in Nagpur was held at what participants called the "samādhi" of Keshav Baliram Hedgewar, the man who founded the RSS in 1925. Samādhi is the term used to refer to the place where a saint permanently leaves his or her body after entering a deep trance, so referring to Hedgewar's memorial as a samādhi accords him the special prestige of a saint. Rajendra Singh (known as "Rajju Bhaiya" to followers), national RSS chief at the time, not only lit the oil lamp at Hedgewar's samādhi to inaugurate the 2000 Kīrtan Sammelan but also gave one of the first speeches at the event. The samādhi shrine is nestled within a meeting center called "Om Bhavan" that houses an RSS school and leases space to various organizations for programs such as the Kīrtan Sammelan (see Plate 5.4).

The organizers of the Sammelan included members of the Akhil Bhāratīya Kīrtan Kula and the RSS, and many participants belonged to both groups.

Plate 5.4.
Students of an RSS school in front of the Hedgewar Samādhī. Nagpur 2000.

Kīrtankārs had varied assessments of the RSS contribution to the Sammelan; those who supported connections between the Kula and the RSS regarded the RSS involvement as quite significant, while those who were opposed to the connection downplayed the RSS's contribution. I asked one Kula member if the Sammelan was sponsored by the RSS and he said no, that they had only rented the space because it was convenient for such a conference. The impression I got from RSS *swayamsevak* (volunteers) was quite different; they described themselves as the real organizers and masterminds behind the event.

At the beginning of this chapter, I mentioned a kīrtankār's statement that the RSS seeks to become involved in "any medium." This sentiment was echoed by other swayamsevaks with whom I spoke at the Sammelan and reflects an important RSS strategy. Through their "volunteer work" with arts and cultural organizations, they attempt to change the discourses of those organizations and contribute to a gradual Hindutva-ization of public discourse. This excerpt from a lengthy RSS Mission Statement highlights the RSS strategy of establishing Hindu nationalist dominance by "engulfing" all aspects of Hindu social and cultural life:

> The aim of the Sangh is to organise the entire Hindu society, and not just to have a Hindu organisation within the ambit of this society. Had it been the latter, then the Sangh too would have added one more number to the already existing thousands of creeds. Though started as an institution, the aim of the Sangh is to expand so extensively that each and every individual and traditional social institution like family, caste, profession, educational and religious institutions etc., are all to be ultimately engulfed into its system. The goal before the Sangh is to have an organised Hindu society in which all its constituents and institutions function in harmony and co-ordination, just as in the body organs.[14]

The Akhil Bhāratīya Kīrtan Kula aspires to become a national entity, despite the fact that its members and officials are Marathi kīrtankārs, its functions are held in Maharashtra, and all of the literature and speeches at Kula events are in Marathi. Token efforts are, however, made to include non-Maharashtrian kīrtankārs—Telugu, Tamil, and Sikh kīrtankārs at the 2000 Sammelan were invited to present twenty-minute kīrtans, and Marathi kīrtankārs performed Hindi, Gujarati, Kannada, and Sanskrit kīrtans in the Marathi nāradīya kīrtan idiom. With the exception of the Sikh kīrtankārs, the visiting kīrtankārs performed to the accompaniment of a "house" ensemble of tablā and harmonium. The expertise of the accompanying musicians led them to play in a nāradīya kīrtan style, which resulted in a "Marathification" of the music in the non-Marathi kīrtans. While Marathi experts were invited to discuss various issues surrounding Marathi kīrtan performance at length and without interruption, the Tamil scholar presenting a lecture-demonstration on Tamil harikatha was allotted only twenty minutes.

The Kula's "All-India" name but Marathi orientation speaks to an ongoing tension between regionalism and nationalism in India that has roots in the colonial era. To mark difference from the British, colonial era, nationalists turned to mother tongues and indigenous artistic media; but because of the vast diversity of languages and cultures in India, "mother tongue" policies threatened the integrity of pan-Indian national identity. Making Hindi a national language was offered as a means to unify India linguistically while maintaining indigenous identity, but this met with only partial success since Hindi remained a second language for many Indians. In Maharashtra, Lokmanya Tilak advocated Marathi language education, media, and performance, and his Gaṇeś and Shivaji Festivals generated national sentiment for Marathi speakers. Similarly, the Akhil Bhāratīya Kīrtan Kula does not attempt to create a nation of Marathi speakers but instead renders Hindu nationalism in a language and idiom with emotional resonance for a particular set of Maharashtrian Brahmans.

The large scale and smooth efficiency of the Akhil Bhāratīya Kīrtan Sammelan attest to the organizational power of the tandem forces of the Kīrtan Kula and the RSS. Most of the 2000 Sammelan events took place on stage in a large semi-permanent tent, with audiences ranging from a few hundred to a few thousand. The whole opening ceremony was structured like the beginning of a Kula kīrtan, beginning with the lighting of oil lamps. Following this inauguration, several kīrtankārs gathered on the stage for a sort of "meta-naman," beginning with the Kula *ghoṣgīt* (repeating song) composed by H. Bh. P. Narayanbuva Kane (see Plate 5.5). This nationalist tune in Raga Kāfi is performed at the beginning of most Kula events. The downbeats in the ghoṣgīt are consistently emphasized, which contrasts with the shifting accent patterns of most devotional songs. The song's militaristic rhythm evokes for me a Scottish 6/8 march[15] that underscores the political aspects of this religious/devotional song, while rāga kāfi indexes Hindustani "light music" and marks the song as distinct from Western marches. Kīrtankār-listeners are asked to increase *deśdharma* (religion of the nation), in which Hinduism is regarded as the original and only legitimate religion of India. This song suggests that "national unity" can be achieved through religious means (see Musical Example 5.1).

Come, let us do harikathā, let us dance to the tune of kīrtan
Let us increase *deśdharma*, the ancient culture //dhru//

Shrihari's advice, Nārad's message
Let us do kīrtan discourse, let us perform the nation's treasure (*bhāgya*)
Let us dance tall, tall, let us raise countless new flags //1//

Let us sing kathās of bravery on religious heroes in kīrtan
Let us plant the seed of dharma in the hearts of the people
This is our duty, let us remember this every moment //2//

Today dharma has been corrupted, it has gone mad
Kindness is depleted, national unity is broken
Let us behave according to true dharma, let us awaken people's hearts //3//

The vision of intelligence, the vision of action, give us complete vision
Let the people be happy, let the world live in peace
Let us pray like this in the tune of kīrtan //4//[16]

The same group of kīrtankārs who sang the ghoṣgīt then performed a standard nāradīya kīrtan naman, a bhajan, and jayjaykārs with enthusiastic audience participation. These songs were followed by the speeches and *satkārs* (felicitations) characteristic of Kula events, many of them tinged with Hindu nationalist content. A vārkarī leader was given a biography of V. D. Savarkar, and other speakers were presented with kīrtan cassettes and books about kīrtan. Most of the speeches that followed the satkārs made reference to kīrtan's nationalist role, and one speaker said that the "object of the Kīrtan Kula is to create national unity."

Babasaheb Salpekar, a Nagpur kīrtankār who hosted the Sammelan, noted that Tilak was the adhyakṣa of earlier sammelans when India was under colonial rule, but argued that Indians are still mentally enslaved by the West. The role of the kīrtankār, he said, should be to help people become free mentally, just as they helped Tilak to achieve political freedom in earlier years.

> Lokmanya graced the sammelan as chairman during colonial times, during slavery. Today we are a sovereign nation and are independent. On the world map, Hindustan is definitely an independent nation, but have we been freed from

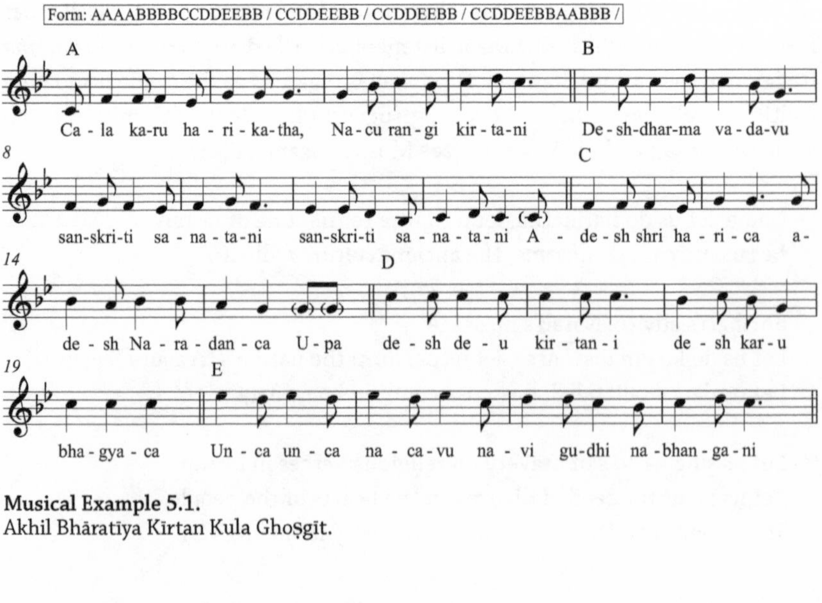

Musical Example 5.1.
Akhil Bhāratīya Kīrtan Kula Ghoṣgīt.

Plate 5.5.
Kīrtankārs singing ghoṣgīt. Nagpur 2000.

> slavery? Today the meaning of slavery is the same. Only the context has changed. By taking the material path, we have become burdened with mental slavery. It is propagated in every home, and society has accepted slavery while sitting at home. So many people believe that television and radio, rather than kīrtan, are the ways to power and social progress, and through these media, our society is being led into an uncontrolled atmosphere. Echoes of this are clearly visible. Every day crime is increasing. Through material means, we try to bring happiness, peace, and tranquility to society; we avoid the path of spiritual self-improvement and turn blindly to the western thoughts and customs. Is this not mental slavery? Once again, the responsibility of bringing society out of slavery has fallen on kīrtankārs. Kīrtan is an excellent medium for awakening people.... Through the doors of this medium, kīrtankārs can raise the thoughts and religion of all levels of society. This means that the haridās is an excellent servant of this nation. Therefore, Lokmanya Tilak said, "If I hadn't become a newspaper publisher, I would have been a kīrtankār." (Salpekar 2000: 168–169)[17]

Salpekar explains first how "mechanical" media lead to mental servitude with relation to the West, and then demonstrates how kīrtankārs act as "servant[s] of the nation" by leading audiences toward mental freedom. In this short segment, Salpekar argues that kīrtankārs are important for achieving the twin goals of nationalism: sovereignty (here mental sovereignty) and creation of a nation (by creating a good "atmosphere" among people from all social classes).

The Shankaracharya of Karveer Peeth, who is the Kula's adhyakṣa, spoke on how the nation needs kīrtan to fight against sociopolitical ills such as the conversion of *ādivāsis* (indigenous people) to Christianity (see Plate 5.6). The master of ceremonies concluded the opening ceremony by saying, "Bhārat Mātā [Mother India] is happy now." Indeed, this ceremony served to contextualize the entire Sammelan as a Hindu nationalist event and the kīrtans performed within as expressions of "national unity."

The remainder of the Sammelan consisted of a long series of twenty-minute Marathi nāradīya kīrtans, though as mentioned earlier, there were a few performances of non-Marathi kīrtans as well as daily vārkarī kīrtans. In much the same way that a kīrtankār collects songs to fit his or her narrative, the organizers of the "meta-kīrtan" collected kīrtans to fit their narrative of a national, Hindu, Marathi culture. Since no kīrtankār was allowed to perform for more

Plate 5.6.
The Shankaracharya of Karveer Peeth.

Plate 5.7.
Vārkarīs at the Akhil Bhāratīya Kīrtan Sammelan. Nagpur 2000.

than twenty minutes, the few non-Marathi performers were mere drops in a sea of Marathi. Vārkarī kīrtankārs took the platform after most people had gone to bed and thus their kīrtans were not well attended. Vārkarīs also gathered daily to recite Jñāneśvar's *Haripāṭh* and to dance in two lines as they do while on the vārī (see Plate 5.7). Again, most of the Sammelan attendees did not go to these gatherings and even seemed to find the loud singing and din of the cymbals to be a bit of a nuisance. Nonetheless, it seemed important to have vārkarīs at the Sammelan—perhaps to make inroads into the relatively unpoliticized world of vārkarī kīrtan and to represent the "pure" devotional tradition.

The three Hindu nationalist kīrtans performed at the Sammelan elicited the most enthusiasm from audience members (see Plate 5.8). Each was presented with intense bravado, and the kīrtankārs went to great lengths to overcome the distance created by the stage to transform their listeners into active participants in Hindu nationalist song. Wearing a bright orange pheṭā tied in the manner typical of swayamsevaks, rāṣṭrīya kīrtankār N. S. Apamarjane engaged the audience in rousing and frequent choruses of "Bhārata Mātā ki jay" (victory to Mother India). Performing in Hindi was a nationalist choice for Apamarjane, who began his kīrtan by saying to the audience, "I appreciate your love for Hindi. You are truly a rāṣṭrīya audience because you like the *rāṣṭrabhāṣā* (national language)."[18] Apamarjane's choice was striking because Marathi kīrtankārs generally perform only in Hindi when they travel to Hindi-speaking areas.

Plate 5.8.
The women's section of the audience at a rāṣṭrīya kīrtan during the Akhil Bhāratīya Kīrtan Sammelan. Nagpur 2000.

As Hindu nationalism became mainstreamed in India, rāṣṭrīya kīrtan was resurgent in venues such as the Akhil Bhāratīya Kīrtan Sammelan as well as in smaller performances on streets and in temples (see Plate 5.9). Two branches of the Kula in and around Pune held weeklong rāṣṭrīya kīrtan festivals in September 2000. One of them, held in Pune's Bharata Natya Maṅdir, a hall that usually presents Marathi plays, was filled almost to its capacity of more than a thousand each night for a week. As the Kīrtan Sammelan clearly illustrates, however, this resurgence of rāṣṭrīya kīrtan and Hindu nationalization of nāradīya kīrtan is at least in part a result of the concerted organizational efforts of the RSS. Kīrtan is just one of many cultural realms that the RSS has attempted to organize and transform, but the RSS found a particularly receptive audience in kīrtankārs and found that the long tradition of rāṣṭrīya kīrtan could be resurrected and remade. In Chapter 7, we will encounter a kīrtan that has been reformed in this way.

GENDER AND THE HINDU NATION: ADVICE FOR OTHER WOMEN

One of the most significant changes in post-colonial nāradīya and rāṣṭrīya kīrtan has been the massive increase in numbers of women who study and perform kīrtan. Schools like Nārad Maṅdir and Akhil Bhāratīya Kīrtan Saṅsthā in Mumbai have opened the kīrtan arena to women by presenting opportunities for them to study kīrtan part-time without neglecting their domestic

Plate 5.9.
Rāṣṭrīya kīrtankār Sinnarkarbuva at the Akhil Bhāratīya Kīrtan Sammelan. Nagpur 2000.

responsibilities. Before Independence, women kīrtankārs were almost unheard of; in the 1970s, about 26 percent of nāradīya kīrtankārs were women; and now that number is approximately 40 percent (Schultz 2002: 321).

Despite the large numbers of women kīrtankārs, some male nāradīya kīrtankārs object to women doing kīrtan and argue that there are very few good female performers. In an interview, I asked an outspoken rāṣṭrīya kīrtankār why he was opposed to women kīrtankārs. This was his response:

> Women can do kīrtan on bhakti and iśvar, but they should not give advice in their kīrtans, no more than that. Most of the women kīrtankārs in Pune are not real kīrtankārs. They were trained at the Nārad Maṅdir... and just learned from [a] book. Women from Nārad Maṅdir are only hobbyists and not professional kīrtankārs. There have been no professional men kīrtankārs from Nārad Maṅdir.

Ironically, he was trained at the Nārad Maṅdir, though admittedly this was before the entrenchment of the Harikīrtanottejak Sabhā's formal curriculum, when students still studied according to the guru-śiṣya tradition. Though this kīrtankār was particularly outspoken, his opinion was not unusual among male kīrtankārs who invoked the feminization of nāradīya kīrtan through kīrtan school education as a sign that these schools didn't train "real" kīrtankārs. Indeed, I know very few kīrtankārs, male or female, who are able to rely on entirely on kīrtan as a professional livelihood. Even Charudatta Aphale, Pune's most successful kīrtankār, makes his living through a combination of art music, saṅgīt nāṭak, and kīrtan.

Female rāṣṭrīya kīrtankār Sudhatai Dhamankar is strong and successful, but she reiterates the claim that women are ignorant of matters of philosophy. Kīrtankārs are evaluated in part on the depth of their Sanskritic knowledge, a field that has traditionally been open only to Brāhmaṇ men. Though women do expound on esoteric religious topics in their kīrtans, most female nāradīya kīrtankārs studied with a kīrtankār, while many male nāradīya kīrtankārs obtained at least part of their religious education through discipleship with a knowledgeable pandit or śāstri. Some kīrtankārs, such Halbebuwa and Kannadebuwa work both as priests and as kīrtankārs, and Kolhatkar was a disciple of a Vedic guru for eleven years. Others, like Ghaisas, Apamarjane, and Koparkar, studied Sanskrit at the university level and the former two made their living as Sanskrit teachers.

Even though many women perform kīrtan today, very few of them are professional or full-time kīrtankārs. Those women who have become successful kīrtankārs, such as Sudha Dhamankar and Manjushree Khadilkar, have negotiated their role in the family in creative ways or have circumvented family life completely. Manjushree Khadilkar, the very popular nāradīya kīrtankār with a government contract discussed in the previous chapter, has been able to negotiate the male-dominated kīrtan world not by redefining family responsibility and power but by allowing her husband to manage those aspects of performing kīrtan that require negotiation with men. The late Mr. Khadilkar was a kīrtan advocate, so for Mrs. Khadilkar kīrtan and family are deeply intertwined. Her daughter is a champion singer and her son sometimes accompanies his mother on the tablā. Mrs. Khadilkar is a trained classical musician who comes from a family of well-known singers, and actors, and her outstanding musical skills have contributed to her success.

Sudha (usually called Sudhatai)[19] Dhamankar was born in the 1940s to a Citpāvan Brahman family in a small Maharashtrian town called Wai, which is where she first heard performances by the famous rāṣṭrīya kīrtankār Govindswami Aphale. She tells me that she learned by imitation as a young girl, teaching herself until her talent was recognized. When she moved to the city of Pune, she pursued a college degree in education and a post-graduate degree in kīrtan from the Harikīrtanottejak Sabhā with Aphale and his colleague G. N. Koparkar, who became her primary guru. Sudhatai flouted convention by going (along with her husband) to stay at Koparkar's ashram,

Plate 5.10.
Sudhatai Dhamankar lecturing at the Rām temple of the Tapodham Ashram. Pune Warje, 2009.

where she assisted Koparkar in managing his *vṛddhāśram* (home for elderly people) and propagating his written and preached messages of Hindutva. With both her husband and her guru now deceased, Sudhatai cares for the ashram alone and performs kīrtan when she gets the time and invitations. She has a dedicated cohort of middle-aged Brahman women and some men who regularly attend her kīrtans, lectures, and other functions (see Plate 5.10).

Sudhatai Dhamankar's kīrtans are intense and skillful, and she attracts sizable crowds in which women outnumber men. Her kīrtan stories are often set in the domestic realm, and she peppers her mythological or historical vignettes with reflections on modern-day arranged marriage, joint families, and motherhood, often with a subversive twist. One of her stories highlighted the male bias in arranged marriage and was met with smiles and nods by women and stony silence by men. Sudhatai sings about brave women from the nationalist past, such as Mainavati Peshva, the daughter of a nineteenth-century Maharashtrian ruler who died at the hands of the British rather than divulge her father's whereabouts. She also performs povāḍā in her kīrtans, as in a 2009 kīrtan in which she narrated an episode from the Shiva Mahapurāṇa depicting the return of Manu's son Nabhag, coming back to his family after he had completed his education in the forest with his guru. Sudhatai described

Nabhag's imposing, dagger-clad appearance and invoked the vīr rasa to describe how he held his own when attacked by robbers.

While the percentage of nāradīya kīrtankārs who are women is increasing, there are still very few female vārkarī kīrtankārs. The Akhil Bhāratīya Kīrtan Kula, the Harikīrtanottejak Sabhā, and the Akhil Bhāratīya Kīrtan Saṅsthā provide instruction only in nāradīya kīrtan. The primary institution of vārkarī kīrtan education in Maharashtra is the Vārkarī Śikṣan Saṅsthā (Vārkarī Education Society) in the small pilgrimage town of Alandi, where boys and young men between the ages of fourteen and twenty-one live and study for four years. Since the founding of the organization in 1917, boys of all castes have joined the Vārkarī Śikṣan Saṅsthā, shaved their heads in the manner of learned men, and practiced madhukari, that is, begging for food while receiving an education. Because the main school for vārkarī kīrtan accepts only boys, it is challenging for young women to learn vārkarī kīrtan. Moreover, even if the Vārkarī Śikṣan Saṅsthā did accept women and girls, it is not clear that women would take part in a full-time course given the expectations of rural home-making and the generally lower rate of female education in the rural areas where vārkarī kīrtan is strongest.

The women who do perform vārkarī kīrtan seem to be drawn to issues of nationalism, and they have rejected or radically redefined home and family in order to become kīrtankārs and bhaktas. Gadge Maharaji kīrtankār Mirabai Shirkar was married but left her husband to travel around performing kīrtan during the Quit India movement.[20] Gayabai Manmadkar and her husband became brahmacaryas in 1925—while they were still young—in order to devote themselves to kīrtan and social change.[21]

A third woman kīrtankār, Jaytunbi Maharaj Sayyid, is a Muslim ascetic who lives mainly in her maṭh in the Maharashtrian pilgrimage center of Pandharpur. She performs Islamic *namāz* every day but is also a devotee of Krishna. Her kīrtans are as syncretic as her religious attitudes, combining sufi *qavvāli*, Hindu bhajan, nationalist povāḍā, and Marathi folk genres like goṅdhaḷ and ovī. Jaytunbi began singing bhajans as a young girl, and during the Quit India movement she and her father traveled around performing povāḍā for Nana Patil, a peasant revolutionary and member of the underground government in Maharashtra's Satara district from 1942 to 1946 (Krishnan 2005: 240–243). Before Patil would speak, Jaytunbi and her father would perform povāḍā on the warrior Queen of Jhanshi, Gandhi, King Shivaji, and women's education. In the post-Independence period, she has transferred these skills to rāṣṭrīya kīrtan. To my surprise, Jaytunbi considers her choice to become an ascetic to be more radical than her choice to combine Hinduism and Islam. I asked her if people troubled her because she was a Muslim performing what is essentially a Hindu genre and she said: "They didn't trouble me for that reason, but I have been troubled a lot for being a brahmacarya and not getting married. It was no problem when I was young, only when I was older and still hadn't gotten married."[22] Jaytunbi has many devotees who travel with her on the pilgrimage from Alandi to Pandharpur twice a year and maintain the ashrams in her absence.

Manmadkar, Shirkar, and Jaytunbi were/are all vārkarīs with maṭhas in the major vārkarī pilgrimage centers, but their kīrtan styles are not entirely vārkarī. Dadamaharaj Manmadkar is dismayed at the degree to which women have been shut out from vārkarī kīrtan, and urged me to use my "influence" to try to create a sentiment of acceptance toward women in vārkarī kīrtan. Manmadkar and Shirkar both followed the Gadge Maharaj tradition, and Jaytunbi employs a nāradīya kīrtan structure with some vārkarī, rāṣṭrīya, and Muslim devotional musical and poetic genres. Within the mainstream vārkarī tradition, I know of three female vārkarī kīrtankārs: Shantabai Deshmukh, who has produced cassettes; Bhagavati Maharaj Satarkar, the daughter of the famous kīrtankār Babamaharaj Satarkar; and Miratai Mirikar.[23]

Despite their personal resistance to normative family lives, female kīrtankārs provide only a partial challenge to these same institutions. In an ambivalent woman-centric discourse, Jaytunbi encourages women to serve their *patidev* (husband god) while also providing examples of strong and powerful women. In the following example, Jaytunbi sings a povāḍā on the freedom-fighting Queen of Jhānsi, while a small group of mainly men join her in the chorus of the povāḍā, which she sings in a loud, aggressive style with her characteristically raspy timbre, beginning the long phrases in the higher part of her range and ending them in the lower part. Following this, she invokes powerful Indian women of the past like Ahilyabai Holkar and Indira Gandhi, asking the women in the audience, "what are we doing?" This segues to an invitation for the women to join her in singing a women's genre called ovī, which they do with great enthusiasm. In this song narrating acts of women's devotion in Pandharpur, home of Lord Viṭṭhala, she describes simple acts of women's devotion in women's language. "Ga," for example, is a term of endearment for women with whom one is close. By moving between these two genres, leading first men and then women, Jaytunbi affirmed a gender binary while embodying her fluency within both identities.

- **Povāḍā**: *Mardānī jhānsicī rāṇī, mardānī jhānsicī rāṇī. Mardānī jhānsicī rāṇī jhānsicī rāṇī jhānsicī rāṇī (etc.). (The masculine Queen of Jhānsi).*
- ***Spoken***: *Like this. Mothers in the world have done everything. What are we doing… let's think about this! Therefore I request that you look at what women are doing today, from jhānsicī rāṇī to [unclear]. Look at what they have done. Look at Ahilyabai Holkar and what she did, and think about what we do. In the present day in our Maharashtra, right? In India our Indira Gandhi went into government, right? She is a woman; we are also women. But what has she done and what are we doing? Think about this. Therefore, I invite you sisters…*

• ***Ovī Sung*** *(with women, call-and-response):*

Paṇḍharilā ātā jāu yā ga,	*Let's go to Pandharpur, ga*[24]
Lavkar calā.(Refrain)	*Let's go quickly (refrain).*
Paṇḍharilā jāu,	*Let's go to Pandharpur,*
Candrabhāge nāu,	*Let's bathe in the Candrabhāg,*[25]
Puṇḍalika darśan gheu yā ga,	*Let's see the image of Puṇḍalika,*[26] *ga,*
Lavkar calā.	*Let's go quickly.*
Hār buka gheu,	*Let's take a garland and vermillion powder,*
Vārilā uḍhi lāu,	*Let's raise the flag of pilgrimage,*
Jāu yā ātā, jāu yā ga,	*Let's go now, let's go now, ga,*
Lavkar calā.	*Let's go quickly.*
Hār buka vāu,	*Let's offer a garland and vermillion powder,*
Ḍoḷā Viṭṭhala pāhu,	*Let's look in Viṭṭhala's eyes*
Viṭṭhal darśan gheu yā ga	*Let's see the image of Viṭṭhala,*
Lavkar calā.	*Let's go quickly.*

• ***Spoken****: See how nicely you are singing. Women are really very smart. Women are smart, but sisters, sing one more ovī. Sing!*

• ***Ovī****:*

Āja kokiḷ ga, kokiḷ kuku gāto. (Today the cuckoo sings, ga, the cuckoo sings *kuku*)
Āja kokiḷ ga, kokiḷ kuku gāto.
Rājā Maṅdiri ga, Maṅdiri Rājā hoto, (The king was in the temple, ga, in the temple he was)

+15 more verses on Rāma and Daśaratha

• ***Spoken****: You are singing it very nicely. Keep on doing this. You have come here to take darśan of Māvlī. Do it after going home to do your duties as a wife and mother in your home. Take darśan of your husband. Every one has to do his/her duties. It must be done. And after doing that you can worship God and do other things. Think of your husband as God and take care of him. It will give you a lot of happiness. So ladies, make it a point to look after your husband. These days, girls don't do their duties properly. That is why I am telling you this. Please follow my advice; it will do you good. Be a pativratā (obedient wife). [asks me if I fall at the feet of my husband]. Remember Tulsivrinda, who worshipped God for the life of her husband for twelve years. And asked for a boon saying that I should never become a widow. And Durvās Rishi gave her the boon. This is the lesson you should learn from this story of Tulsivrinda. She was a great pativratā. Call your husband a God, serve your husband, and then take Parameśvar's name. Don't do anything else, (unclear), and do bhajan with love (last two words... starts chant tone).*

As if to underscore the notion that brave women are the stuff of history and mythology, Jaytunbi Maharaj followed the ovī by telling women to cultivate pride in these female heroines but to serve the world by fulfilling their duties as wives and mothers. Despite championing women's service to men, Jaytunbi has herself rejected family life to live the life of a female ascetic (*sādhvī*) and has rejected many markers of womanhood. She does not wear a woman's salvār kuḍtā or sāḍī, but a man's white kuḍtā payjāma and vest (see Plate 5.11). In order to become a successful sādhvī and full-time kīrtankār, she has abandoned key markers of female identity and is known by a male honorific, "Mahārāj" (king). Sonically and physically, she positions herself within the realm of brave women from history, those exceptional women who enter the male domain like the "masculine Queen of Jhānsi."

WOMEN AND THE VĪR RASA

Tucking in the end of one's sari, "padar ghaṭṭ karaṇe" is a gesture of feminine courage and resolve often performed in Marathi kīrtans about brave women. As my friend Ajay explained after such a performance, it would be undignified

Plate 5.11.
Jaytunbi Mahārāj performing kirtan. Alandi 2000.

for a woman's sari to start slipping off her shoulder in the middle of a heated argument. I became intrigued by the possibility that the vīr rasa, or heroic essence, may not be as masculine as its typical narrative contexts of battle suggest and wondered if there are analogous musical gestures of female bravery. In rāṣṭrīya kīrtan, I never found an exact sonic parallel to the tightening of the padar, but did learn that female rāṣṭrīya kīrtankārs use vīr rasa to mold the sentiments of audience members in ways that are less jarring than one might expect given the novelty of women's participation in rāṣṭrīya kīrtan. Although men and women perform the same heroic song genres in rāṣṭrīya kīrtan, the dialogue between rasas in Marathi kīrtan is gendered, and it is at these intersections that women are claiming a heroism of their own. Given the masculine orientation of current Hindu nationalist formations in India, this is a process with profound political implications. The re-gendering of the vīr rasa makes possible an empathetic mode of listening to heroic stories that can produce a uniquely engaged national subjectivity, reproducing masculinist nationalism while sneaking feminist counternarratives in through an aesthetic back door.

Though any type of Marathi song can appear in rāṣṭrīya and nāradīya kīrtan, rāṣṭrīya kīrtans include a heavier dose of those genres coded as "nationalist." These songs appear at moments of heightened excitement, they employ third-person narrative texts, they have strong, driving rhythms in duple meter (usually a laggi), and they are melodically repetitive to facilitate prolonged narration. The genre most characteristic of rāṣṭrīya kīrtan is povāḍā, which is used to tell stories of battle and the bravery of heroes of previous centuries. The gendered quality of povāḍā is expressed by this comment on a youtube clip of a povāḍā from a 1951 Marathi film, "Maharashtras politicians should surely listen to this song or else should wear saree, they already r wearing bangles."[27] Given the masculine orientation of these povāḍās, which anchor the narrative of rāṣṭrīya kīrtans and occupy a good deal of space within them, it is not surprising that very few women perform rāṣṭrīya kīrtan.

In the summer of 2009, I engaged several kīrtankārs in discussions about whether women perform the vīr rasa in the same way as men. Most understood this to mean whether men or women *can* perform vīr rasa, to which the unanimous answer was yes. Only Smita Deshpande, a kīrtankār trained at a kīrtan school in Pune, told me that there is "a little bit of difference. Because men are bigger and their voices are deeper, they can do it a bit more powerfully."[28] She said there are women who sing the vīr rasa in this manner and they're more like men. Indeed, in listening to a povāḍā sung by Ms. Deshpande and five other women in a new type of kīrtan called *samyukta kīrtan* (collective/united kīrtan), I noticed a thinner, more flute-like vocal timbre associated with what is sometimes called the "head voice," which is quite different from the "chest voice" that characterizes the singing of Sudhatai and Jaytunbi Maharaj.

Audiences are used to hearing men sing povāḍā and it is likely that rāṣṭrīya kīrtankārs like Sudhatai and Jaytunbi are more readily accepted because their voices are lower and raspier than many women's voices. As Smitabai said, these women's voices are more like men's, but I argue that they stake their own female heroic aesthetic territory through soliciting audience empathy. Vaman Kolhatkar explained to me that both vīr and *karūṇa* (sad/compassionate) rasas are employed in rāṣṭrīya kīrtan because the same force can lead to either sadness or bravery. "If you control these two, you can have a good kīrtan."[29] It is more common to find male characters depicted through songs in the vīr rasa, while the karūṇa rasa is often expressed through a first-person song in the character voice of a woman. While kīrtankārs described karūṇa rasa to me as "sadness" or "dukh," dictionary definitions more often prioritize "compassion" or "mercy" (e.g., Molesworth). Embedded in the vīr-karūṇa pair, then, is an additional pairing of the perspectives of performer and listener in karūṇa rasa—when a kīrtankār performs sadness successfully, compassion is excited within the listener. Interestingly, no such ambiguity surrounds the vīr rasa. In other words, the listener of the karūṇa rasa has an active, transformative role in the aesthetic experience while the listener of the vīr rasa is assumed to receive the rasa as it is performed.

Sudhatai Dhamankar, when discussing vīr rasa with me, explained that women can combine bravery and sorrow in a way that men can't because—although men feel sad—they don't know how to express it. In a kīrtan performed in 2009, she spent a good portion of the uttararaṅga in the voice of a crying Nabhag who did not want to leave his guru and who was overcome with emotion when he met his family after a long absence. In contrast, Jaytunbi Maharaj employed very little of the affect of crying in her kīrtan, nor did she include many songs in the first-person voice, but her narrative did couple violence and sadness, as in the short, first-person song in which a mother expresses grief that her son has been killed at the hands of his brother, crying "for you I became a mother." This strategy for encouraging audience empathy in performance is less common for Jaytunbi Maharaj, who more often transforms audience members by making them co-participants, leading them in songs and chants typical of Marathi devotionalism.

Sudhatai is an advocate of Hindutva but is on the margins of the alliance between the Akhil Bhāratīya Kīrtan Kula and the RSS, and Jaytunbi Maharaj is completely removed from it. Despite these profound differences, both women have strong local followings and are creating their own nationalist narratives within a host of possibilities. Hansen, Bacchetta, and others have interpreted the gender work of Hindu nationalist women in light of how they operate within the limited discursive realm established by organizations like the RSS or its women's branch, the Rashtriya Sevika Samiti. This perspective is of little usefulness in understanding Sudhatai, who contributes to Hindu nationalist discourse without the need to reconcile her stance with the "party line." I read her Hindu nationalist performances—which are certainly based in deeply felt sentiments—more as a means to attract her own following than to garner support for organized Hindu nationalism. Jaytunbi's younger years were characterized by a strong link with nationalist groups, but these connections have become more tenuous since Independence, and she told me that she has become increasingly interested in "*iśbhakti*" (devotion to God) rather than "*deśbhakti*" (devotion to the nation). Jaytunbi's upbringing as a performer was deeply connected with grassroots anti-colonial nationalism, but the vīr rasa of her povāḍā on the Rani of Jhansi is now used more to incite women to be strong at home than to provoke people to fight for the nation.

Both Sudhatai and Jaytunbi use a variety of techniques to reach audience members, skillfully combining rasas to create a shared aesthetic experience for singer and listener. As is typical in the rural Maharashtrian devotional milieu, Jaytunbi engages the audience through songs that are sung collectively, while Sudhatai generally (though not exclusively) downplays participation in a manner typical of nāradīya kīrtan. They share two ways to engage female audience members: first, they speak to women from a position of common experience; second, they temper the forceful renderings of vīr rasa with karūṇa rasa in a way that invites participants to imbibe their gendered but not sexualized rasas.

To understand nationalism beyond the parties, we must engage with the aesthetic systems that render a performance effective. It is not enough to know that both men and women perform the same songs in the vīr rasa; we must also position these songs within a broader aesthetic context. By doing this, we learn of a heroic aesthetic that is not entirely masculine, producing nationalist subjectivity through empathetic listening. We know from Partha Chatterjee and many others that women have presented a ground upon which nationalist positions are staged, but we don't yet know much about women like Sudhatai and Jaytunbi, for whom nationalism is a path to rethink gender.

CONCLUSION

While previous chapters emphasized the failures of kīrtan institutions, this chapter highlights their renaissance. The kīrtan universities of the 1980s in some sense represented a swan song for Tilak's vision of a learned and systematic kīrtan that would appeal to "modern, educated people." What the administrators of these universities learned is that for the cosmopolitan urbanites of the time, kīrtan appeared outdated and anachronistic, and devoting long hours to Sanskrit scholarship and esoteric song genres only guaranteed its impenetrability to the intended audience. In turn, the relatively small audiences made it difficult for graduates to eke out middle-class livings as professional kīrtankārs and thus minimized their motivation to study.

Other institutional models were better tuned to post-colonial economic and social realities, while also effecting profound changes in those realities.

The kīrtan schools at the Harikīrtanottejak Sabhā of Nārad Maṅdir in Pune and the Akhil Bhāratīya Kīrtan Kula of the Viṭṭhala Maṅdir in Mumbai have been thriving since the 1930s and 1940s. Founded during and just after the anti-colonial movement, they expanded during the 1950s by adapting to the habits of a growing Maharashtrian middle class. A large percentage of Marathi nāradīya kīrtankārs received some training at one or the other of these institutions, and their classes continue to attract new students. The schools' success is built in part on a realistic understanding of the amount of time students will spend learning kīrtan, and the class schedules accommodate people who can commit only one solid month per year and/or intermittent evenings. The Nārad Maṅdir śibīr schedule is timed perfectly for students on summer vacation, and the afternoon and evening classes offered during the rest of the year are convenient for people who work during the day. The curriculum includes memorization of Sanskrit and Marathi scriptures, memorization of a kīrtan, and a basic knowledge of the song genres, meters, and rhetorical techniques of nāradīya kīrtan, but instruction in the finer philosophical and Hindu scriptural points that one might learn from a guru or from a "university" is abbreviated at Nārad Maṅdir.

One result of this method of instruction is that it has opened the field of nāradīya kīrtan to women who previously had fewer opportunities to learn from an older (female) family member or a guru, leading to a flood of female kīrtankārs who alter the aesthetics of nāradīya kīrtan and feminize its discourses. Those with nationalist leanings are introducing a feminine aesthetic of heroism to the masculine realm of rāṣṭrīya kīrtan. These women, as well as their exceptional analogues in the vārkarī orbit, preach traditional gender roles while subverting those same norms through their life choices. Some navigate a delicate line between domesticity and public leadership, while others abandon conventional femininity.

The Akhil Bhāratīya Kīrtan Kula has enacted sweeping changes to the recent culture of Marathi kīrtan. While the Kula in some sense represents a culmination of processes set in motion by Tilak's 1918 speech, it also introduces new and highly successful strategies for achieving Tilak's goal of making kīrtan relevant in contemporary life. The kīrtan universities of the 1980s sought to bring the content of kīrtan up to date without significant changes in performance practice, but the Kīrtan Kula later realized that seemingly anachronistic kīrtans can be encapsulated and objectified on proscenium stages for powerful (Hindu) nationalist effect. These "cultural performances," to use Milton Singer's term, display what traditionalists and Hindu nationalists believe is best in their culture using the formal devices of non-kīrtan "functions" (Singer 1972). The cosmopolitan concert format is comfortable for urban, middle-class Indians, and extra-performance allegiances and motivations are displayed through introductory speeches and felicitations. Given the similarity between this framing display and other political events, it seems likely that an alliance between the Kīrtan Kula and the RSS has contributed to this change. While earlier rāṣṭrīya kīrtankārs used the devotional context to spread political messages, in Kīrtan Kula contexts, the devotional sphere is itself becoming nationalized. The changes in content and musical style that have accompanied this change are vast and are addressed in the remaining chapters.

PART THREE

Performing a Hindu Nation

6

Performance, Genre, and Politics in Rāṣṭrīya Kīrtan

The first two parts of this book addressed the relationship of Marathi kīrtan to changing strands of nationalism throughout the twentieth century, and culminated with an ethnographic account of kīrtan institutions at the turn of the millennium. In this part, we focus on rāṣṭrīya kīrtan as performance, first by introducing its song genres, form, and themes in this chapter, and then through close readings of two rāṣṭrīya kīrtan performances in Chapters 7 and 8. Temporal tensions are key to most rāṣṭrīya kīrtans, and the complicated dance of "then" and "now" constitutes a major theme of the final chapters of this book. It could be argued that rāṣṭrīya kīrtan is resolutely about the present moment. kīrtankārs provide sociopolitical "current events" commentary and they engender ephemeral moments of heightened experience, but this presentness is paradoxically colored and constructed by embodied, sung, and narrated evocations of pastness. An idealized past sets the troubles of the present in relief, and the prestige of pastness is embodied through sonic markers of performance lineage (*paṭhaḍī*).

Rāṣṭrīya kīrtan unfolds according to a conventional form, but within that form a kīrtankār has infinite scope to combine genres and generate unique experiences of nationalist devotion. In the process of creating a performative moment, the kīrtankār also negotiates her position vis-à-vis performance lineages, religious sects, and political affiliations. The rich semiotic play of rāṣṭrīya kīrtan links kīrtankārs to pasts that they imagine through storytelling and pasts that they embody sonically through paṭhaḍī. For the performer, as well as for other kīrtankārs and some aficionados, references to paṭhaḍī are meaningful, but not all audience members understand the subtle shades of paṭhaḍī style. They do, however, respond to the creative combinations of genre and rhetoric that communicate many things at once.

THE RITUAL STAGE: SETTING AND DRESS

The influence that kīrtankārs have on listeners through the skill of their performance is compounded by the respect they are accorded for their role as mediators of tradition. When a nāradīya or rāṣṭrīya kīrtankār stands to deliver a kīrtan, he or she is standing on Nāradānci gādī, a space imbued for the time of the kīrtan with the presence of Nārad (Plate 6.1), the divine sage of the purāṇas who traveled the three worlds singing God's praises while accompanying himself on the vīna.[1] Once the kīrtankār has invoked Nārad's presence, he or she may not sit until the devotional frame has been closed at the end of the kīrtan.[2] The ritual significance of Nārad's mat is enacted in the middle of the kīrtan, when the host of a kīrtan garlands the kīrtankār and touches her feet ("does namaskār"), and at the end, when all members of the congregation do namaskār and make offerings of money and food (Plate 6.2). When children performed kīrtans at the Bāḷkīrtan Mahotsav organized by the Akhil Bhāratīya Kīrtan Saṅsthā, even elderly people touched the child's feet, attesting to the power that accompanies standing on Nārad's mat. As Manjushree

Plate 6.1.
Image of Nārad at Nārad Maṅdir, Pune.

Plate 6.2.
Listeners touch the kīrtankār's feet after a kīrtan.

Khadilkar described in one of her kīrtans: "Kīrtan has been going on since Nārad. When someone stands to do kīrtan, they are standing on Nārad's mat, so when you do namaskār at the end, it is to Nārad."[3]

On any day of the year, one can open a Marathi newspaper to find listings for that day's kīrtans being performed in Pune temples, homes, tents, and concert halls.[4] The daily kīrtans at Nārad Maṅdir (Plate 6.3) are a reliable staple, as are the semi-regular kīrtans at Modī Gaṇapati Maṅdir in Pune's old Narayan Peth neighborhood. Temples, families, and religious or social organizations additionally sponsor kīrtans on Hindu festival days. I have heard a kīrtan on the feminine divine hosted by a family in their home during *Navrātra* (festival for the Goddess), a kīrtan on the half-lion avatar of Viṣṇu in the Nṛsiṅha Maṅdir, and a *Krāntikārak Caritra Mahotsav* (Freedom Fighter Biography Festival) at the Bharat Nāṭya Maṅdir (a theatrical hall) sponsored by the Akhil Bhāratīya Kīrtan Kula. Daily kīrtans at Nārad Maṅdir tend to be sparsely attended, but kīrtans commemorating special events and festivals attract larger crowds. Rāṣṭrīya kīrtans are performed in all of the contexts in which nāradīya kīrtan is performed, although one would be less likely to hear a rāṣṭrīya kīrtan in a temple during a festival for a deity.

The performance ensemble of rāṣṭrīya kīrtan is the same as that of nāradīya kīrtan (kīrtankār, tablā, harmonium), but the kīrtan can be identified instantly as nationalist by the dress of the kīrtankār (if he is a man). While nāradīya kīrtankārs wear a red *pagaḍī*, the type of hat worn by Vasudeo Burse in Plate 6.3, most rāṣṭrīya kīrtankārs wear a saffron *pheṭā* (turban) like the one

Plate 6.3.
Vasudeo Burse performing nāradīya kīrtan at Nārad Maṅdir.

donned by Narahari Apamarjane in Plate 6.4. The color saffron is highly charged with both religious and political significance. In Maharashtra, pilgrims who walk by foot to Pandharpur carry saffron flags to identify themselves as vārkarīs, and many Hindu ascetics dress entirely in saffron. Hindu nationalists have appropriated these and other religious associations of saffron, wearing saffron pheṭās and carrying saffron flags. There is no standard dress for female rāṣṭrīya kīrtankārs, who wear either five-yard or nine-yard saris of any color in silk or cotton.

FROM VĀRKARĪ TO NĀRADĪYA TO RĀṢṬRĪYA

When nāradīya kīrtan crystallized into a distinct style in the nineteenth century, it offered a presentational, virtuosic, and entertainment-oriented alternative to vārkarī kīrtan, but it continued to incorporate many elements of vārkarī kīrtan. Rāṣṭrīya kīrtan, as a subtype of nāradīya kīrtan, articulates the same relationship to vārkarī kīrtan. Nāradīya kīrtankārs throw the theological net much wider than do vārkarī kīrtankārs; they embrace both *jñān* (knowledge) and *bhakti* (devotion), and they worship saints and deities of both Vaiṣṇava and Śaiva traditions. They also sing devotional songs composed by non-saints, while vārkarī kīrtankārs restrict themselves to the words of vārkarī saints. Nāradīya kīrtan's philosophical syncretism is matched by its musical eclecticism. Many songs in nāradīya kīrtan are rāga-based and

Plate 6.4.
Saffron pheṭā of rāṣṭrīya kīrtan worn by Narahari Apamarjane.

kīrtankārs undergo at least some training in Hindustani art music, but segments of nāradīya kīrtan are dedicated to communal singing, and any type of Marathi light music or folk song can find its way into a nāradīya kīrtan. Nāradīya kīrtankārs worship multiple saints and draw on an eclectic bank of songs and literature, so it does not require radical restructuring for them to infuse their performances with stories of nationalist heroes and patriotic songs. For this and other reasons, rāṣṭrīya kīrtan grew easily out of the nāradīya saṁpradāya while vārkarī kīrtan has resisted politicization.

Rāṣṭrīya kīrtan is basically identical to nāradīya kīrtan in most matters of structure, style, and music, but differs from ostensibly apolitical nāradīya kīrtan in its use of nationalist themes in the nirupaṇa and stories of nationalist or historical figures in the ākhyān. Rāṣṭrīya kīrtan pūrvaraṅgas focus on such topics as honesty, adherence to a *sadguru* (true teacher), the need to recognize enemies, and serving the nation. Some of these topics are easily recognized as nationalist, while the nationalist relevance of others is revealed only in the ākhyān section. The major defining characteristic of rāṣṭrīya kīrtan is that the uttararaṅgas are not based on hagiographies of Marathi saints as in nāradīya kīrtan, but instead are patterned on the lives of nationalist leaders and revolutionaries such as Lokmanya Tilak, Vinayak Damodar Savarkar, Vasudeo Balwant Phadke, Subhashchandra Bose, and Madanlal Dhingre. Other stories involve earlier Hindu kings and soldiers who fought against the Mughals such as Shivaji, Tanaji, and Rana Pratap Sinha. Stories about these

Maṅgalācaraṇ (Introductory songs)

1. Kīrtankār recites Sanskrit ślokās. Audience members participate if they know the ślokās.
2. Kīrtankār sings *naman* to greet the deity
3. Some kīrtankārs sing the *pad*, "Bālakṛṣṇa Caraṇī Lakṣa Lāgo"
4. Kīrtankār leads the audience in singing a bhajan **(usually a Rāma bhajan)**
5. Kīrtankār leads the audience in jayjaykārs **(+ jayjaykārs to Bhārata Mātā (Mother India), Rāmdās, and/or Ārya Sanātan Vedic Dharma (Eternal Aryan Vedic Religion)**
6. Kīrtankār sings the muḷpad, which is usually an abhaṅga and usually by Saṅt Tukārām **(on courage, taking decisive action, or protecting religion).**

Pūrvaraṅga

1. Kīrtankār intones the muḷpad
2. Kīrtankār discusses the abhaṅga line by line **(a link is made between a devotional concept and the nation, nationalism, or patriotism)**
3. While expounding on the abhaṅga, the kīrtankār may use Marathi and Sanskrit ślokas, abhaṅgas, and ovīs.
4. The kīrtankār ends the pūrvaraṅga by singing a portion of the muḷpad while being garlanded by the host or hostess.

Interval

1. Announcements are made by host and by the kīrtankār
2. The harmonium player or an audience member is invited to come to the front to sing a devotional song
3. The kīrtankār leads the audience in singing a bhajan

Uttararaṅga

1. The kīrtankār tells a story about a saṅt or an event from the epics or purāṇas. This story illustrates the philosophical concepts discussed in the pūrvaraṅga. **(The kīrtankār tells a story about a nationalist leader or other Marathi historical hero.)**
2. The storytelling is interspersed with various Marathi songs, such as āryā, sākī, diṅḍī, jhaṁpa, aṅjanī gīt, filmī gīt (film song), *nāṭya gīt* (songs from plays), abhaṅga, bhajan, and ovī. **(Most rāṣṭrīya kīrtans also include povāḍā, rājahaṅs, and kaṭhāv, which are metered song genres used for historical storytelling in non-kīrtan contexts.)**
3. The kīrtankār sings the muḷpad in bhairavī

Closing

1. The kīrtankār and audience stand and sing the Tukārām abhaṅga, "Hecī Dāna Degā Devā"
2. Waving of an oil lamp and communal singing of āratī. The āratī is for Ganeś, the temple deity, or the deity to whom the kīrtan is dedicated.
3. Communal singing of the bhajan, "Hari Rām Hari Rām Rām Rām Hari Hari"

Figure 6.1.
Nāradīya Kīrtan Structure (with Rāṣṭrīya Variations or Additions in Bold).

kings express fierce pride in Hindu identity and strength in action, and they cast Muslims or "outsiders" as the enemy. In pre-independence era kīrtans, the narrated enemy was meant to stand for the British, while in contemporary kīrtans the enemy represents living Muslims.[5] The same song genres are used in rāṣṭrīya kīrtan as in nāradīya kīrtan, though rāṣṭrīya kīrtankārs make more frequent use of povāḍā, *kaṭhāv*, and *rājahaṅs*. The variations that transform a nāradīya kīrtan into a rāṣṭrīya kīrtan are noted in Figure 6.1.

PAṬHAḌĪ AND POLITICS IN THE MAṄGALĀCARAṆ

A kīrtan begins only after the kīrtankār has bowed to the *mūrti* (divine image) by touching the ground in a gesture of respect. Both nāradīya and rāṣṭrīya kīrtankārs begin with a set of songs and chants—ślokas, naman (also called namanāca pad), bhajan, and jayjaykar—known collectively as maṅgalācaraṇ. Rāṣṭrīya kīrtankārs learn kīrtan ākhyāns and songs from many different sources, but the maṅgalācaraṇ is learned from the guru. More than any other point in the kīrtan, these songs are inscribed with the kīrtankār's paṭhaḍī both in repertoire and in performance style. The maṅgalācaraṇ also allows the kīrtankār to generate audience participation, display solo singing skills, and frame his or her political sympathies.

The first items in the maṅgalācaraṇ are prayers or ślokās, recited very quietly and without any musical accompaniment (audio example 3, 0:00–1:10,). The prayerful gestures, solemn expression of the kīrtankār, and quiet atmosphere help cue the devotionalized frame and separate it from mundane life. The Sanskrit ślokās are sung by the kīrtankār with harmonium accompaniment and some participation from listeners. While members of a single paṭhaḍī use the same śloka texts, rāga and melody may differ depending on the musical background or personal preference of a particular kīrtankār. Each kīrtan paṭhaḍī uses a particular set of ślokas reflecting the devotional and political allegiances of its proponents. For example, kīrtankārs of the Nārad Maṅdir paṭhaḍī (see Figure 6.2) chant ślokas for Gaṇeś (1), Sarasvatī (2), Nārad (3), and Guru (4).[6] Gaṇeś and Sarasvatī, deities of learning and the arts, are invoked at the beginning of most Hindu devotional events and performances, and the final śloka, for gurus, is common to all nāradīya and rāṣṭrīya kīrtan paṭhaḍīs. Nārad Maṅdir kīrtankārs are unique in the invocation of Nārad (3), the sage (and their temple deity) for whom nāradīya kīrtan is named.

The Gangadharbuwa Koparkar rāṣṭrīya kīrtan paṭhaḍī (Figure 6.3)[7] is connected with the Nārad Maṅdir paṭhaḍī,[8] and kīrtankārs of Koparkar's tradition similarly begin by invoking Ganesh with the śloka "Yadā laṁbodaram haṅti," which they follow with praises to Śaṅkarācārya (2), Rām (5), and

1 - Yadālaṁbodaram haṅti satāpratyuhasaṁbhavam/
Tadālambe dayālaṁbam laṁbodarāpadāmbujam//

2 - Śaradā śaradāmbhojavadana vadanāmbuje/
Sarvadā sarvadāsmakam sannidhim sannidhim kriyāt//

3 - Namastasmei bhagavate Nāradāya mahātmane/
Kāmakrodhavihināy ṛṣinām pravarāyaca//

4 - Gururbrahma gururviṣṇuh gururdevo maheṣvarah/
Guruh sākṣāt parabrahma tasmei shrigurave namah//

Figure 6.2.
Ślokās, Nārad Maṅdir Paṭhaḍī.

Kṛṣṇa-Arjūna (6).[9] The first Śaṅkarācārya articulated the philosophical and spiritual concept of nondualism (Advaita Vedāṅta) in the eighth century and founded four maṭhs in north, south, east, and west India[10] that would be headed by four heirs to the title of Śaṅkarācārya (Balasubramanaya 1987: 3804–3805). Koparkar credits Śaṅkarācārya with restoring strength to a failing Hinduism and creating a proto-Hindu nation as demarcated by the large area encompassed by the heir Śaṅkarācāryas, and he erected a small *tapascarya* ashram (he translated this as "penance ashram") in Śaṅkarācārya's honor on the grounds of his compound. On the festival celebrating the first Śaṅkarācārya's birth, Koparkar sponsored a function at his ashram that was attended by the current Śaṅkarācārya of Karveer Peeth, a Hindu religious figurehead who was formerly a kīrtankār named Ramchandrabuva Karhadkar (Shevde et al. 2000: 37). The śloka recitation ends with an homage to Rama, who has become the primary deity of many Hindu nationalists.

kīrtankārs perform ślokas in a variety of ways, ranging from chants on three or four notes to a rāga-based style encompassing an octave or more. Of the performances I have recorded, most are in the chanted style that remains within a range of a third or fourth, with most syllables chanted on a single note. One might assume that kīrtankārs trained in Hindustani music would be more likely to perform ślokas in a sung style, but this not always the case (Badave, at the beginning of audio example 5, sings ślokas). Charudatta Aphale, Narahari Apamarjane, and Vijay Apamarjane have undergone extensive classical music training, but they all perform ślokas in the more austere chanted style that indexes their Sanskrit education. Indeed, several kīrtankārs have studied Sanskrit. Ghaisas Guruji is a retired Sanskrit teacher, and rāṣṭrīya kīrtankār Narahari Apamarjane is a retired Sanskrit professor whose kīrtankār son Vijay Apamarjane teaches Sanskrit at the New English School in Pune, a Marathi-medium school founded by nationalist leader Lokmanya Tilak. Gangadharbuwa Koparkar studied at a Vedapāṭhśāḷā[11] (Joshi 1982: 25), and Vaman Kolhatkar studied the Vedas for eleven years as a boy.

1 - Yadālaṁbodaram haṅti satāpratyuhasaṁbhavam/[i]
Tadālambe dayālaṁbam laṁbodarāpadāmbujam//

2 - Śankaram śankarācāryam keśavam mādharāyanam/
Sukathāśabaravante bhagavān namo….//

4 - Gururbrahma gururviṣṇuh gururdevo maheṣvarah/
Guruh sākṣāt parabrahma tasmei śrigurave namah//

5 - Rām rām rameti rame rāme manorame/
Sahasranām tatulyam rāmanāma varaname//

6 - Yatra yogeṣvara kṛṣṇo yātra partho dhanurdharah/
Tatra srī vijayo bhutir dhruvā nītir matir mama//

Figure 6.3.
Ślokās, Koparkar paṭhaḍī.

Ślokas are followed immediately by the naman (song of obeisance), which maintains the meditative mood of the ślokas and assures that the audience's attention becomes fixed on the kīrtankār. Sudhatai Dhamankar explained to me: "Just like a child prepares for school by taking a bath and getting dressed, the kīrtankār and *śrote* (audience/congregation) make their minds (*man*) ready with naman."[12] The text, tune, and performance style of the naman indicate the paṭhaḍi of the kīrtankār. Most nāradīya kīrtankārs use the naman, "Jayjay Ramakṛṣṇa hari" (see Figure 6.4) but kīrtankārs of the Kolhatkar paṭhaḍi sing "Vandu Tula," those of the Shirwalkar paṭhaḍi sing "Rāmdās māulī," and those of the Aurangabadkar paṭhaḍi sing "Kṛṣṇatiricyā vasanarya" (Kolhatkar 1995: 7–8). Yashwant Pathak also notes that there are two versions of "Jayjay Ramkṛṣṇa hari" that share a refrain but have different verses, and that these versions correspond to different paṭhaḍis (Pathak 1980: 96).

The first version, sung by kīrtankārs of the paṭhaḍī of Nanabuwa Badodekar, Murlidhar and Lakshmanbuwa Nizampurkar, Vasudeobuwa Joshi, and Kavishwarbuwa, begins with the text "Heci rasāyana sevana karita." kīrtankārs of the other paṭhaḍī, such as Dattopant Patwardhan (the first recognized rāṣṭrīya kīrtankār), Kashikarbuwa, and Gautambuwa Pathak incorporate a verse with the text "Govardhana dhara, Gopālanaratha" (Pathak 1980: 96). The former naman seems to have fallen out of fashion, and most rāṣṭrīya or nāradīya kīrtans I attended used the version of "Jayjay Ramakrishna Hari" with this text (audio example 3, 2:05–8:34,).

Most nāradīya kīrtankārs sing this Kṛṣṇa naman text but employ a variety of tunes, rāgas, and performance styles. Some kīrtankārs, such as Moreshwarbuwa Joshi, sing the naman with little improvisation, but classically trained kīrtankārs (such as Shreeyash Badave) begin by emphasizing the naman's words through an unadorned statement of the text and tune before improvising on both within the parameters of the chosen rāga. This naman is suited to classical improvisation since it comprises two melodies: a refrain—

Jayjay Rāmkṛṣṇa Harī// (refrain) (Victory to Rāmkṛṣṇa Hari[i])	
Navanīradasama navanītapriya/	(The one who loves butter and is the color of dark clouds)
Navala vinoda vihārī//1//	(The one who performs miracles and plays games).
Govardanadhara, Gopālanarata/	(The one who held up Mount Govardhan and conquers disease)
Gokula sankaṭa hāri//2//	(The one who defeated disaster in Gokula.)
Durvāsonuta, dukhavimocaka/	(The one who removes hatred and sadness)
Durjana saṅgama hārī//3//	(The one who destroys all the wicked people.)
Sharaṇāgata dīnā, caraṇī neī/	(The one whose feet bring protection to the poor)
Karuṇādṛṣṭi nihārī//4//	(Behold His compassionate gaze.)

Figure 6.4.
Naman, "Jayjay Rāmkṛṣṇa Harī."

called *dhrupad* by Marathi musicians and *sthāi* by Hindustani musicians—and a verse sung at a higher tessitura (the *antarā* of Hindustani music). In his 2009 performance, Badave sang only two verses, improvising extensively on each line either with the text or using "ah," straying further from the original melody as his improvisation progressed. Other kīrtankārs diverge from the text by singing *sargam* (solfège) within the raga of the naman, and some follow the naman with a *tarāna*. Tarāna is a Hindustani art music genre in which the singer performs quick-tempo rhythmic and melodic improvisations on the syllables "ta" and "na."

The naman "Jayjay Rāmkṛṣṇa Hari" is most commonly performed in Rāga Yaman, but I have also heard performances of the same naman in Rāgas Hamīr, Caṅdrakauṅs, Bilāval, Multānī, and Bhūp. The author of a 1925 biography of the nineteenth-century nāradīya kīrtankār, Govindbuva Hoshing, mentions that Govindbuva performed the pad "Jayjay Rāmkṛṣṇa Hari" in Rāgas Yaman and Multānī (Dhole 1925: 7, 26). Of the namans in Rāga Yaman that I have transcribed, half are in one melody and half are in another. kīrtankārs told me that they choose rāgas appropriate to the kīrtan's time of day, and Yaman—an evening rāga—is particularly appropriate since kīrtans are usually performed in the evening. The Kolhatkars similarly sing "Vaṅdū tūlā" in various rāgas, depending on time of day and personal preference. Vaman Kolhatkar taught me to sing the naman in Rāga Bhūp, though he performed it in this and many other rāgas. At a morning kīrtan for the Gaṇapati festival, he performed the naman in Rāga Asāvarī, a morning rāga, and in one of our lessons he demonstrated how the same naman can be sung in Rāga Mālkauṅs if the kīrtan is after 9:30 at night. His father typically performed the same naman in Rāga Khamāj, an evening rāga used for nāndī, an invocatory song similar to naman in Marathi sangīt nāṭak.

Some kīrtankārs follow the naman with an additional pad that may also indicate the kīrtankār's paṭhaḍī. kīrtankārs in Aphale's paṭhaḍī use the vārkarī abhaṅga, "Rūpa pāhatā locani" ("To see your form") by Jñāneśvar after the naman, a practice that Dilip Dabir and Shreeyash Badave employ to reference a melding of vārkarī and nāradīya styles (audio example 3, 8:35–13:03,). The most common pads sung following the naman are "Bāḷakṛṣṇa caraṇi" (The feet of baby Kṛṣṇa) and "Ye sadguru rāy." According to Dhole's biography of Govindbuwa Hoshing, "Bāḷakṛṣṇa caraṇi" was written by Anyagosavi Trimbakkar, a great kīrtankār of Pune's Peshva court who taught the pad to Hoshing's father. As a proponent of his father's paṭhaḍī, Govindbuwa learned and further popularized the pad (Dhole 1925: 39). As the originator of modern nāradīya kīrtan, Hoshing's wide-reaching influence has made this pad a common component of maṅgalācaraṇ in various kīrtan paṭhaḍīs. Some late-twentieth-century rāṣṭrīya kīrtankārs sing this pad but change the words "Bāḷakṛṣṇa caraṇi lakṣa lāgo" ("My attention is on the feet of young Krishna") to "Rājarāma caraṇi lakṣa lāgo" (My attention is on the feet of Lord Rama"), which resonates with the Ram focus of Hindutva discourse. Today, "Bāḷakṛṣṇa caraṇi" is strongly associated with the Karhadkar paṭhaḍī (among others), a lineage known for producing nāradīya kīrtankārs who are also skilled singers. Rambhau Karhadkar, the son of the famous Haribhau Karhadkar, taught successful kīrtankārs such as Joglekarbuva, Milinda Barve, and Dattadas Ghag before accepting the position of Śaṅkarācārya of Karvir Peeth. The Karhadkar lineage is not known for the performance of rāṣṭrīya kīrtans, but Śaṅkarācārya has been involved in Hindu nationalist activities.[13]

Following the solo performance of naman, the kīrtankār leads the audience in a spirited, participatory bhajan, a devotional song in which the names of a deity are set to a repeating melody of one or two short musical phrases.[14] Bhajans in rāṣṭrīya and nāradīya kīrtan might be for any deity, while vārkarī bhajans are typically in praise of Viṭṭhala. Shreeyash Badave departs from nāradīya kīrtan to sing a vārkarī bhajan, "Viṭṭhoba Rakhumāi" (audio example 3, 13:12–13:50,). In both vārkarī and nāradīya bhajans, the tempo increases with each repetition of a musical phrase, though this increase is more pronounced in vārkarī kīrtan than in nāradīya kīrtan. The opening bhajan in rāṣṭrīya kīrtan foreshadows the primary subject matter of the kīrtan or reflects the ideological position of the kīrtankār. Bhajans in nāradīya kīrtan may be for any deity, but the majority of bhajans in rāṣṭrīya kīrtan are for Rāma. Devotion to Rāma has been a cornerstone of the nationalist movement in India, from Gandhi's use of the notion of *rāmrājya* (Rāma's rule) to invoke an inclusive and independent nation, to the *rāmjanmabhumī* (Rāma's birthplace) issue that has preoccupied Hindu nationalists and incited communal violence (Van der Veer 1994: 174–178).

To illustrate the shifts in tempo, range, and rhythmic density characteristic of a typical performance of bhajan within nāradīya kīrtan, I again return to Manjushree Khadilkar's 1999 performance. She invited the audience to sing a bhajan on the text "Jayjay Rāmkṛṣṇa Hari" (different from the naman above) and they enthusiastically sang and clapped along. The single melodic phrase of Khadilkar's bhajan was repeated several times at increasingly high tessituras and with a gradual increase in tempo. Box 6.1 is a transcription of Khadilkar's rendition of the bhajan, "Jayjay Rāmkṛṣṇa Hari." During the first six repetitions of the bhajan, the tempo increased from 96 to 100 beats per minute (bpm). This tempo remained constant as the singers moved up to and beyond the high tonic, and increased to 104 bpm after the bhajan returned to its original tessitura. The tempo ended at 108 bpm, having increased by 12 bpm since the beginning of the piece. The slight tempo increase in this short bhajan contrasts with the pronounced quickening of tempo in vārkarī kīrtan bhajans, which are more open-ended and are likely to triple over the course of one performance. Intensity in nāradīya kīrtan is generated more through increasing the rhythmic density of jhānj and tablā patterns than by increasing the tempo of the vocal line as in vārkarī kīrtan. At the beginning of the bhajan, Khadilkar accented the quarter note with jhānj, but by the end she had doubled the rhythmic density to accent every eighth note. In vārkarī kīrtan, the congregation actively helps generate the gradual increase in tempo, while nāradīya kīrtankārs assume more control for guiding the intensity and emotional impact of bhajans.

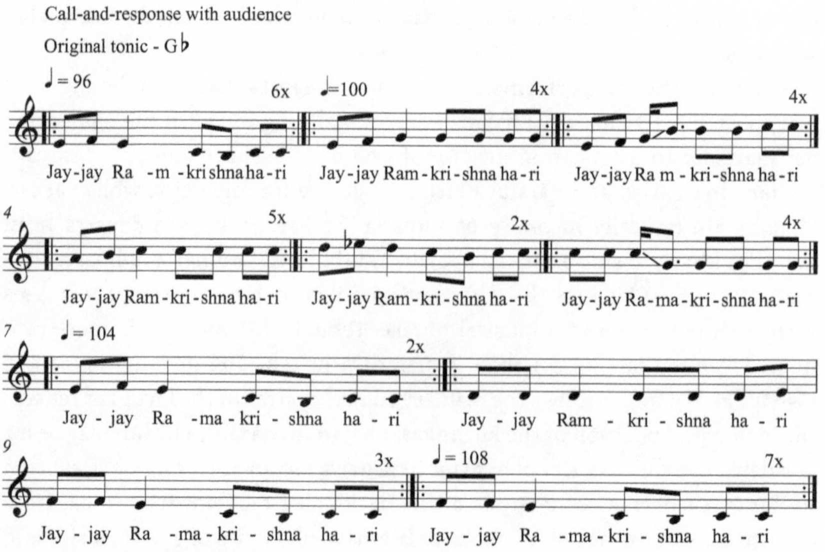

Musical Example 6.1.
Bhajan, "Jayjay Rāmkṛṣṇa Hari." Performed by Manjushree Khadilkar.

Having generated collective excitement with bhajan, the kīrtankār leads the audience without pause into jayjaykār, an enthusiastic intoned and shouted list of "victory to!" (*ki jay!*) various deities and saints (audio example 3, 13:49–14:25,). While ślokas and naman indicate the performance style and paṭhaḍī of the kīrtankār, jayjaykar allows the kīrtankār to express political opinions that may diverge from those of the guru. Rāṣṭrīya kīrtankārs exclaim jayjaykārs to deities that connote nationalism and a fierce Hindu identity, as well as to deities and saints associated with the kīrtankār's devotional tradition and the kīrtan's venue. In a kīrtan on the Hindu nationalist pioneer V. D. Savarkar, Manjushree Khadilkar located the kīrtan in a hall dedicated to Viṭṭhala by first paying homage to Viṭṭhala and his devotees Jñāndev and Tukārām[15] (See Musical Example 6.2). She then praised Jagadaṁbā Mātā (Durgā) and Sadgurunāth Mahārāj, probably because they are associated with her performance tradition (lines 2–3). Most jayjaykārs are based on repeated chant tones, except for the "ki jay" that is shouted in unison with the audience. "Maṅgalamūrtī Morya," an invocation of Gaṇapatī, is typically the final line in a set of jayjaykārs, providing closure with a slight rallentando and a descent to the middle tonic. Khadilkar breaks from this model by descending to the tonic in the previous line, and ending this section by singing "Maṅgalamūrti Morya" and "Jayjay Raghuvīr Samartha" on the fifth (lines 4 and 5). Samartha Rāmdās (line 5) is often invoked in rāṣṭrīya kīrtans as the spiritual advisor to King Shivaji and as an advocate of a united field of religion and politics. Unlike other Marathi saints, Rāmdās was a devotee of Rāma rather than of Viṭṭhala, making him an especially attractive figure for Hindu nationalist kīrtankārs who support the Rāmjanmabhumī project. Accordingly, Khadilkar includes a jayjaykār for Rāma (line 6) and one for his bhakta Hanumān (line 7). She slows and cadences with a jayjaykār to Kṛṣṇa (line 8), but an audience member who apparently shared my interpretation of this final section as nationalist, added "Bhārata Mātā ki jay"(victory to Mother India), the jayjaykār most frequently used in rāṣṭrīya kīrtans (line 9).

PREACHING IN THE PŪRVARAṄGA

Having thus completed the mangalācaraṇ, a muḷpad cues the beginning of the kīrtankār's pūrvaraṅga. Vaman Kolhatkar described the muḷpad in this way:

> The pūrvaraṅga begins with a small abhaṅga of a saint, which is authentic and unchallengeable. This first abhaṅga is the principal abhaṅga and is known as the muḷpad, or message by an immortal. It must be something given by a person of God and must be universally true. The pūrvaraṅga takes the message from the main story of the uttararaṅga and explains it, beginning with the muḷpad.[16]

Musical Example 6.2.
Jayjaykar. Performed by Manjushree Khadilkar.

As Kolhatkar's explanation suggests, the primary abhaṅga serves to anchor the discourse of the pūrvaraṅga, and the authority of the saint-composer supports the words of the kīrtankār. An abhaṅga is a song by a saint in which the final line of text begins with the name of the poet.[17] Like the naman, this is in a dhrupad-pad form, with the first half of the dhrupad serving as the refrain and the pad (verse) sounding at a higher tessitura than the dhrupad. Nāradīya kīrtankārs perform abhaṅgas in a variety of Hindustani rāgas and improvise using Hindustani musical techniques such as *tān* (rapid melismatic passages), *ālāp* (rhythmically free improvisation on "ah"), and *sargam* (improvisation using solfège syllables). Shreeyash Badave's muḷpad begins at 14:46 in audio example 3( ).

Rāmdās was the first Marathi saint to advocate a combined notion of politics and religion, but rāṣṭrīya kīrtankārs use Tukārām's abhaṅgas more often than those of any other saint; of the seventeen rāṣṭrīya kīrtans I have transcribed, fourteen are by Saint Tukārām, one is by Saint Sūrdās, one was composed by the kīrtankār, and one is by Saint Eknāth. Tukārām, a simple businessman and farmer from a non-Brahman caste, is probably the best-loved Marathi saint, and rāṣṭrīya kīrtankārs choose his straightforward abhaṅgas advocating decisive action. Tukārām may have intended these abhaṅgas to mean that one should avoid spiritual lethargy, but they are interpreted by rāṣṭrīya kīrtankārs to mean that one should become involved in nationalist activities.

In the pūrvaraṅga, which lasts between a half an hour and an hour, the nāradīya kīrtankār elaborates on the primary message of the abhaṅga, periodically intoning individual lines from the song. In contrast to European fairy tales that leave the moral of a story to the end, nāradīya and rāṣṭrīya kīrtan pūrvaraṅgas begin with an ethical lesson, which is followed by an illustrative story in the uttararaṅga. In the kīrtan by Manjushree Khadilkar mentioned earlier, she begins by expounding on the first line of the abhaṅga, "nāma gāu" ("let's sing the name") by describing the various contexts in which one does bhajan, kīrtan, and *nāmasmaraṇ* (repeating God's names). With each example, she briefly sang the songs appropriate to those contexts, beginning with the vārkarī kīrtan chant, "Viṭṭhala, Viṭṭhala," as an example of bhajan. "Viṭṭhala, Viṭṭhala" was the only song in the pūrvaraṅga in which audience members sang along, though they did clap in accompaniment to some of the others. She also sang a few bhajans (without audience participation) and recited several ślokas in both Marathi and Sanskrit. Khadilkar sang most songs in the pūrvaraṅga too briefly for group song to develop, and she sang a few others in an elaborate improvisatory style that was not conducive to unison singing. At the end of the pūrvaraṅga, Khadilkar sang the muḷabhaṅga in a different rāga than the one with which she had begun.

Pūrvaraṅgas in rāṣṭrīya kīrtan are identical in form to nāradīya kīrtan, but rāṣṭrīya kīrtankārs insert nationalist perspectives in both explicit and subtle ways. In some rāṣṭrīya kīrtans, the pūrvaraṅga is almost indistinguishable from a nationalist lecture, as in a pūrvaraṅga by Charudatta Aphale on Chandrashekar Azad. Aphale began by paraphrasing a line of a Tukārām abhaṅga as "speak nicely, do nicely," and then he went on to say that one should do things not only to achieve personal satisfaction but also to help others. Specifically, he said that one should serve the Hindu nation: "Every citizen should try to lead a good life and try to make at least three people good in their lives. I will try to make a Hindu *samrājya*, to try and serve Hindu dharma and culture."[18] His language of "citizens" and "Hindu samrājya" (Hindu rule), which evokes the rhetoric of Hindutva political rallies, is common in rāṣṭrīya kīrtans. Other rāṣṭrīya kīrtankārs reveal the nationalist import of the pūrvaraṅga in the uttararaṅga, as in a kīrtan by Bhaskar R. Ghaisas on Lokmanya Tilak.[19] In the pūrvaraṅga, Ghaisas expounded on the idea that honesty enables one to face death without fear, citing examples from the *Mahābhārata* and the *Rāmāyana*, and defining "honesty" in detail. It was only in the uttararaṅga that Ghaisasbuva related his scriptural accounts of honesty to the life of Tilak by demonstrating the honesty of Tilak's actions.

By returning to the complete muḷabhaṅga, a kīrtankār signals that the pūrvaraṅga is complete; listeners shift their positions on the floor and the host approaches the kīrtankār carrying a metal plate. On the plate are a garland of flowers and a small box of black powder known as *bukā*. The host first honors the kīrtankār by garlanding him and applying bukā to his forehead, after which the kīrtankār in turn applies bukā to the host's forehead. The host then bows to touch the kīrtankār's feet before returning to the back of the room to pass bukā around for listeners to apply to their own foreheads. After the exchange of bukā between kīrtankār and host, some kīrtankārs motion for the host or hostess to apply bukā to the foreheads of specific distinguished listeners.

The application of bukā signals the beginning of the interval, when the kīrtankār gets some respite while the host takes the microphone to make announcements. Although the kīrtankār gets a break from performing during the interval, she is still on Nārad's mat and may not sit down or leave the area. Usually, the kīrtankār then invites one of the accompanists, a student, or an audience member to the front to sing a devotional song. The interval ends when the microphone shifts back to the kīrtankār and he says, "let's do bhajan!" The communal singing of bhajan indicates that the interval is over and that the uttararaṅga will begin.

ARRANGING GENRES AND INDEXING MEANINGS IN THE UTTARARAṄGA

The uttararaṅga (also called *ākhyān*) is the second half of a nāradīya kīrtan, in which the kīrtankār tells a story from the life of a saint or an episode from the epics or purāṇas that illustrates the philosophical concepts introduced in the pūrvaraṅga. Shreeyash Badave's uttararaṅga follows his invitation for the audience to sing bhajan with him (audio example 4). Songs figure more prominently in the uttararaṅga than they do in the pūrvaraṅga. While the songs of the pūrvaraṅga are limited primarily to abhaṅgas and ślokas, almost any genre of Marathi song can be found in the uttararaṅga, though some song types (such as āryā and sākī) are found in most kīrtans. Throughout the course of the uttararaṅga, the audience listens quietly, and participation is limited to laughing at appropriate moments and clapping with a few of the songs. Songs are inserted to describe situations in the story or express a character's feelings. For example, a kīrtankār may evoke the women's sphere by singing women's ovīs, which are strophic, metered songs comprising two short musical phrases that acquire new but related texts with each repetition. Other song genres commonly found in nāradīya kīrtan include āryā, sākī, diṅḍī, abhaṅga, and jhaṁpa, though any Marathi (or Hindi) song genre (including film or drama songs) can be used if it is appropriate to the story. Āryā, sākī, and ovī are short declamatory genres used to narrate important events in the story, while padas or bhāvgīt ("emotional songs") are strophic songs that allow the kīrtankār to express the emotions of characters in the story in the first person. Diṅḍī and jhaṁpa are metered genres; diṅḍī is in six-eight time and jhaṁpa is

Musical Example 6.3.
Āryā tune.

in ten-eight time, and—like āryā, sākī, and ovī—they are used to narrate key events in the story. In the following insert, I briefly introduce some of the genres commonly heard in nāradīya kīrtan.

Description of Genres Commonly Sung in Nāradīya Kīrtan Uttararaṅgas

Āryā: A short, unmetered song used in kīrtan to narrate important events or describe inner emotions. Moropant, an important Marathi poet of the eighteenth century, wrote almost exclusively in āryās, and the genre is strongly associated with him. Āryās are couplets, each line of which is composed of two *caraṇ* (phrase, lit. foot). The first caraṇ of each of the two lines in a Moropanti āryā has twelve mātra, while the second caraṇ has eighteen mātra.[20]

Two standard tunes are usually used for singing āryās, both of which are characterized by gradual melodic descent. In a common āryā tune, the main text is sung without tablā accompaniment, but after the two lines of text are complete, the tablā joins the singer in performing a short coda with tāl. Some kīrtankārs omit the coda with tāl. Musical example 6.3 is the outline of an āryā tune without coda.

Pad: A generic term that can loosely be translated as "song." Pads are metered, are often newly composed, and are not attributed to a saint or other spiritual authority from the past. Any rhythmic structure, number of lines, or melody can be used.

Nāṭya gīt: A general term referring to songs from Marathi saṅgīt nāṭak. Various song genres are used in saṅgīt nāṭak. Many of them (sākī, āryā, diṅḍī, etc.) are in the same recitation molds common in nāradīya kīrtan, while others do not fit into any predetermined structure.

Sākī: Sākī is strongly associated with both saṅgīt nāṭak and kīrtan. In nāradīya and rāṣṭrīya kīrtans, sākī is often sung to depict the emotions or actions of a character making a brave decision. Sākī, sung loudly and at a high tessitura, is said to convey the *vīr rasa* (emotion of bravery) (Gurumurthy 1994: 71).

A metered couplet genre, sākī consists of fourteen poetic mātras per line (total of 28 mātras) (Joshi 1980: 91, 140–141). A variety of tunes were used to sing sākī

Musical Example 6.4.
Sākī tune.

in the past, but nāradīya kīrtankārs of today use a particular tune in Rāga Bhairav almost exclusively (Joshi 1980: 91). Sākī is sung to an eight-beat Dhumālī Tāla, and each line begins decisively with a single syllable per tablā stroke (Figure 6.4).

Diṅḍī: A song genre sung to dādra tāl (a six-beat tāl) comprised of at least two couplets. The same melody is used for each half of the couplet, though the second half is sung up a fifth.

Ovī: This is one of the oldest Marathi song genres still performed today. Jñāneśvar's *Amṛtānubhav* and *Jñāneśvari* were written in ovī (Gurumurthy 1994: 67, Joshi 1980: 102–103). There is a wide variety of ovī structures, but they are all composed of four caraṇ, the first three of which share the same number of mātras, while the fourth has fewer mātras. So, for example, the first three caraṇ of *Jñāneśvari* ovīs comprise eight mātras, while the fourth caraṇ contains four or six mātras. There are two main categories of ovīs performed today: literary ovī and women's ovī. Literary ovī, which kīrtankārs sing without tāl, encompasses all of the ovīs by saints such as Jñāneśvar, Eknāth, and Nāmdev. Women have sung a separate type of ovī for centuries when they gather together for work or pleasure, and these ovīs are sung with tāl (Gurumurthy 1994: 67).

Rāṣṭrīya kīrtan uttararaṅgas usually consist of a story of a nationalist hero that may be buttressed by one or more subsidiary stories about the same hero. Many uttararaṅgas that I heard in 1998–2000 and 2009 were on early twentieth-century (Hindu) nationalists such as B. G. Tilak; Hedgewar, the founder of the RSS; Subhashchandra Bose, the Bengali revolutionary; and V. D. Savarkar, the founder of the Hindu Mahasabha. Other rāṣṭrīya kīrtan uttararaṅgas were on Hindu kings and warriors such as Shivaji and Rana Pratap. The nationalist hero of the uttararaṅga is portrayed as an exemplar of the ideal described in the pūrvaraṅga. For example, Vasudeo Burse performed a rāṣṭrīya kīrtan in 2000 in which *dayā* (benevolence) was the subject of the pūrvaraṅga. He said that there are two sides to dayā: being kind to good people and punishing bad people. In his uttararaṅga on Madanlal Dhingra, Burse discussed how Dhingra's shooting of the British Lord Curzon was an expression of dayā—he was shouldering the responsibility of protecting "good people" from "bad people."

As in nāradīya kīrtan, rāṣṭrīya kīrtan ākhyāns consist of a spoken story interspersed with short songs used to convey the emotions of a character, to advance the story, or to simultaneously index various contexts and ideas. In addition to āryās, sākīs, diṅḍīs, abhaṅgas, and other genres used in nāradīya kīrtan, rāṣṭrīya kīrtankārs sing povāḍā, rājahaṅs, and kaṭhāv. These genres index nationalism and have strong, driving rhythms that provide an exciting rhythmic undercurrent to spoken or sung text and unite the genres of speech and song. The only type of kīrtan in which povāḍā is heard today is rāṣṭrīya kīrtan, and, even after almost 100 years of rāṣṭrīya kīrtan performance, povāḍā still carries its original associations of war and masculine bravery.[21] Kaṭhāv is often used to show the large scale of a battle, and a kīrtankār may use it to list many types of battle implements or to present a long list of delicacies to show the lavishness of a feast put on by a warrior king. The following insert describes song genres characteristic of rāṣṭrīya kīrtan uttararaṅgas.

Genres Sung in Rāṣṭrīya Kīrtan Uttararaṅgas

Rājahaṅs vṛtta: a genre that has its roots in drama music and is now a mainstay of rāṣṭrīya kīrtan. One rāṣṭrīya kīrtankār told me that rājahaṅs is used "to create fervor or say a lot in a short time,"[22] a sentiment echoed by other kīrtankārs. The quick, short, repeating phrases consisting primarily of staccato repetitions of a single note are iconic of something that one sees or experiences repeatedly and are accompanied by a *laggi* on the tablā with emphasis on the last half beat of the cycle that drives the rhythm insistently forward. A laggi is a quick rhythm in a four-beat meter (kīrtankārs often use the first half of keharva tāl or bhajani ṭheka) that repeats cyclically without much alteration.

Povāḍā: Povāḍā continues to index the historical storytelling of śāhīrs when used in rāṣṭrīya kīrtan. The outdoor performance context of povāḍā has contributed to a loud, forceful singing style (Ranade 1978) that reiterates the mood of strength and force—a mood that is maintained when povāḍās are sung indoors for kīrtans. Povāḍās are composed of long, flexible musical phrases based on a handful of stock melodies. Since povāḍā lyrics are partially improvised, the flexible melodic and rhythmic structure allows the singer to change the melodic rhythm by inserting and omitting syllables without disrupting the metric cycle. Povāḍā laggis provide an insistent rhythmic ostinato that sustains musical tension in long battle stories even as the performer periodically switches into speech.

Kaṭhāv: A song genre used for quickly listing items. The word kaṭhāv also refers to "an imposing display; firm and showy array (of troops, of a retinue, etc.),"[23] thus the term itself has associations of militarism. It consists of very short, quickly sung musical phrases that, in their unaltered repetitiveness, convey a feeling of infinite sameness or large quantities. Musical example 6.5 is a kaṭhāv sung by Charudatta Aphale listing the various vehicles upon which a group of people traveled—an elephant, a horse, a camel, and a swan.

lilting laggi accompaniment
Hat - ti varu - ni ko - ni cha - la
Gho - da uda - vit ko - ni pa - la - la
Un - ta var - ti ko - ni ba - sa - la
Houn - sa var - ti ko - ni sa - ja - la
Sa - re ge - le pra - dak - sha - ne - la

Musical Example 6.5.
Kaṭhāv.

When the story of the uttararaṅga is finished, the kīrtankār finishes with a closing moral that unites the themes from the pūrvaraṅga and uttararaṅga and leads back to the muḷpad in Rāga Bhairavi, a morning rāga performed at the end of concerts. In the kīrtan discussed in the next chapter, Sudhatai Dhamankar encapsulates her pūrvaraṅga on sadguru (great teacher) and her uttararaṅga on Tukārām as sadguru with these words: "When you find a sadguru, listen to his advice and behave accordingly. I give you my prayer that you will find this sadguru and I will pray to God that you get the sadguru" (audio example 6). This ends the uttararanga and commences the standard set of nāradīya kīrtan closing songs: Tukārām's abhaṅga, "Hecī dāna degā devā" (what a gift god has given us); *āratī*; and the bhajan, "Hari Rām Hari Rām Rām Rām Hari Hari." During the āratī, a small oil lamp is waved in front of an image of the deity, and all participants stand and sing the āratī song in three-quarter time (see Plate 6.5). The most commonly sung āratī is for Gaṇeś, but different texts are used depending on the occasion or the deity of the temple. During the āratī, audience members touch the kīrtankār's feet and place a few coins on the āratī plate or give her a donation of 1 to 50 rupees, then take *prasād* (a token of food consecrated by the deity and event) and leave.

CONCLUSIONS

The musical and narrative structures of nāradīya and rāṣṭrīya kīrtan do not promote participation to the same degree as vārkarī kīrtan. Nāradīya kīrtankārs have no ṭāḷkarīs to serve as leaders of group song, and their narratives are not peppered with familiar songs that lend themselves to unison performance. Instead, they compose or choose songs that fit the kīrtan being performed, and sing them in an improvisatory style using techniques from Hindustani music. There are moments in the beginning, middle, and end when the kīrtankār invites audience members to join her in singing bhajan, but these bhajans do not have the significant increases in tempo and dynamics that characterize vārkarī bhajans, nor do they last as long. In the

Plate 6.5.
Āratī after a Rāmdāsī kīrtan by Gajananbuva Railkar. Pune 2009. Photograph by Mark Nye.

uttararaṅga of nāradīya kīrtan, the kīrtankār becomes a storyteller, performing *for* rather than with the audience. The introduction of a story section as an integral part of nāradīya kīrtan in the nineteenth century not only facilitated entertainment-oriented kīrtan but also provided a structure conducive to politicization.

Rāṣṭrīya kīrtankārs combine Brahmanical and vārkarī methodologies and literatures, and traditionalize their political discourses with songs by the most loved of vārkarī saints, Tukārām. Within rāṣṭrīya kīrtan's devotional context—keyed at the beginning by the invocation of Gaṇapatī and the guru and at the end by āratī—political philosophies and stories of nationalist heroes acquire new religious significance. Nāradīya and rāṣṭrīya kīrtankārs appeal to audience members using their skill as musical soloists and their prowess in philosophy, and they combine the complex and somewhat exclusive path of jñān with the open and accessible path of vārkarī bhakti. Dress and mangalācaraṇ songs position the kīrtankār within a devotional and/or political lineage, but it is within the performative artistry of the pūrvaraṅga and uttararaṅga that songs and genres converse and collide to bring embodied nationalist meaning to this history. This is the subject of the next two chapters.

7

Sudhatai Dhamankar

Embedded Embodiments

During the congregational singing of a *devī* (goddess) song led by rāṣṭrīya kīrtankār Sudhatai Dhamankar at a temple in Pune, an elderly woman became so overwhelmed that she swayed vigorously and hyperventilated with eyes closed, attracting the concern and admiration of her neighbors until her trance subsided.[1] The intensity of this experience was unusual, but less ecstatic engaged responses like cheering, throwing rice, singing, crying, and clapping are common in nāradīya and rāṣṭrīya kīrtan. The power of kīrtan to affect listeners in profound ways led to its censure during the colonial era and more recently to the imprisonment of a Hindu nationalist kīrtankār who is prone to springing animatedly across the stage while shouting "Bhārata Mātā ki jay!" (victory to Mother India). How are these responses engendered and how do they operate in the service of the nation?

In this chapter and the next, I discuss the primary points of narrative and emotional impact in the uttararangas of two rāṣṭrīya kīrtans, one performed by Sudhatai Dhamankar in 1998 and the other by Yogeshwar Upasani in 2000, and examine how such moments lead to the notion that serving the Hindu nation is a legitimate means of *bhakti.* Rāṣṭrīya kīrtankārs use two general strategies for combining nation and devotion: nationalizing devotion and devotionalizing the nation. The former technique, outlined in this chapter's discussion of Sudhatai Dhamankar's kīrtan, involves creating a scene of worship using devotional song genres like bhajan, abhaṅga, and ovī before introducing a nationalist figure into that environment. Devotionalizing the nation, more popular in recent years, is exemplified by Yogeshwar Upasani's kīrtan and is discussed in Chapter 8. In this approach, genres like povāḍā and rājahaṅs generate a mood of militaristic excitement that is justified by the bhakti rasa of devotional abhaṅgas and bhajans. Both of these techniques involve the manipulation, juxtaposition, and resignification of song genres' indexical and iconic associations to create new meanings.

In his study of emotion and meaning in Zimbabwean musical nationalism, Thomas Turino proposes that "music, dance, clothing, food, and performative speech, in contrast [to propositional speech], typically function semiotically as icons and indices, and the indexical nature of these media especially augments their emotional potential" (Turino 2000: 174). Indices are particularly powerful because they are imprecise and have multiple simultaneous referents that resonate with people's past experiences without the potential hindrances of "language-based reflection" (Turino 2000:174). This assessment is certainly true for songs in kīrtan, which are "compact symbol[s]" (Wadley 93) that communicate through the messages in song texts, through the iconic nature of rhythms and melodies, and by indexing contexts in which the song genres are usually heard. When I asked listeners what makes rāṣṭriya kīrtan nationalist, they usually mentioned the song genres povāḍā, rājahaṅs, and kaṭhāv, all of which are associated with extra-kīrtan panegyric performances extolling the bravery of kings and soldiers. The indexical associations of these genres are reinforced through musical structures iconic of quick action and force, underpinned as they are by fast rhythmic ostinatos that drive the rhythm forward and imitate the speed and constant motion of the battle scenes they narrate. Rāṣṭrīya kīrtankārs play with song genre connotations to transform nationalist events into religious memory and they intersperse songs indexing devotion and nation in ways that generate new, complex, and succinct meanings.

The indexical and iconic associations of genres and styles reveal only part of the story of rāṣṭriya kīrtan's performativity. Just as important are the complex layers of subjective, intersubjective, and divine embodiment produced within kīrtan's ritual context. If the same genres and styles were combined in a performance coded as theatrical rather than religious, the emotional range and expectations would be quite different. As in other Hindu spiritual and devotional practices, the body performs a paradoxical but crucial role in achieving heightened states of consciousness. If we start, as phenomenologists Merleau-Ponty and Csordas have advocated, with what Scheper-Hughes and Locke call the individual body ("lived experience of the body-self"), we note that poet-saints danced, sobbed, and were infused with strength during kīrtan, and that kīrtankārs today cry, sweat profusely, and display unconventional bodily movement (Merleau-Ponty 1962, cf. Csordas 1990: 8–10, Merleau-Ponty 2003: 95, Scheper-Hughes and Lock 1987: 7). Thomas Csordas, in his paradigm-shifting piece on embodiment, argued for a phenomenological anthropology that begins with pre-objective (cultural) experience and moves outward to what Bourdieu calls the "socially informed body," a methodology that can be productively applied to rāṣṭriya kīrtan (Bourdieu 1977: 72, Csordas 1990: 8–12).

The pre-objective heightened experience of kīrtan is informed by social conventions that demarcate certain gestures as "acting" and others as "real," but ambivalences within the goals and form of kīrtan render this a difficult distinction. Kīrtankārs are dramatic storytellers who *also* have the potential for divine embodiment, and the aesthetic success of a performance is dependent on a kīrtankār's ability to traverse the delicate boundary between entertainment and authenticity. She must both entertain the audience as a singer and performer and also convince them of the sincerity of her emotion while providing an embodied link to the saints. Collective, authentically engaged bodies are the mechanism of spirituality, but the goal is a loss of bodily sensation that accompanies divine embodiment or "deep listening" (Becker 2004). The "body politic" (Scheper-Hughes and Lock 1987: 23–27) that emerges from this process is shaped by the power of the experience, the political-devotional content of the narrative, and the semiotic richness of the signs.

FROM KING TO SAINT: THE CONFUSION OF NATIONALIST AND DEVOTIONAL SELVES

Sudhatai Dhamankar (see Plate 7.1), in her rāṣṭrīya kīrtan on Tukārām and Shivaji, embeds a largely participatory vārkarī kīrtan within her performance-style rāṣṭrīya kīrtan, promoting audience participation in a way that would not have been possible without the embedding. The main players at the embedded kīrtan are a saint and a nationalist, who she and the audience embody through the mutual performance of ecstatic worship songs. The result of this embodiment is a confusion of the identities of saint, nationalist, kīrtankār, audience, and the divine, and the recreation of "Hindu nationalism" through performance.

This kīrtan was held in the Maharashtrian pilgrimage center of Pandharpur, where Dhamankar and her guru, the late G. N. Koparkar, had taken approximately forty people for an eight-day religious retreat in celebration of Kṛṣṇa's birthday. Dhamankar and Koparkar are regarded as religious authorities, and most of the people attending the kīrtan and retreat were there to participate in devotional activities and to receive religious instruction. All of the participants on the retreat as well as a few local people attended the kīrtan, which was held in an open-air hall on the grounds of the home of one of Pandharpur's saints.

Sudhatai based the purvaranga of her kīrtan on a poem by Saint Tukārām on the topic of finding a *sadguru* (true teacher), and how one should submit one's self completely to that sadguru once found. The uttararanga centers around two stories from the life of Shivaji, a seventeenth-century Marathi king. Shivaji Bhonsle has come to be regarded as a Marathi and/or Hindu "national" hero by many Maharashtrians, though he lived long before India's nationalist movement and had both Hindu and Muslim soldiers and noblemen (Ranade 1961: 15). By the seventeenth century, Mughal rulers had captured much of north India, but Shivaji provided a significant challenge to the unity

Plate 7.1.
Sudhatai Dhamankar performing kīrtan. Pune, 2009.

of Aurangzeb's sovereignty in the Deccan. Communalist historians and rāṣṭrīya kīrtankārs of the twentieth century have portrayed Shivaji as a freedom fighter working to rid the Hindu nation of Muslim oppressors. I will discuss the second of the two stories on Shivaji, in which Dhamankar explores how Shivaji worshipped Tukārām as a sadguru, and how this faith gave him political and military strength.

The story begins with Tukārām commencing his kīrtan in a temple in Pune by singing "Jayjay Viṭhobā Rakhumāi," a bhajan commonly used by vārkarī kīrtankārs. Sudhatai's singing of this bhajan indexes vārkarī kīrtan and cues the beginning of a vārkarī kīrtan within her rāṣṭrīya kīrtan. The bhajan consists of only one repeated line sung in a call-and-response fashion with the audience, allowing them to participate in both Sudhatai's rāṣṭrīya kīrtan and in the embedded vārkarī kīrtan of Tukārām that she is performing.

As is common with these types of bhajans, the music gradually becomes louder and faster as the rhythmic density increases. The cyclical structure encourages participation since the audience can join in at any point, and provides scope for ecstatic worship since the intensity of tempo and dynamics can increase unhindered by the restrictions of closed forms. In this first rendition of the bhajan, the tempo increases slightly—from ♩ = 112 to ♩ = 120—but the rhythm of the jhānj doubles in density. Participatory and cyclical songs such as these are found infrequently in nāradīya kīrtan but are very common in vārkarī kīrtan. By reenacting a vārkarī kīrtan cued by this bhajan, Sudhatai is able to harness its participatory potential and increase the ability of the audience to identify with the audience of the embedded kīrtan. This bhajan is for the vārkarī deity and the tune is a vārkarī one, but the technique of generating intensity more through rhythmic density than through quickened tempo is characteristic of nāradīya kīrtan. As the kīrtan proceeds, the increases in tempo become more pronounced, which generates excitement and brings the performance closer to vārkarī kīrtan (audio example six, 0:00–1:36,).

SPOKEN: Shivaji Rājā came to Pune and inquired with people where the sadguru was. He wanted the blessings of his sadguru. In that manner, in a Viṭṭhala Maṅdir in Lohagav—Tukārām Mahārāj's kīrtan was under way in that Viṭṭhala Maṅdir.... Maharashtra has had two great treasures: one was Samartha Rāmdāssvāmi and the other was Dehu's Saint Tukārām Mahārāj. Shivaji decides to go to his kīrtan and says, "Let's go to get guru's *darśan*."[2] ... Tukārām Mahārāj's kīrtan had begun.

BHAJAN: *Jayjay Viṭhobā Rakhumāi* (Victory to Viṭhobā and Rakhumāi)[3]

While Tukārām/Sudhatai is singing this song, Shivaji enters and is seated at the kīrtan. Tukārām notices his arrival and Sudhatai says, "Tukārām notices that Shivaji Rājā has arrived and is pleased and sings louder." As is typical in nāradīya/rāṣṭrīya kīrtan, when Sudhatai is narrating in the third person she speaks (or shouts) and when she is embodying Tukārām or someone else, it is usually through song or dance. After Tukārām resumes singing the bhajan along with the audience, he continues to increase the tempo to 138 beats per minute and stops the leisurely call-and-response pattern. Sudhatai/Tukārām begins to sing on every repetition, as though Tukārām had become so engrossed in the music that he could not wait for the audience to sing their line. At the end of the bhajan, Shivaji comes to the front of the temple and "falls at the feet of Tukārām," a gesture that solidifies the reversed roles of king as devotee and devotee/saint as king. From this point on, Tukārām begins advising Shivaji in tactical matters and demands his strict obedience (audio example 6, 1:37–2:24,).

SPEAKING: Tukārām notices that Shivaji Rājā has arrived and is pleased and sings louder.

BHAJAN: *Jayjay Viṭhobā Rakhumāi*

SPEAKING: When the bhajan was over, Shivaji Rājā fell at the feet of Tukārām Mahārāj, and with all of the people around, Tukārām Mahārāj begins the kīrtan with the abhaṅga chosen for the nirupaṇa.

Sudhatai then sings Tukārām's abhaṅga, "Janma yeuni kāy keli" ("What have you done since birth?") from Tukārām's perspective (audio example 6, 2:27–5:33,). At this point, her embodiment of Tukārām breaks down a bit because she sings his abhaṅga in a style that is decidedly nāradīya rather than vārkarī. It is in Rāga Bihāg, performed with classically inspired ornamentation in a deep, mellow voice. Following Hindustani vocal music performance practice, she sings the antarā[4] at a higher tessitura than the sthāi and introduces increasingly more ornamentation with each rendition of the antarā. Her rendering of this abhaṅga is unlike the high, tense, loud method of singing employed by vārkarīs. In a style that indexes "nāradīya" and "classical performance" like this, she could not hope to convince the audience that she is an ecstatic Tukārām.

> *Janma yeuni kāy keli/* After birth, what have you done?
> *Tuva muddala gamavile//* You've squandered all your capital//
> *Gelī gāṭhodicī madaci/* Lost the treasures you had tucked away/
> *Puḍhe bhikācī māgasī/* You will beg in the future//
> *Cālelā phirasī māghāra/* Then you will turn back/
> *Ajuna tari phajiṭa kohaḷa//* Still you're not ashamed/

This abhaṅga serves as a means for Dhamankar to traditionalize her kīrtan through a demonstration of her knowledge of the saint literature and to contextualize her message as "nationalist" because this abhaṅga has come to be associated with nationalist kīrtans.[5] "Janma yeuniyā"—and abhaṅgas with similar meanings—are interpreted by rāṣṭrīya kīrtankārs to mean that we (the audience) should actively work for the nation while we are physically able.[6] By using this abhaṅga in a rāṣṭrīya kīrtan context with Shivaji as a listener, Sudhatai is interpreting the abhaṅga as other rāṣṭrīya kīrtankārs have: after birth we should work for the nation. Of course, this is not the only possible interpretation of this abhaṅga and is probably not the one that Tukārām intended, given that there was no "nation" in the modern sense during Tukārām's era. Interpreted in a strictly spiritual light, this abhaṅga condemns those who are concerned only with amassing wealth and who turn to God only when they have lost all else.

After "he" is through singing this abhaṅga, someone tells Tukārām that the soldiers of the Nabāb of Chinchwad, a nearby Muslim ruler, have arrived to capture Shivaji and have surrounded the temple. When Shivaji gets up to leave, Tukārām, in his role as "king," orders the people to stay where they are. Tukārām is making a tactical plan of battle to keep Shivaji from being harmed, and his telling Shivaji to stay seated is the first step in the plan. Sudhatai then says that Tukārām stops the discourse of the kīrtan and begins singing a bhajan in praise of God, "Jayjay Pāṇḍuraṅga Hari." Jay means "victory to," and Pāṇḍuraṅga is a name for Viṭṭhala of Pandharpur (audio example 6, 5:35–8:59,).

SPEAKING: *Tukā mhaṇe kāy jāsi āpulyā.* Shivaji Rājā was listening, everyone was sitting in rows and listening. A thousand tāḷkarīs were standing in the back.

The Chinchwad Nabāb is spying on him. During the nice atmosphere of Tukārām Mahārāj's kīrtan, someone whispers in his ear that the army has surrounded the temple. Why? To catch Shivaji. Somebody tells Tukārām what is happening. Shivaji is about to leave. So Tukārām tells him that if he leaves, he'll be captured. "If you leave the kīrtan, Viṭṭhala will be angry!! Do not stand up!"

PAD: *Tukā he*... [text unclear]

Nāmāca gajar soḍu nāhi (Don't stop proclaiming God's name)

SPEAKING: Do not stop doing *gajar*[7] and no one leave! Don't stop doing gajar! And Tukārām Mahārāj stopped the nirupaṇa of our kīrtan and on the kīrtan platform...

BHAJAN: *Jayjay Pāṇḍuraṅga hari.* (Victory to Viṭṭhala Kṛṣṇa) (Musical Example 7.1)

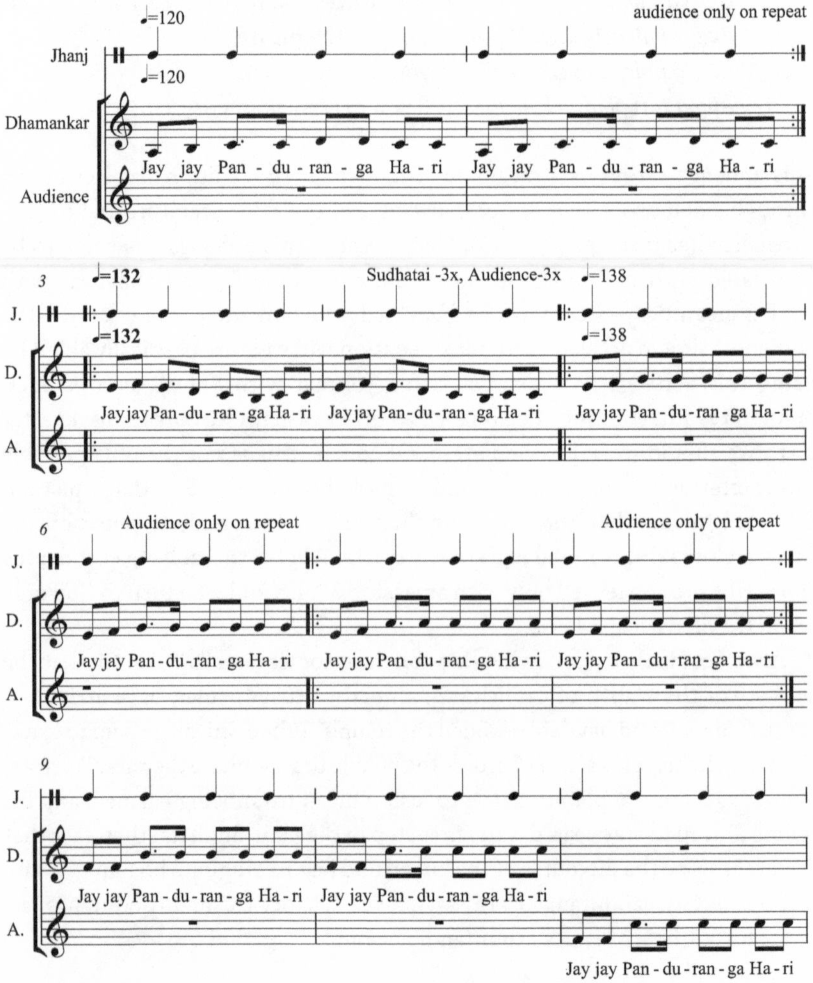

Musical Example 7.1.
Bhajan, "Jayjay Pāṇḍuraṅga Hari." Performed by Sudhatai Dhamankar.

We are nearing the climax of the story, and the amount of time Sudhatai spends using the third person speaking voice diminishes and the amount of time spent singing in the voice of Tukārām increases. She sings this bhajan in much the same way she sang the previous one, raising the pitch, rhythmic density, and dynamics. The pitch shifts to a higher point in this bhajan than in the previous one; Sudhatai incrementally works her way up to the high tonic here, while she had only progressed as far as the fifth in the previous bhajan (Musical Example 7.1). As Sudhatai sings "Jayjay Pāṇḍuraṅga hari," she dances, which is rare in nāradīya kīrtan, turning around in circles with eyes closed as she sings praise to Pāṇḍuraṅga. The audience echoes her enthusiasm with their own singing and clapping, and this portion of singing ends with nine repetitions of the last phrase. Later in the kīrtan, Sudhatai alludes to the transformative power of this musical/textual intensity when she says, "This power is in the words, in the intensity of bhakti . . . it got people engrossed."

The narrative and musical climax occurs when Tukārām motions to Shivaji to leave the temple (Musical Example 7.2). For the first time, the genres of speech and song collide; the actual audience identifies with the narrated audience and no longer relies on Sudhatai's sung prompts. Dhamankar interjects speech into the audience's singing of the bhajan, explaining how the soldiers outside also became engrossed in the music and began singing and dancing, using their shields and swords to beat out the rhythm. By speaking *over* the singing of the audience—rather than initiating a complete transition into speech mode—Sudhatai does not have to interrupt the excitement and flow of the music. When Sudhatai narrates over the singing, the pitch of the bhajan is at its highest point and the tension of the strained voices is not released until Shivaji escapes. The audience has hijacked the singing, no longer following the kīrtankār in the event, but independently enacting the embedded and embedding events.

After Shivaji has escaped, Sudhatai narrates, saying, "Shivaji Rājā escaped and reached Shivapur. After one hour, Tukārām Mahārāj began bringing down the . . . singing." When she resumes singing, she begins on the middle register tonic rather than the high tonic where she had paused, and gradually makes a decrescendo. Having begun this last rendition of the bhajan "Jayjay Pāṇḍuraṅga Hari" at 126 beats per minute, she slows to 120 beats per minute over the course of the performance. She explains that "when the singing came down and was stopped, people dropped their swords and shields" and stopped dancing. After the main discourse is finished, she notes that people are fooled by supposed sadgurus who perform miracles. What Tukārām did was not a miracle but was simply because "Tukārām Mahārāj was very alert, knew just what was happening, and gave the signal at the right time and freed Shivaji Mahārāj. It was only the power of the word that got people engrossed." Sudhatai and the audience at her kīrtan became similarly "engrossed," with the audience usurping the singing of the bhajan, and Sudhatai becoming immersed in dance (audio example 6, 8:58 until end of track,).

SPEAKING: Outside of the temple the soldiers were listening and dancing. They read the Jñāneśvarī and were Viṭṭhala bhaktas but were serving the Moghul rulers. Why? For work. They worked for Muslims, but they were Hindus, they were bhaktas. Outside of the Mandir, they were taking shield in one hand and sword in the other and playing them like ṭāḷkarīs.

BHAJAN: Jayjay Pāṇḍuraṅga Hari, jayjay Pāṇḍuraṅga Hari

SPEAKING: The people outside took their shields in one hand and swords in the other and were dancing...

BHAJAN: *Jayjay Pāṇḍuraṅga Hari, Jayjay Pāṇḍuraṅga Hari* (Musical Example 7.2).

BHAJAN: Jayjay Pāṇḍuraṅga Hari (ends on high tonic)

SPEAKING: He signaled to him and Shivaji Rājā escaped and reached Shivapur or wherever he was going. After one hour, Tukārām Mahārāj began bringing down the gajar.

BHAJAN: Jayjay Pāṇḍuraṅga Hari

SPEAKING: When the gajar came down and was stopped, people dropped their swords and shields. In Jñāneśvar's pālkhī the horses dance along with the ṭāḷ [she claps jhānj a couple of times and drum joins in]. But when the mṛḍang stops the horses stop dancing. The same was true for the soldiers.

BHAJAN: *Jayjay Viṭhobā Rakhumāi*

SPEAKING: Just like when horses stop dancing in the pālkhī when the bhajan stops, the people inside and outside of the temple stopped dancing when the gajar stopped. Then suddenly they got up. After taking *prasād*[8] and a blessing, they left the temple. The soldiers checked everyone leaving, but none of them were Shivaji. "You are not Shivaji! Go! You are not Shivaji! Go! You are not Shivaji! Go!" They checked each and every person, children, Tukārām, everyone. When the *pujāri* (temple priest) finally left and locked the temple they still never found Shivaji. How did it happen that Shivaji escaped safely? Because he had the mercy (*kṛpā*) of the sadguru. The job of the bhakta is to protect servants of dharma.
Another time everyone in a temple is made to look like Shivaji. Women, men, children, tall, short, wide. "How was he able to make everyone look like Shivaji?," someone asks. Because of his devotion to God, he receives these kinds of miracles. This power is in the words, in the intensity of devotion. This is how the devotee acquires it. This type of devotion is selfless.

In this instance, though, there was no miracle. Tukārām Mahārāj was very alert, knew just what was happening, and gave the signal at the right time and freed Shivaji Rājā. It was only the power of the word that got people engrossed. That is why Tukārām Mahārāj says in the first line:

Musical Example 7.2
Bhajan, "Jayjay Pāṇḍuraṅga Hari" with speech. Performed by Sudhatai Dhamankar.

ABHANGA:
Sadguruvānconī sāmpaḍenā soy/ Dharāve te pāy ādī ādī//1//
Tukā mhaṇe kaise āndhole he jana/ Gele visarun kharyā devā//4//

[Without a sadguru there is no way to find knowledge / One should devote one's self to the sadguru first // Tuka says, how blind these people are who have forgotten the real God //][9]

At the end of her kīrtan, Sudhatai comments on how her discussion of the concept of sadguru relates to politics today:

> Now be aware of imposters (*bhondhus*). Don't follow them with blind faith (*andhaśraddhā*). Keep your eyes open. This is what is happening in democracy. People are blindly following some politicians for what they'll get. This faith (*śraddhā*)... if it's gone from the world, it would be terrible. If you start questioning, "is she really my mother? Is he really my father? Is he really my brother? Is this really my house?" you'll go insane. You'll go crazy if you start questioning everything. There is no trust or belief anymore. What will help you in this is to look for the sadguru, and you will find him if you look for him. You have to believe. Look! Once you get his blessings, you will also get to Paramātma.

Dhamankar argues that the problem with democracy is that people follow politicians with blind faith, but the problem is also that people don't have enough faith, which makes them crazy with uncertainty. She is equating nondemocratic politics and following a sadguru, shifting between a discussion of politics and a discussion of religious faith. Dhamankar uses no linking phrases to indicate some *way* in which politics and religion are related, assuming a relationship not of similarity but of one-ness. Nondemocratic politics is not *like* following a sadguru; it *is* following a sadguru. Just as Shivaji submitted to Tukārām in his role as tactical advisor, Sudhatai encourages the audience to submit to the sadguru and to have faith in (certain) political leaders.

I did not interview audience members about Sudhatai's kīrtan when it was finished, but I spent eight days living with them and noticed a marked difference in their attitudes toward her after the kīrtan. Before the kīrtan many women had questioned Sudhatai's authority and complained about her strict running of the retreat, but they spoke about her in glowing, respectful terms after the kīrtan. No one said anything to indicate that they might take exception with any aspect of her performance. The audience members, who had come to the kīrtan primarily for religious reasons, unexpectedly took part in the performance of a devotional-political event.

BETWEEN TRANCE AND DRAMA

Most kīrtans fall between "trance" and "drama" at a place I am calling "devotional embodiment." While performing kīrtan, a kīrtankār invokes and speaks as a representative of the divine sage Nārad, and may even feel a merging with the divine, but this process falls short of "trance." Kīrtankārs are what Judith Becker might call "deep listeners," that is, "people who are profoundly moved, perhaps even to tears, by simply listening to a piece of music" (Becker 2004: 2). This is related physiologically and processually to more acute experiences of trance, which she defines "as a bodily event characterized by strong emotion, intense focus, the loss of the strong sense of self, usually enveloped by amnesia and a cessation of the inner language" (Becker 2003: 43). Although most kīrtankārs do not experience amnesia while performing kīrtan, they may capture fleeting moments of trance-like awareness and subjectivity, and they reference trance subjectivity by singing the songs of poet-saints who describe intense emotion and loss of self during kīrtan. Saint Eknath, in his sixteenth-century translation of and commentary on the *Bhāgwat*, described the ecstasy, intense emotion, and loss of sensory awareness that accompany kīrtan and bhakti (Eknath 1936: 49, my translation).

> Concentrating on that which does not change,
> The mind is overcome with love,
> Insistently crying,
> Sobbing intensely, breathing heavily//93// (A3, shloka 31/32)
>
> The loving confusion of bhakti,
> Untainted by the fatigue of *sādhana*,[10]
> Set free by the complete confusion of emotion,
> Awareness of the senses is gone //60// (A3 shloka 31/32)

Although kīrtankārs act out scenes from the lives of saints or Gods, a kīrtan is only called "drama" as an affront to the sincerity of the kīrtankār. Indeed, although many kīrtankārs told me of the importance of dramatic skills and oratory for kīrtan (see also Pathak 1980: 11–17), I also heard occasional whispers that such-and-such kīrtankār is "just acting." Tilak alluded to the difference between kīrtankārs and actors in his 1918 address to the Nagpur Kīrtan Sammelan:

> Today, efforts are made to preach religion through theater by writing and presenting dramas on the life of saints like Tukārām. But, according to me, the goal will be achieved through kīrtan better than theater. I believe that the actor performing as Tukārām is in one sense ridiculing the great saint. The majority of the audience knows very well about his activities behind the screen. So, even if in the play he presents a great religious analysis, people know that it is not real and is only a play. So, even regarding religion and morality, I give more importance to kīrtan. Basically it is religious and moral in form. (Tilak 1976: 821)

Kīrtankārs, conversely, are entitled to "perform as Tukārām" because they are thought to have higher moral standards than actors and are revered as divine representatives of Nārad while performing kīrtan. In an unpublished kīrtan instruction book, Vaman Kolhatkar writes that "the objective of kīrtan should be to teach people good behavior, so the kīrtankār should also behave well" (Kolhatkar 1995: 1). The minimum requirements of good behavior, according to Kolhatkar, include offering food to gods, Brahmans, and guests; being virtuous; doing sandhya twice a day; avoiding vice; speaking without lies, boasting, and empty words; protecting justice; serving gurus and the elderly

(Kolhatkar 1995: 1–4). Moreover, while an actor can perform the role of Tukārām (or some other saint) without devotion, a kīrtankār must perform with emotions of love and devotion. Tukārām and Namdev, saints who are often quoted in kīrtans, were harsh critics of devotional insincerity and lambasted kīrtankārs (*haridās*) and pravacankārs who feign sincerity and perform for money. This Namdev abhaṅga expresses this sentiment in no uncertain terms (Inamdar et al. 1979: 133, my translation):

> Name on the tongue, ṭāḷ in hand,
> The Black One[11] grants mercy.
> What do those songs do?
> Shame, shame they are shameful acts!
> The honor of the haridās is diluted,
> He breathes for money.
> The haridās's feet wallow around,
> How to stop from cutting his throat?
> Nama says he's a complete crook,
> One *harināṃ*[12] is too much.

In this discourse of authenticity, kīrtankārs with genuine devotion tell stories and sing songs of saints as a devotional exercise, and the bodily manifestations of devotion (sweating, dizziness, crying, detached expression) signal its veracity. Because bhakti was the main concern of vārkarī saints, vārkarī kīrtankārs emphasize devotion over other spiritual practices, and vārkarī kīrtans sometimes approach the trance-like abandon described by the saints. Toward the end of a kīrtan, when the cumulative excitement of collective song is at its height and the nirupaṇa is completed, audience and ṭāḷkarīs enthusiastically clap and sing bhajan, and the ṭāḷkarīs spin and jump in a coordinated dance. At this point, I have occasionally seen a kīrtankār close his eyes or become engrossed in the image of the divine for many minutes. The contrast of his quietude and the charged energy of the audience suggest that his mind and attention are elsewhere, indeed, that the collective energy has brought him to that place.

The vārkarī poets are commonly regarded as saints who represent, to borrow a phrase from Karen Prentiss (1999), "the embodiment of bhakti." The saints signify ideal devotion and their songs provide a means for ordinary devotees to reach the ultimate goal of bhakti, communion with the divine. In terms equally applicable to Marathi poetry, Norman Cutler (1987) refers to the process of communion in Tamil bhakti poetry as a "theology of embodiment."

> It is useful to think of Tamil bhakti poetry as a poetic corollary of a theology of embodiment. . . . Just as the presence of divinity is thought to be literally embodied in a properly consecrated stone or metal image or god, similarly the saints' communion with divinity is literally embodied in the recitation of his or

her poetry in a consecrated ritual environment. All who participate in the ritual performance of the saint's poem reenact the saint's experience of communion with the deity. (Cutler 1987: 113)

Cutler argues that audiences at recitations of Tamil bhakti poetry identify with the imagined audience of the original text as well as with the poet, while the poet identifies with God, creating an environment in which the audience can also identify with God (Cutler 1987: 37). The ultimate aim then is communion between God, saint, and audience that results from this series of identifications. Though Cutler indicates interest in the enactment of embodiment in temples, the burden of his analysis is on the poetic texts themselves and on the relationship defined by the poet with his or her intended audience, whether the poet takes the voice of devotee or of God. I am interested in the *performance* of bhakti and how series of identifications are created through performed songs that can lead to a blurring of distinctions between real and invoked participants. To achieve devotional embodiment in kīrtan, kīrtankār and participants sing, dance, and clap with vigorous bodies until sensation recedes and selves merge with the formless divine. In other words, divine communion begins phenomenologically with the experience of collective song and the visual-aural pleasure of experiencing the kīrtankār's transformation. Tukārām Mahārāj described in an abhaṅga how, through "sounds of love" and "swaying dance," the kīrtankār (or perhaps the kīrtan's audience) embodies Viṣṇu.

Kīrtan is good, kīrtan is good,
The body takes the form of Hari.
Sounds of love, swaying dance,
Consciousness of the body disappears. (Patil 1964: 108, my translation)

In nāradīya and rāṣṭriya kīrtan, the audience and kīrtankār experience the kīrtan's messages through the embodiment of saints and other figures in the story. In Dhamankar's kīrtan, the roles of devotee and ruler are temporarily reversed when Tukārām orders Shivaji to stay in the temple despite the fact that the Nabāb's soldiers are surrounding it. When the bhajan reaches its highest pitch and fastest tempo, Sudhatai's eyes close, and she waves her hands in the air while spinning around in circles. She is embodying an ecstatic Tukārām as the audience moves from the realm of performance to that of embodiment. No longer relying on her for call-and-response, the audience sings the bhajan, actively and independently recreating the kīrtan. Because everyone, even the soldiers, lost consciousness of their bodies, Shivaji was able to slip away without anyone noticing. Identities are lost and regained in ways that create a confusion of nationalist, saint, and observer.

The phenomenological experience of individual bodies during kīrtan emerges collectively and is led by the kīrtankār, who is responsible not only for choosing songs that inspire participation but also in gaining the attention and trust of the audience. She must entertain and engage, while also demonstrating that the emotions of devotion and love she embodies are genuine. While a gestural semiotics of kīrtan authenticity is beyond the scope of my research, it appears that kīrtankārs are deemed "real" if they experience some degree of abandon in the context of a highly formalized event, as Sudhatai did when she spun and danced until she became "less Sudhatai" and—with the help of singing participants—more Tukārām. The socially informed [kīrtankār's] body, to use Bourdieu's term, is one that can balance on the line between entertainment and ecstasy to engage listeners in a collective experience that further pushes the group toward devotional embodiment. It is on this precarious line between drama and trance that a kīrtankār can mold the body politic, in Sudhatai's case, toward an embodied feeling of natural belonging to a Hindu nation.

THE EMBEDDING OF EMBODIMENT

My interpretation is informed by Richard Bauman's (1992) analysis of a poem embedded within a narrating Icelandic legend about a magic-poet who recites a poem that kills his adversary. Bauman is interested in the dialogue of the genres verse and story, arguing that genres are rarely "pure" and are more often found in combination and communication. Bauman writes that the embedded text, though it may be radically set off from the main narrative by differences in dynamics, rhyme, meter, and figurative language, has an effect on the grammar and metaphor of the surrounding text (Bauman 1992: 132–135).

As in Bauman's example, the genres in Dhamankar's kīrtan are in communication with one another and the embedded event spills over into the embedding event, but the effect of the embedded event on the surrounding narrative is more extreme in Dhamankar's case than in the Icelandic legend. The genres of vārkarī and rāṣṭrīya kīrtan collide and compete, with vārkarī kīrtan usurping time from the rāṣṭrīya kīrtan and eventually invading the persona of the narrator. Sudhatai does not simply say what Tukārām said, but embodies him through song and movement until the narrative of Sudhatai is minimized and superseded by the ecstatic singing voice of Tukārām.

The enactment of a vārkarī kīrtan also gives Dhamankar license to abandon the more rigid decorum of nāradīya/rāṣṭrīya kīrtan and provides her with a method for encouraging audience participation. The vārkarī kīrtan is cued by her use of the bhajans "Jayjay Viṭhobā Rakhumāi" and then "Jayjay Pāṇḍuraṅga Hari." The audience understood that these songs indexed "vārkarī kīrtan" and participated in singing them as they would have at a vārkarī kīrtan. Since audience participation is only minimally built into the structure of nāradīya and rāṣṭrīya kīrtan, the use of a vārkarī kīrtan within the rāṣṭrīya kīrtan enabled Sudhatai to engage the audience in the performance.

Ultimately, it is the genre of the embedded kīrtan that allows the accomplishment of *collective* embodiment in Dhamankar's kīrtan. While performance of or participation in any type of kīrtan is considered a major method to achieve *mokṣa* (liberation from the cycle of rebirth), rāṣṭrīya kīrtankārs generally follow the path of jñān more vigorously than that of bhakti. They study the ancient Sanskrit texts, the poems and biographies of the poet-saints, and nationalist histories as preparation to preach to audiences through classically inspired song about the major messages of Hinduism and nationalism. Dhamankar is able to subvert the limitations of presentational performance in her rāṣṭrīya kīrtan by embedding within it a participatory vārkarī kīrtan in which "consciousness of the body disappears." The disembodied selves can then re-attach in new ways, and a king becomes a devotee, a devotee becomes a king, and "Hindu" becomes attached to "nationalism."

This technique of embedding a vārkarī kīrtan within the nāradīya kīrtan framework is used frequently by nāradīya and rāṣṭrīya kīrtankārs. For example, in a kīrtan on Saint Eknāth performed in Pune in April 2000, Gangadhar Vyas embedded a kīrtan of Eknāth within his own nāradīya kīrtan in a way that served to entertain and to increase audience participation.[13] In the re-creation of Eknāth's kīrtan, Vyas not only commented on Eknāth's saintly character and behavior, but also joked about the greediness, inattention, and lethargy of kīrtan audiences. The audience laughed at the stereotyped portrayal of themselves and eagerly joined Vyas in singing bhajans like "Jayjay Rāmkṛṣṇa Hari," echoing the participatory quality of vārkarī kīrtan. Moreshwarbuva Joshi, in a kīrtan on the nationalist revolutionary Vasudeo Balvant Phadke, briefly described how Phadke hid in a temple where a bhajan session of vārkarī bhajans and abhaṅgas was being held.[14] This was only a brief moment in a long kīrtan, but it served to characterize Phadke as a devotee, much as Shivaji was portrayed as a devotee of Tukārām in Dhamankar's kīrtan.

Embedding a vārkarī kīrtan within a performance is only one method for generating excitement in rāṣṭrīya kīrtan; kīrtankārs blend disparate song genres in their kīrtans in endless ways, deftly structuring audience members' sonic reminiscences and inducing emotional/behavioral responses. The basic structure of rāṣṭrīya kīrtan is standardized, but there is a great deal of personal variation in narrative style, choice of songs, and degree of interaction between performer and audience.

CONTEXTUALIZING KĪRTAN IN THE NATIONALIST ARENA

Sudhatai's kīrtans promote the discourse of Hindu nationalism espoused by organizations and parties such as the BJP, RSS, and VHP, but she is not affiliated with them in any direct way. In response to my survey question regarding her political party affiliation, Sudhatai wrote that "my only party is god-religion (*dev-dharma*)."[15] Although she speaks disparagingly of politicians and does not approve of democracy, her mistrust of secularism and of other religious communities intersects with the rhetoric of Hindu nationalist parties. Western cultural and economic structures threaten Brahmanical and "traditional" patterns of culture and knowledge, and people from other places and religions are scapegoated as the cause of cultural disjunctures. Dhamankar and the BJP blame a feeling of insecurity in a changed and changing India on Christians (Western economic and cultural practices in the global economy) and Muslims (with whom power is shared in a secular system). Despite the Hindu rhetoric of the BJP, their Hindu nationalist policies are diluted by a desire to appeal to as many people as possible, as well as by India's secular-democratic constitution and political structure. This dilution, as well as the common and understandable perception that politicians are corrupt, is probably the cause of her distance from party politics.

The goal of rāṣṭrīya kīrtan, Dhamankar wrote, is to "awaken people," and she does kīrtan because "if the nation is illuminated, then god, religion, and nation will be protected."[16] In interviews and in writing she does not specifically say what the nation needs to be protected from, but her sentiments become clear in speeches and kīrtans. In a short speech that she gave following Vasudeo Burse's kīrtan at her ashram, she asserted that "we need to keep a space for Hindus!" because (according to her) Muslim families consist of one husband, two wives, and eight to ten children, while Hindu families consist of a husband, a wife, and two children. Kīrtan is the remedy, she continued, and "If we do kīrtan in the streets, alleys, and intersections, Hindu religion and society will be like an elephant!"[17]

CONCLUSIONS

In the kīrtan described earlier, Sudhatai Dhamankar reaffirms and enacts a combined interpretation of religion and national politics. She uses music as a means to associate political and devotional concepts, as a way to engage the audience in her performance of Hindu nationalism, and as a vehicle to embody a saint and encourage the audience to embody a nationalist.

At the moment when Sudhatai's self merges with Tukārām's, and the audience's merges with Shivaji's and those devotees at the embedded kīrtan, the kīrtan is no longer a re-enactment. When we see Tukārām before us, unfazed by the fact the he is a woman in a sāḍī, and we feel Shivaji sitting among us, we have internalized the political message that Sudhatai is trying to convey. Nationalism, as personified by Shivaji, is devotion, and religion, as personified by Tukārām, is the ruling force that requires our submission and absolute adherence. Religion and politics are just distinct enough for this reversal of standard roles to be meaningful, but they are not tightly bound categories and become less so through the singing of ecstatic worship songs and the temporary loss of self. The audience at Sudhatai's rāṣṭrīya kīrtan becomes part of this process as their identities merge with those of Sudhatai and Tukārām, and through the unison singing of songs that led to the series of embedded embodiments that began with the kīrtankār.

8

Yogeshwar Upasani

The Collision of Genres and Collusion of Participants

Wise people live for themselves, but mad people live for the nation. Wise people have written the history of the nation, but mad ones have created it. You should become mad along with them.

———Yogeshwar Upasani, 2000

With these words, Yogeshwar Upasani ended his virtuosic performance of rāṣṭrīya kīrtan. His story—stocked with a standard repertoire of Hindu nationalist tropes—depicted a battle in which an impassioned seventeenth-century Hindu soldier fought and killed an elephant during a battle with a Muslim king. The soldier emerged bloody and half-dead, but victorious. In this chapter, I address the creation of madness through musical communication that Upasani alluded to in his final directive, and will use his kīrtan as my primary example. I am interested in the process through which discourse is transformed into personal, immediate experience, which is activated—at least in Upasani's case—by the use of dialogism in the service of monologism.

Upasani gave a dizzying performance, in which he moved adeptly between speech and song, between "pure" Marathi, Mumbai Marathi, Hindi, Urdu, and English; between genres; and between voices. He used this heteroglot format to actively engage the audience of about 1,000 people and invoke a religio-political world that existed outside that hall. In interpreting this complex performance, I enlist Bakhtin's notion of "dialogue," that is, the notion that a word, utterance, genre, or work is always colored and deflected by potential or previous utterances of the same word, by other utterances that surround it, and by the real or imagined responses of interlocutors (Bakhtin 1981:271–282, 1986: 73ff). Bakhtin's attention to multiple, intersecting voices and genres within the novel provides a set of interpretive tools that can help address the communicative strategies of the similarly multivoiced rāṣṭrīya kīrtan, but because his analyses were based primarily on written media, his treatment of context and performance are understandably limited. This bias toward text is perhaps one reason that Bakhtin's notion of dialogism has been more influential in historical musicology and music theory (e.g., Fast 1996, Heile 2004, Reynolds 2003) than in ethnomusicology, which has traditionally been concerned with orally transmitted music and with musical performance in cultural context. Folklorist/anthropologist Richard Bauman has filled a practical gap by applying Bakhtin's notion of dialogism to oral performance, but since his analyses are primarily of spoken genres, he is more concerned with syntax and semantics than with rhythm and melody (Bauman 2004). The present study is inspired by Bauman's use of Bakhtin, but engages more directly with musical sound than Bauman does.

Three types of dialogue—primarily between genres, but also between songs and modes of discourse—are relevant to the present discussion. In addition to the interpersonal dialogue in performance between performer and participants, I address the dialogue between adjacent genres in the text as well as the dialogue that emerges between a given performance of a genre and past/future performances of the same genre (intertextuality). In kirtan, adjacent genres often transition from dialogue to a more intense interpenetration of form and meaning that I term "collision," a process with profound political implications and emotional resonance. In referring to the second type of Bakhtinian dialogue, I use the term intertextuality[1] more often than other related terms (such as indexicality or associativity) because I find it useful to think about not only how past usages infuse texts with particular connotations but also about how texts from the present constrain the meanings of related texts of the future. Though the term "text" is used to refer to both written and oral instances of art and communication, some residue of the more literal meaning of the term seems difficult to avoid in musical studies. When analyzing texts qua texts, interpretations are limited only by the imagination of the scholar, but when texts are interpreted as an element of emergent performance contexts, we see how meanings are constrained by performers, participants, and listeners.

To address the larger narrative contours of this performance, I engage with Bakhtin's notion of the ongoing tension in communication between monologism and dialogism. The former refers to attempts by those in power to silence the dialogism of utterances in order to present a unified, "official" point of view, while the latter provides templates for multiple interpretations (Allen 2000:21–30). Bakhtin argued that certain large-scale genres are more dialogic than others. Poetry, for example, is less dialogic than the novel because the author's stylistic voice never becomes subsumed by the centrifugal forces of characters and speech styles threatening to de-center the voice of the author (Bakhtin 1981:277–278, 285–287). Similarly, kīrtan is most powerful when its dialogic qualities are emphasized and the body and voice of the kīrtankār recede, but it is precisely this invisibility that allows him or her to (re)produce a monologic master narrative that leads audience members toward particular interpretations and emotional responses. I believe that if we focus on performance, we find that performers often carefully limit possible interpretations so as to privilege certain signifieds over others, thereby creating monologism out of apparent and/or potential dialogism. It is the illusion of dialogism, I argue, that renders rāṣṭrīya kīrtan particularly powerful. In this presentation, I will use Richard Bauman's term for the role of the performer in this process: "manager" (Bauman 2004:2).

ARRIVING AT THE KĪRTAN

Upasani's rāṣṭrīya kīrtan was held in a concert hall in the middle of the Sadashiv Peth neighborhood of Pune, known as one of the old, established neighborhoods populated primarily by Brahmans. I attended the performance with a college student named Anupama, whom I had met while visiting a friend's Dale Carnegie Training course. Though she was raised in Pune, Anupama had never been to a kīrtan, and her curiosity about this local practice led her to join me on one of my outings. We entered rather late and thus had to take a seat in the balcony overlooking the concert hall, which was packed with about a thousand people of all ages. As we arrived, a man was in the middle of an introductory lecture on the nationalist importance of kīrtan, and when I whispered to Anupama that I was glad we hadn't missed the beginning of the kīrtan, she answered with, "oh, this isn't the kīrtan?" While rāṣṭrīya kīrtan is a performance medium that is exceedingly popular among certain people, it is far from being central to the lives of all—or even most—Punekārs, particularly young cosmopolitans like Anupama.

Temples are still the primary setting for kīrtans, but this rāṣṭrīya kīrtan was performed on a concert stage and was presented by the Akhil Bhāratīya Kīrtan Kula. The kīrtan began only after a series of speeches by senior members of the Kīrtan Kula, scholars, and Hindu nationalist political activists. This need to "frame" the kīrtan as emblematic of Marathi or Hindu culture is absent in temple kīrtans like Sudhatai's, which typically begin without introduction or speeches. Once Upasani had taken his place on "Nārad's mat" and bowed to the images of deities to his right side and to the musicians on either side of him, he began his invocatory prayers and songs, some of which he sang solo and some of which he sang with the audience.

Following temple kīrtans, the ritual significance of Nārad's mat is enacted as each member of the congregation comes to the front of the temple to touch the kīrtankār's feet and present him or her with an offering of money or food. Also, the host of the kīrtan garlands the kīrtankār and touches his or her feet between the pūrvaraṅga and uttararaṅga. Aspects of the ritual context were retained in Upasani's kīrtan, but they were re-framed by a proscenium stage that objectified the performance and separated listeners and performers. In this context, no audience members came to the front of the hall to touch the kīrtankār's feet, and donations were made while entering the hall rather than as a personal presentation to the kīrtankār after the performance, mirroring the economic behavior of the secular dramas that normally take place in that hall. The ritual importance of the kīrtankār was instead performed in the intermission between the two sections, when an officeholder of the Kīrtan Kula garlanded Upasani.

In addition to singing, Upasani also played jhānj and was accompanied by tablā and harmonium players, as well as by an ancillary percussionist who switched between several instruments, including a tambourine and a barrel drum (*ḍholak*). In this performance, the percussionists and the harmonium player were themselves musically talented rāṣṭrīya kīrtankārs who shared Upasani's Hindu nationalist inclinations. They comprise a close-knit group and represent just one of the several factions within the Kīrtan Kula formed on the basis of political orientation, musicianship, knowledge of Sanskrit scriptures, and degree and manner of engagement with politics.

BHAJAN: INTERTEXTUALITY AND THE COLLUSION OF PARTICIPANTS

The first excerpt I'll describe was performed at the beginning of Upasani's kīrtan. In this example, Upasani carefully managed the intertextuality of songs to include audience members in an affectively powerful experience of Hindu nationalism. After concluding a series of invocatory prayers and songs, he invited the audience to join him in a bhajan. Though rāṣṭrīya kīrtan is primarily presentational rather than participatory, there are a few instances in which audience participation is expected, including this first bhajan, and Upasani used the affective potential of shared performance to its maximum effect here. This bhajan allowed him to transition seamlessly from an indexing of devotional to political contexts. Upasani cued his bhajan through an introduction: "Let's sing so loud that our voices will reach each and every one of our homes. That's a lot. Everyone clap, clap with your hands, and in a loud voice take the name, Rāmrām. Sing!"[2] With this, he initiated a performance of the bhajan, "*Rāmkṛṣṇa hari, jay-jay Rāmkṛṣṇa hari*" (Musical Example 8.1), which translates as "Glory to Rāma, Kṛṣna, and Viṣṇu." This is a common bhajan, sung by people of all castes and classes in informal song sessions, while on pilgrimage, and while in temples, to name just a few settings. After singing this bhajan in call-and-response with the audience (measures 1 through 4), he gradually increased the rhythmic density of the percussion, and then sang the bhajan in double-time (measures 5 and 6) before switching to a Rāmajap (*Śrirām Jayrām Jayjay Rām*) characterized by a

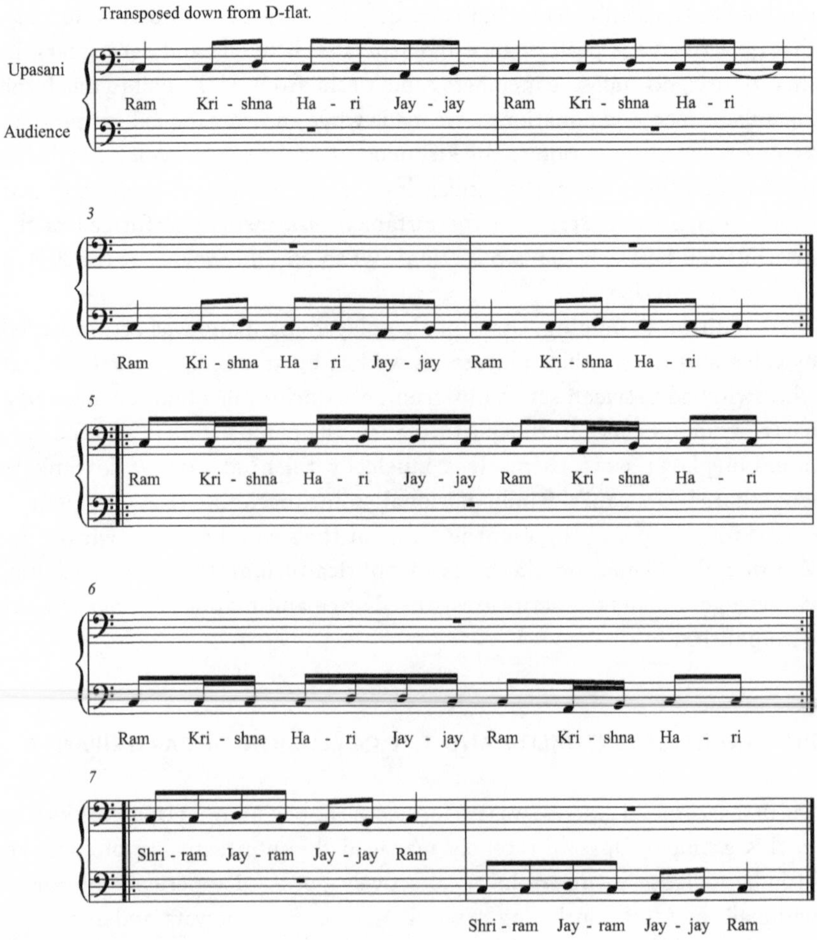

Musical Example 8.1.
Bhajan, "Rāmkṛṣṇa hari." Performed by Yogeshwar Upasani.

melody sharing the bhajan's contour and pitches that fits into the new metric cycle (measures 7 and 8). Jap is a chanted repetition of a deity's name as an act of penance and/or devotion, much like the recitation of the rosary. He has transformed the jap into a bhajan by eliding it rhythmically and melodically with the preceding bhajan (audio example 7,).

How do we interpret this experience? Why did the audience join in with such exceptional enthusiasm, and with what meanings did they interpret it? With what other performances of the bhajan genre and this song in particular is this performance intertextually related? As a genre that lives in the oral tradition, there is no "original" performance, and, at least for the first bhajan in this medley of two, it is so universally sung by Hindus in Maharashtra, that I doubt that it references any single context more than others. The second song, however, into which Upasani skillfully transitions through a compression of the melody, has stronger resonances with Hindu nationalism.

While the first bhajan is for three deities (though the first two are incarnations of the third), the jap is devoted solely to Rāma. Hindutva activists tore down a mosque in Ayodhya in 1992 that Hindu nationalists claim was built on the exact site of Rāma's birth, a symbolic act that provoked deadly Hindu-Muslim riots throughout India. One of the campaign promises of the ruling BJP was to build a Rāma temple on that site, but temple construction was not permitted until 2010 because of the possibility that it could lead to further communal unrest (Bhatt 2001:170–178, Hansen 2001:121–126, Mitta 2010). The indexical associations of bhajans and jap are highly context-dependent, and it is impossible to say that Rāmajap *necessarily* implies Hindu nationalism. For many people it evokes feelings from religious festivals or images of a grandmother's morning devotion, but it is precisely these memories that add emotional weight in a Hindu nationalist context. Though the meanings attached to Rāma are varied, this specific jap, "Śrirām Jayrām Jayjay Rām," has been flamboyantly appropriated by the VHP. A mass chanting of this jap was called by the VHP on November 26, 2001, to try to achieve support for the movement to build the Rāma temple on the site of the demolished mosque (Panicker 2001), and when Rajendra Singh, the former chief of the RSS, passed away in 2004, his funeral was marked by the mass chanting of this same jap (Express 2003).

To ensure that the Ayodhya-related interpretation of the Rāma jap was the dominant one, Upasani managed the intertextuality of this performance after the bhajan had concluded. In a loud voice, he said, "Who says it won't happen? If you just hear the voices of Punekārs, you will know that this is enough to build the Rāma temple," a comment that met with vigorous applause. Upasani is referring to the Ayodhya issue, and the bhajan included audience members in a shared and familiar experience that simultaneously indexed religious and nationalist sentiment. By increasing the rhythmic density of this melody, he was able to skillfully merge bhajan and jap such that their differences were downplayed, and the primarily religious associations of the first become intertwined with the complex, political/devotional associations of the second. Through all of this, he enlisted the help of tempo increases that promote ecstatic devotional experience in other contexts. The audience members were transformed into participants and as participants, into colluding enactors of Hindu nationalist discourse.

According to Irving Goffman, collusion is "the controlled systematic use of the multiple meanings of words and phrases in order to conceal speech behind speech, thereby effecting collusive communication between the very persons who are excolluded" (Goffman 1986: 514–515). In a footnote on the same page, he continues: "A simpler version of this controlled use of ambiguity is found in public political speeches wherein the speaker addresses special publics by means of second meanings that are not discernible (he hopes) to the larger audience. This technique in turn is to be distinguished from another framing possibility: a speaker's use of special voice and kinesic markers to openly direct his words temporarily to a special public" (Goffman 1986: 515). In this complex landscape of possibilities, Upasani ends with the most transparent of options, but that transparency provides a satisfying reward for the concealed collusion activated by the "special voice and kinesic markers" of genres with ambiguous associations. Indeed, by pulling back the curtain to publicly reveal his intended associations, he celebrates that collusion.

DIALOGUE/COLLISION OF GENRES

Having addressed the intertextual, intertemporal dialogue of genres, I now turn to a selection from the main part of Upasani's two-hour kīrtan to interrogate his engagement with "history" and his construction of dialogue between adjacent genres. Here, I found that kīrtan genres not only inform one another; they sometimes become indistinguishable. I term this complex interplay of sung and spoken genres—which I believe accounts for much of a performance's transformative power—"collision of genres." When genres collide, they rupture and are reformed—a sung genre becomes dissociated from its text and recombined with spoken narrative to surpass the "dialogue of genres" (Bauman 1992: 132–135) in which the syntax and style of quoted verse bleed into a surrounding narrative speech. In the previous chapter, we addressed how this process can activate the merging and transformation of subjectivities, while we attend now to the formal and rhetorical qualities of this transformation, theorized as collision.

The aggressive connotations of the term "collision" seem particularly appropriate for describing the interplay of genres in rāṣṭrīya kīrtan, since genres in kīrtan are most likely to collide when they narrate violence. Indeed, all of the genres that bring (Hindu) nationalism to rāṣṭrīya kīrtan (povāḍā, kaṭhāv, rājahaṅs) are used in combination with narrating speech. As a kīrtan progresses in time, spoken and sung genres alternate, competing for time, until eventually they collide and join, one no less important than the other. The ability of multi-participant music to collapse genres in this way sets it apart from the solo storytelling that Bauman discussed. Collision would be impossible without the capacity for some musicians and audience members to perform one genre while the kīrtankār becomes free to juxtapose it with another genre. The metaphor of collision suggests a combination of genres through their simultaneity without the implication of fusion or hybridity. If I collide with a tree branch, I may become bruised and scratched by the tree, and I may likewise leave some clothing threads on the branch, but I am not in a state of becoming the tree (nor, for that matter, is the tree becoming me). Similarly, the distinctness and impact of both genres is heightened through their simultaneity.

Upasani's pūrvaraṅga was structured around a devotional song (*abhanga*) by Eknath,[3] the sixteenth-century Brahman saint who composed Marathi songs (abhanga and *bhārūḍ*)[4] and a translation-commentary on the *Bhagvad*

Gītā in verse (*ovī*) form. The Eknāth abhanga chosen as the muḷpad for this pūrvaraṅga was similar in meaning to the Tukārām abhanga sung by Sudhatai Dhamankar, that is, "What have you done for people since taking birth?" The text of the Eknath abhanga is this:

By being born, what have you achieved, man? What have you achieved, man?
You've grown older; you have nourished your body with curd and milk.
    You have enjoyed pleasures of the flesh, but what have you achieved?
    May all that is virtuous remain with Janārdan.[5]

The crux of Upasani's pūrvaraṅga was that we should take stock of our worldly contributions, and since a nation comprises individuals, each individual's choices affects the entire nation. A particular set of choices that one should avoid, Upasani stressed, are those that favor the West over "our own culture." Instead, he said that one should "live for the nation" by nurturing pride in traditional culture and honoring the bravery of nationalist heroes. Kīrtankārs performing earlier in the twentieth century emphasized the insights of their pūrvaraṅgas, but many kīrtankārs of today (Upasani included) perform only very brief and straightforward pūrvaraṅgas, choosing instead to captivate audiences through the skillful performance of songs and stories in their uttararaṅgas.[6] While some kīrtankārs use the pūrvaraṅga to expound on subtle paurāṇik understandings of terms such as "truth" or "guru," Upasani made his points about patriotism concisely, elaborating mainly through brief anecdotal stories about why the audience should eschew Western values to follow the examples of selfless Indian saints. For example:

> "By being born, what have you achieved, man?"
>
> There comes one moment in every person's life, when he loses his way. Then he does not understand what a nation is. If it happens to an individual, it is okay. But when the whole society does it, then it is a matter of concern. Today we all are after Western culture, which is not a good thing for us. If only a few persons are doing it, it does not matter. But when many people are doing it, then it is a matter of concern. Why are you leaning towards the West? Look at the sun, now it is going towards the west, and as a consequence the whole world will have to stay in the dark for twelve hours. So stay where you are, don't lean towards the West. This means, follow your own culture and denounce Western culture. What have you done in your life? Have you done something for the good of the people? If some one asks you the question, "why are you born?" is there a good answer to that question? There must be some purpose behind the birth of every human being. What one achieves in life is important.
>
> Every one looks at life from different viewpoints. Saints have different views about it than politicians or social workers. Saints like to look at it as an opportunity to make the life of other people better. Everyone's life has some meaning

> and he should try to understand it and act accordingly. Saints have made the life of the people belonging to lower caste society better. They tried their best to teach them and make them understand their problems. They asked them to understand the purpose behind their life. After spending many years in penance, the saints have learnt that life must be lived for others and not for oneself. One gets happiness in living such a life, because that is why we are born. We should live not for ourselves but for others. The saints have helped our people to retain human values and the meaning of human life.
>
> These days every thing has changed. Now the girls born in the house of Sanskrit pandit are dancing in films in scanty clothes. When I see this it makes me sad. All of us have forgotten our glorious past and are dancing to the tune of Western culture. But we should go back to our own culture. We should listen to kīrtan, in which you can hear the old values and biographies of good people.
>
> No one asks oneself the question, "why am I born?" let alone answer it.

Following the pūrvaraṅga, a few announcements, and a brief participatory bhajan, Upasani embarked on the uttararaṅga, a story set in Shivaji's seventeenth-century kingdom that illustrated and enlivened the pūrvaraṅga's notion that one should follow the example of heroes who lived for the nation and honor them through the remembrance of storytelling. Common themes in rāṣṭrīya kīrtan include the *śaurya* (bravery) with which Shivaji killed Afzal Khan or the *rāṣṭrabhakti* (patriotism/devotion to nation) that was his weapon against Qutub Shah, all framed in stark Hindu-Muslim terms. In Upasani's kīrtan, the focus is on the bravery and single-minded nationalist devotion of one of Shivaji's soldiers, but he sets the scene with a lengthy song extolling the virtues of Shivaji himself.

The song Upasani chose for his panegyric to Shivaji was povāḍā (audio example 8,). As discussed in Chapter 6, the employment of povāḍā distinguishes rāṣṭrīya kīrtan from other styles of Marathi kīrtan, and when I asked kīrtankārs to list nationalist song genres heard in rāṣṭrīya kīrtan, povāḍā invariably topped their lists. Povāḍā rhythms, with their driving emphasis on the last beat of a metric cycle, provide an insistent rhythmic ostinato that sustains musical tension in long battle stories when the performer periodically switches into speech. The tāla used in povāḍā is only four beats long (as opposed to the more common eight beat meters used in most Marathi devotional music), so a singer can rest for a cycle without leaving a long melodic gap. Povāḍās are sung in a handful of stock tunes, all of which are characterized by abundant note repetition, stepwise motion, a swung rhythm, and long, descending, stepwise phrases spanning at least an octave at the end of narrative sections. Singers of povāḍā often utter the word "jī" ("yes," borrowed from Hindi) at the ends of some phrases.

The povāḍā commences after Upasani narrates a dialogue in which Shivaji asks his advisor if the army is ready for battle. Upasani then sings the advisor's response in a standard povāḍā tune and the action has begun: "We have gathered together 30,000 soldiers. King, we are completely ready for the attack."

After singing these phrases for a few minutes, Upasani switches into a speaking voice. While he speaks, the tablā and harmonium player continue playing the meter and melody associated with povāḍā. As the melody continues, Upasani uses a poetic recitation genre to invoke Ramdas, the Marathi saint who many conservative (particularly Brahman) kīrtankārs say was Shivaji's guru. He quotes Ramdas as saying, "*Śivarāyace kaise cālaṇe, Śivarāyace kaise bolaṇe* (How King Shivaji walks! How King Shivaji talks!)." Povāḍā has collided with poetic recitation, and the frenzy of preparing for battle lingers in the povāḍā rhythms and melodies even as the battle is justified by the admiration of a saint.

After a few such transitions between sung povāḍā and spoken narrative/instrumental rendering of povāḍā, the battle preparations have become firmly attached to their melodies and rhythms. When Upasani periodically returns to spoken narrative (as the tune continues on harmonium), he situates the battle within what he describes as a supremely idyllic time, when even the horses of kings and queens were more honest than people are today. He also uses these moments of speech to interweave Shivaji's narrative with those of the saints Jñāneśvar, Eknāth, Tukārām, and Rāmdās, and to state that Shivaji "was the protector of these saints and the creator of history in this country." He depicts an idyllic era, when the elderly didn't live in nursing homes, women were safe, Brahmans and cows were protected, and rulers were Hindu. The past is invoked through povāḍā and contextualized through spoken narrative—when spoken and sung genres collide, so do temporalities. Pastness—in this povāḍā within a kīrtan—becomes a metaphor for what is lacking in contemporary society and serves as a model for an "alternative civil society."

This practice of collision is just one strategy employed by kīrtankārs to destroy generic boundaries and lend the emotional resonance of devotion to politics (and vice versa). Most of the rāṣṭrīya kīrtans I attended employed this technique at least once in the course of performance, and the povāḍā genre often enabled the juxtaposition of speech and song, but it should be noted that all of the song genres most often cited as nationalist by my consultants had the rhythmic and melodic prerequisites for this process. The songs used to express pure devotion or familial love, on the other hand, were typically either unmetered or underpinned by longer tālas and more complex melodies that rendered the transitions between speech and song more problematic.

As discussed in the previous chapter, Sudhatai Dhamankar, in her kīrtan on Tukārām and Shivaji, did not employ political or historical genres, but she did collide spoken and sung genres in a manner similar to Upasani (albeit much more briefly). The main difference is that Sudhatai merges religion and politics by politicizing a devotional, temple scene while Upasanibuva devotionalizes a battle scene. Sudhatai's approach is much less common in contemporary rāṣṭrīya kīrtans, for which povāḍā, kaṭhāv, and rājahaṅs have become de rigueur. Instead, her performance is a remnant of an older style of rāṣṭrīya kīrtan, when the genre's practice had not yet become standardized and when Hindu nationalism did not yet necessarily imply aggressive action.

In addition to enacting a similar, albeit inversely related, combination of religion and politics, how does the collision of genres operate affectively in each kīrtan? First, musical tension is generated when accompanists maintain repeating musical patterns indefinitely, creating a sense of elongated time or uncertainly paused action, as in a moment later in Upasani's kīrtan when the harmonium player transitions from a three-note melody to the repetition of a single note while Upasani narrates dancing. Second, the exciting rhythms that produce embodied responses like dancing or clapping continue as the kīrtankār speaks over the harmonium and tablā. In both kīrtans, this technique is used to narrate scenes characterized by physical action and movement: in Sudhatai's kīrtan, dancing in devotional ecstasy, and in Upasani's kīrtan, recreational dance and the movement of soldiers across a battlefield. Perhaps the most significant difference is that Upasani's juxtaposition of speech and song in povāḍā functions to create a vivid image of a battle from days gone by, to which the spoken narration lends contemporary significance. Sudhatai, on the other hand, engages not just the accompanists, but also the audience in the performance, so that the past becomes present through their participation.

KILLING THE ELEPHANT: RELIGIOUS ARCHETYPES IN SPEECH AND SONG

The scene of the uttararaṅga's main story, in which King Qutub Shah challenges Shivaji's soldier Yesaji Kanka to fight an elephant, is set by descriptions of Shivaji (through the povāḍā discussed earlier), Yesaji (through a march-like narrative song), and Qutub Shah (through a parody of how he is introduced in court in Urdu, painting him as vain and frivolous). After the povāḍā, which shifts between third-person narrative and first-person dialogue, Upasani begins to move toward songs sung exclusively in the first person, lending a sense of immediacy and dramatic embodiment to the kīrtan. The primary action of Upasani's story centers on Yesaji fighting and ultimately killing an elephant, and builds on the metaphor that "all of Shivaji's soldiers were as strong as elephants." The battle is initially narrated with speech and then through a song describing Yesaji's devotion and bravery. Yesaji eventually collapses with an injury after fighting the elephant almost until exhaustion, causing someone to think he is dead and cry out "*melā*!" which is Marathi for "he died" (audio example 9,). The Punjabis associated with Qutub Shah are portrayed as dim-witted traitors who, on hearing the word "melā," think that it is the Hindi noun meaning festival or celebration (pronounced *meḷā* in Marathi). Upasani then sings and dances a *bhangra* of celebration in an embodiment of the Punjabi characters' callous joy (audio example 9, 0:33–3:00,). Bhangra is a dance genre originally associated with *baisaki* (the harvest celebration) in Punjab, which has now achieved a transnational, year-round audience of young diasporic South Asians. Upasani's bhangra tune is actually from the 1956 Hindi film, *Jagte Raho*. The swung rhythmic pattern, characteristic bhangra bravado, and invocation of "melā" identify this piece as bhangra, but the mixture of Punjabi and Marathi lyrics and the replacement of the large dhol drum with tablā, harmonium, and jhānj indicate that it is mediated by and for Marathi people.

Upasani speaks over the bhangra, first depicting the celebrations and Yesaji's diminishing strength, and then switching to a description of his renewed resolve, the continuing rhythm underneath the spoken text maintaining the vitality of the dancing even as the subject is changed. Following the bhangra, Shivaji's concern and devotion to the goddess are expressed through his singing of a goṅdhaḷ, a Marathi genre sung in praise of the Devi (goddess) by male hereditary musicians employed by temples and neighborhoods (audio example 9, 3:00 through the end of the track,). This goṅdhaḷ is characterized by a denser rhythm and less swing than the bhangra, but its melodic contour, tempo, and repeated notes are similar.

Both the bhangra and the goṅdhaḷ are sung in the first person in a downplaying of the distinction between narrator and narrated that allows the audience to have a more direct experience of the re-created event. The similarities in melodic contour and tempo of the bhangra and the goṅdhaḷ enable Upasani to move from one to the other almost without pause, much as Upasani had moved fluidly from the bhajan to the nāmjap at the beginning of the pūrvaraṅga. Despite the similarities in sound, the goṅdhaḷ, the text of which pleads, "Protect my child," contrasts pious concern and prayer with the evil celebration of dancing at a time of death. Almost as soon as the song is finished, Yesaji kills the elephant with a single blow of his club, and the audience bursts into applause (audio example 9, 5:29–end,).

During this battle episode, Shivaji is portrayed as caring and pious through his singing of songs for the Devī, while Muslims and Muslim-supporters are represented as foolish and insincere through their singing of secular songs of celebration. Bhangra has particular resonance with younger audiences; this Punjabi song/dance style has gained all-India appeal through its use in popular Hindi films, and Upasani's tune is actually borrowed from a "golden age" Hindi film. The kīrtan audience clapped, smiled, and laughed while Upasani sang the bhangra—simultaneously enjoying its infectious rhythms and imbibing a condescending view of its performers. Upasani maintains the tension of battle by creating rhythmic continuity between speech and song; and he uses song genre connotations to portray Hindus as both the heroes of this battle and as the only community with bhakti for both *dev* and *deś*.

The emotional impact of this denouement of the kīrtan is intensified by the convergence of multiple modes of dialogue. Adjacent genres are in dialogue—sonic differences between bhangra and goṅdhaḷ are downplayed while the partying and piety of religious communities are set in relief. As narrating speech and sung speech collide, the narrative voice slowly recedes in favor of first-person embodiment of diegetic songs. This in turn encourages a more active dialogue between audience and kīrtankār—listeners contribute to the performance by clapping to the bhangra rhythm and cheering for Yesaji as though they were spectators at his fight.

MARATHI IDENTITY, PERFORMANCE, AND NATIONALIST EMOTION

My primary concern in this chapter has been with the performance of political ideologies as acts of musical communication, but I have spent more time addressing the *hows* than the *whats* of communication. This is intended primarily as a corrective to folkloristic studies that minimize the importance of musical sound, analyzing sung genres with little treatment of how melody and rhythm contribute to narrative. Rāṣṭrīya kīrtan comprises both narrative and song, so to ignore narrative structures and meanings leads to an incomplete portrait of performance. Based on Upasani's allusion to the Bābri Masjid/Rāmjanmabhūmī issue after the initial bhajan, and his appearance during a festival organized by the faction of the All-India Kīrtan Kula that supports the RSS, it can safely be said that his views are in line with those of contemporary Hindu nationalist politics. This is, however, not simply a Marathi reiteration of narratives and ideologies that were created by centralized political parties/organizations such as the RSS, BJP, and VHP. Marathi-centric nationalism has never represented a separatist regional movement or a simple translation of centrally produced discourses. Maharashtrian nationalism in the late nineteenth and early twentieth centuries articulated a space for Maharashtrians in the nation-state, while rallying the "emotive resources" of regional identity (Deshpande 2006:37). In rāṣṭrīya kīrtan, these emotive resources are intensified through the strategic use of Marathi song genres. For less cosmopolitan audience members, evocations of Marathiness help assure them that there is a space for Marathi people within the nation, while also attracting them through the power of familiar and emotionally resonant songs, stories, and drama.

Upasani's pūrvaraṅga poses a distinction between "The West" and "India," in which "The West" (girls dancing in scanty clothing, children out of wedlock, apathy) represents a threat to "Indian culture" (saints, kīrtan, "the past," martyrdom for the nation, respect for elders). This dichotomy is further elaborated in the povāḍā section of the uttararaṅga, in which pastness stands for an essential Marathi/Indian valor and is articulated through the interplay between povāḍā and narrative speech. Pastness becomes associated with sung povāḍā, and Upasani switches to speech both to narrate the significance of Shivaji in Maharashtrian history and to draw contrasts with the current situation. Temporality enhanced the dichotomization of East and West, and the collision of narrating speech and song in the povāḍā enabled Upasani to foreground these imagined temporal/spatial disjunctures. For example, after having established the size and grandeur of Shivaji's army through povāḍā, Upasani switched to narrative speech to contrast this image with contemporary life: "The horse of Queen Laxmibai of Zhansi created history. But today even the human beings of our country have become dishonest. What a time this is!" A stark East-West binary is a feature of the colonial orientalist discourse that was mirrored by all-India elite nationalist leaders at the turn of the last century (Chatterjee 1993), but it was a less pervasive element of rāṣṭrīya kīrtan from that time period than it has become today. The new RSS-inspired kīrtan generates a sonic manifestation of "Hindu culture" in need of protection, an idea that is communicated through the introductory speeches and the kīrtankār's narrating voice. Staged kīrtans sponsored by institutions such as the Kīrtan Kula have been leading to the use of kīrtan as an objectified symbol of Hindu-ness rather than as an active conduit for nationalist/devotional discourses.

Though I can guess at the communicative motivations and narrative-musical techniques of the kīrtankār (dialogue, collusion, and collision), it is more difficult to gauge how the audience is actually receiving his performance. It is nearly impossible to determine whether a kīrtan such as Upasani's has a lasting influence on listeners and whether it was received in the way the singer intended. Although audiences are predisposed to accept what a kīrtankār says—given that he is speaking from Nārad's mat—performances are nonetheless met with differing degrees of appreciation, and kīrtankārs are not beyond criticism.

In the case discussed here, audience enjoyment was palpable; I observed most audience members responding to Upasani's jokes by laughing, his rhythms by clapping, and his depictions of shocking events by gasping. Even my young cosmopolitan friend said that she had really enjoyed the performance and only seemed aware of its exclusionary politics after I mentioned that I disagreed with his remarks against Christians and Muslims. Of the many glowing responses I heard, one comment—made to me by an office bearer in the Kīrtan Kula—was particularly memorable. He sought me out to tell me with uncharacteristic enthusiasm, "Now, *this* is what rāṣṭrīya kīrtan really is!" I responded by telling him that yes, it was rāṣṭrīya, as was the entire festival, to which he answered, before moving away to talk with other friends, "Yes, but this is truly rāṣṭrīya, which the others weren't." Without further explanation, I was left to speculate on what he might have meant. Given that stories of Shivaji's protection of Marathi honor are commonplace in rāṣṭrīya kīrtan, the subject matter of this kīrtan was not unusual, nor were the techniques he used to generate participation and to conflate religion and politics, though Upasani is a particularly skilled performer. When comparing this kīrtan to those that the commentator did not consider "truly" rāṣṭrīya, I see one major difference: Upasani aligned himself in explicit ways with projects—such as the Ayodhya controversy—of Hindutva organizations. Nationalism, in other words, refers to a particular type of Hindu nationalism, based on the actions and ideologies of

Hindutva groups and communicated through a Marathi idiom. Some kīrtankārs, such as Jaytumbi Maharaj (a Muslim woman) or Ghaisas Guruji, advocate service to a non-Hindutva nation, and still other rāṣṭrīya kīrtankārs index an ambiguous Hindutva identity while eschewing association with contemporary parties and organizations. Upasani, on the other hand, ultimately leaves little room for multiple interpretations.

CONCLUSIONS

My primary motivation in this chapter has been to achieve some understanding of the processes through which Hindu nationalism is created and communicated in performance. When kīrtankārs perform particular genres, they do so in relation to past and future performances of the same genre and in relation to surrounding genres, as well as in relation to the anticipated and actual responses of listeners and participants. In his analysis of novels, Bakhtin regarded competing voices and genres as threats to the unitary vision presented by the author, pulling it centrifugally toward a multiplicity of interpretations. In kīrtan, it is precisely when dialogue and centrifugal forces appear strongest—such as when kīrtankār and audience merge during the bhajan or when narrative speech and sung povāḍā collide—that the actual monologic control of the kīrtankār emerges. When monologue wears the cloak of dialogue, the performer can almost imperceptibly, and thus more powerfully, manage the interpretations of audience members. Upasani was a particularly skilled manager of interpretations, leading participants from bhajan to Hindu nationalist chant, transforming a sung historical narrative into a backdrop for his contemporary social and political criticism, and dancing to the music of an Indian religious minority. His ability to transform the dialogic texts in this performance to a shared monologue with the audience speaks both to his temporary ritual authority and to his unique power as a performer.

To conclude, I believe that a nuanced treatment of the many axes on which dialogue in performance is presented, managed, and experienced can allow us to approach a glimpse of the power of song and speech to generate emotion and devotion. By focusing on performance, we are reminded that master narratives such as Hindu nationalism must be communicated to individuals in particular contexts, and it is in these unique contexts that Hindu nationalism becomes both personally felt and locally articulated. When we read about the effects of Hindu nationalism in histories based on written document of political leaders, we miss the lived experiences by which nationalist sentiment is produced and reproduced. To become devoted to the nation, even willing to die and kill for it, people experience nationalist ideas in sonic and physical ways: they create the mad history of the nation.

9

Conclusion

Throughout the twentieth century, kīrtankārs have used compelling narratives, their own spiritual authority, and the words of the Marathi saints to convince Maharashtrians of the spiritual benefits of working for the nation. Rāṣṭrīya kīrtankārs sing a Hindu nation to audiences ranging in size from just a handful of listeners in neighborhood temples to crowds of thousands in packed concert halls, providing an embodied experience of nationalism from the auspicious position of Nārad's mat. They sing and preach in idioms that are emotionally resonant only for Marathi speakers, aligning themselves with all-Indian leaders when interests converge and staking their own territory when they don't. Over the past hundred years, some audience members have turned to rāṣṭrīya kīrtan because it is an integral part of their family histories, others enjoy kīrtan as a conscious rejection of things "Western," and still others are attracted to the fiery zeal of nationalism in performance. Rāṣṭrīya kīrtan has been shaped by forces that are unique to Maharashtra: Brahman patronage of Marathi arts since the eighteenth century, Marathi cosmopolitan intellectuals' leadership in the anti-colonial movement, an insular conservative Brahmanism following Gandhi's assassination, a vibrant theatrical tradition, and strong rural support for the Congress party and Maratha leadership.

This political, caste, social, and artistic landscape has contributed to the development of Marathi rāṣṭrīya kīrtan, but Maharashtra is not alone in staking out an artistic regional voice within broader Indian nationalism(s). Indeed, rāṣṭrīya kīrtan is only one of several regional nationalist performing arts in India. North Indian *rāṣṭrīya gīt* (nationalist song), for example, has been performed by professional and semi-professional rural folk singers since the anti-colonial movement. Edward Henry recorded nationalist *birahā* songs in Bhojpuri-speaking Uttar Pradesh, India, in the early 1970s (Henry 1988: 202–206), and singers from Rajasthan and Uttar Pradesh can be heard performing rāṣṭrīya gīt about khādī, national unity, and the nation on the beatsofindia.com website.[1] In the 1950s, *harikathā kālakśepama*, a Tamil genre derived from Marathi kīrtan, was performed to promote the five-year plans (Singer 1972), and North Indian *nāuṭankī* theater artists between 1895 and 1920 incorporated Rajput martial sangīts and ālhās (Hansen 1991). These heroic songs depicted Rajput victories over Mughal kings using regional tropes and depictions of Rajput chivalry, bravery, and virtue that, as argued by Kathryn Hansen,

> may have helped disseminate a new strand of nationalism, insofar as they proposed armed combat as the appropriate means of righting society's wrongs. Their model of active struggle paralleled the nationalist ideology emerging from leaders such as Bal Gangadhar Tilak and later Subhash Chandra Bose. The Alha Nautankis' representation of the forcible redress of injustice thus reinforced the agenda of the activist wing and may in circular fashion have gained in popularity because of the ascendance of such leaders. (Hansen 1991: 133)

Regional musical idioms throughout India have been used to rally support for the anti-colonial movement, to construct national identity, and to arouse nationalist sentiment. Taken together, they comprise a nationalist patchwork of regional performances that reference regional heroes, social practices, and generic meanings. Further research in these traditions would illuminate whether these singers served as regional nationalist *leaders* in a manner akin to rāṣṭrīya kīrtankārs.

Because I was trained as an anthropologist rather than a historian, my method for approaching the past was informed by my approach to the present, with one person (or source) leading me to another until I had a sense for the range of perspectives on a belief or practice. Kīrtankārs in the new millennium tell oral histories and perform historical kīrtans that feature kīrtankārs from the past as nationalist leaders. These highly positioned accounts are not "objective" sources, but they do tell us about how leadership is constructed in a conservative Hindu community. They are remarkably similar in style and metaphor to accounts of national leadership by pre-Independence rāṣṭrīya kīrtankārs as documented in their autobiographies, biographies, published kīrtan texts, and pedagogical books. These sources, along with magazine and newspaper articles, comprise the data for the early portion of the book. Missing are recordings of performances from before the 1950s, accounts (other than a few newspaper articles) by kīrtan attendees written before the 1950s, and government reports on the activities of kīrtankārs. I was unable to find recordings and first-person accounts, but Prachi Deshpande refers to colonial intelligence reports on a nationalist singer named Haribhau Bhandare in the Maharashtra State Archives (Deshpande 2007: 147–148). My ethnography of the past has resulted in omissions of some sources, particularly those of a more "official" nature, but it offers a route to the past charted by kīrtankārs and kīrtan enthusiasts. This is an account of historical memory (Deshpande 2007: 6–7), or to be more precise, of the historical memories of historical memory that form the core of rāṣṭrīya kīrtan.

The differences between the historical approach of Chapters 2 through 4 and the ethnographic method of Chapters 5 through 8 has led me to interpret pre-Independence and late twentieth-century rāṣṭrīya kīrtan differently. Since I did not have access to any recordings (or live performances) of early rāṣṭrīya kīrtans, my comments are based on oral histories and written documents. Historical memory tends to mythologize and idealize, and thus my account of anti-colonial rāṣṭrīya kīrtankārs may weigh too heavily in favor of the spiritual while paying inadequate attention to the more mundane aspects of these kīrtankārs' performances and personas. When I explored rāṣṭrīya kīrtan in the present day, on the other hand, I could see the sharp details of recent experience without rose-colored glasses. Moreover, by attending and recording live kīrtans, I was able to gain a sense of kīrtankārs' lives outside of kīrtan and their feelings regarding politics and performance, while witnessing the aesthetic power of kīrtans and analyzing the musical structures of kīrtan as they emerge in semi-improvised performance. The most difficult aspect of the ethnographic portion of this work has been that audience members can seldom be coaxed into detailed verbal responses to performances, so my understanding of how and why kīrtan affects audiences has emerged mostly from my own observations and the thoughts of the performers themselves rather than from the people for whom they are creating an aesthetic experience. Moreover, although participants became quite accustomed to my presence at kīrtans, I unavoidably altered the dynamics of kīrtans I attended and was a frequent topic of conversation and subject of the discourse within kīrtans. Rather than inserting an entirely new variable, though, my presence elicited remarks on topics that were already salient for rāṣṭrīya kīrtankārs, such as the turning of Indian youth to things Western, their disinterest in "Indian culture," and the spiritual inadequacy of Americans.

This project turns the historical lens on individuals who operate outside the classically "political" sphere, which shifts the ground of the nationalist landscape considerably. Nationalist leaders such as B. G. Tilak and V. D. Savarkar appear reformist rather than conservative, and noncosmopolitan kīrtankār/nationalist leaders such as Gadge Maharaj and Vasudeo Kolhatkar challenge characterizations of nationalist leaders as cosmopolitans. One reason that historians overlook the nationalist leadership of religious preachers and musicians is practical: it is more straightforward to study well-documented political and governmental meetings and the prolific writings of Westernized elites than it is to piece together the words of people who led through an oral medium. Rāṣṭrīya kīrtankārs were popular promoters of nationalism during their lifetimes because they spoke directly to people in language and idioms that were familiar and authoritative, and because they were skilled at controlling emotion through musical performance. The written remnants of this oral performance medium are not nearly as compelling as the original kīrtans would have been, nor are these remnants as persuasive as the words of nationalist elites who composed for the printed page.

I also hope to have contributed a new perspective on the relationship between music and nationalism in India. Musicologists of nationalism have emphasized the appropriation and classicization of Indian art music by high caste Hindus who strove to retain moral leadership and political power while producing a form of nationalist expression that was "systematized" and purged of "degenerate" elements. Rāṣṭrīya kīrtan (of the nāradīya type) was different because kīrtankārs shared caste status with the nationalist elite, who considered them to be upstanding, moral Hindus and thus acceptable nationalist representatives, thereby enabling kīrtankārs to continue propagating nationalist ideas without dissent or appropriation. The two chapters in Part I address the same period from two perspectives—the first presents the now well-rehearsed notion of artistic reform in the interest of national identity by nationalist elites, and the second addresses how kīrtankārs responded in song and action to those attempts at reform and to the broader nationalist movement. While other works on music and nationalism have illustrated how musicians responded artistically to attempts at state or elite reform, my research suggests that their responses were not only artistic but also political, and that they went beyond critique or acceptance to generate their own performative nationalisms.

The formation of an independent Indian nation-state did not lead to the demise of nationalism or rāṣṭrīya kīrtan—in many ways the work had only begun in 1947. At the time of Independence, large groups of people remained unincorporated by the nation, the colonial state needed to be replaced by the Indian state, and the character of the Indian nation was very much in dispute. In Maharashtra, these issues were compounded by intense caste conflict following Gandhi's murder, which contributed to the marginalization and insularity of Brahman-oriented Hindu nationalist groups and to the more conservative rāṣṭrīya kīrtankārs. Meanwhile, the Nehruvian state found useful allies in rural rāṣṭrīya kīrtankārs from lower castes, whose participatory songs generated support for rural development, family planning, and educational policies. The post-colonial withdrawal from Hindu nationalist rāṣṭrīya kīrtan by some kīrtankārs is indicative not only of a discursive shift toward secularist socialism but also demonstrates an "officializing" of nationalist leadership within the state. In the Indian state, nationalist leaders were cosmopolitan, reform oriented politicians, which left little room for a nationalist leadership that resisted discourses of modernity. Indeed, the rāṣṭrīya kīrtankārs who met with the most success during that era were those who understood their subordinate position in the nation-state.

The rebirth of rāṣṭrīya kīrtan in the 1990s can be attributed at least in part to a resurgence of Hindutva, but also to the Akhil Bharatiya Kīrtan Kula's remaking of kīrtan within modern, politicized performance contexts. Conservative kīrtankārs are again attracting huge crowds but are now explicitly supporting (however veiled) the programs of Hindu nationalist political parties. The speeches and felicitations that frame these new kīrtans mark them as "modern" and provide a venue for organizers to outline the nationalist significance of the genre. Along with this change in context and framing has come a change in performance style, with greater emphasis on genres of aggression and bravery and less on the elaboration of the pūrvaraṅga philosophies. The older, perhaps gentler, rāṣṭrīya kīrtans are still performed, but the newer trend is to infuse uttararaṅgas with metered genres that generate a driving sense of action.

Kīrtankārs sonically and physically guide listeners toward pastness in ways that have profound spiritual and political implications. In thinking about genre, meaning, and the body, I explore interpretive approaches from a variety of disciplines. In both of my main examples, the emotional climaxes occurred when boundaries were blurred to generate new meanings; in Dhamankar's case, subjectivities were blurred through the multiple political and devotional embodiments initiated through participatory song, and in Upasani's case, indexically rich spoken and sung genres were collided to maintain the excitement of battle while narrating its significance for contemporary Hindu nationalism. In both cases, the blurring of boundaries is meaningful because the indexical associations of genres and styles are so embedded in memory that their emotional resonance is felt immediately, allowing the kīrtankār to alter meanings without the need to enlist more precise but less affectively potent semantico-referential speech. Emotion in musical performance emerges through the generation of profound experiences of transformative embodiment, by tapping into memories of such experiences, or (ideally) by a combination of the two. My interpretations emerged from careful listening to rāṣṭrīya kīrtan, but they affirm a more general politics inherent in performative boundary crossing, and my approach to embodiment, subjectivity, and genre has wider applicability for studies of music, politics, and emotion.

Although Hindu nationalist discourse has become dominant in the nationalist arena as well as in the restricted world of rāṣṭrīya kīrtan, kīrtankārs continue to promote a variety of nationalist visions through their kīrtans. Intellectual descendents of Gadge Baba support peaceful international solutions, oppose the nuclear bomb, provide shelter for orphans, and work against wasteful spending. Other rāṣṭrīya kīrtankārs performing in the nāradīya style, such as Jaytunbi Maharaj, sing of nationalist heroes in their kīrtans as metaphors for human resolve and persistence rather as battle cries against religious minorities; indeed, she actively combines Hindu and Muslim genres in her performances. Still other kīrtankārs perform squarely in the nāradīya-style rāṣṭrīya kīrtan idiom, but their political perspectives—though conservative—stop short of chauvinism against minorities.

Though doing fieldwork with Hindu nationalists was at times complicated, it provided me with new perspectives on *why* and *how* people gain allegiance to Hindutva ideologies. In kīrtan, I witnessed how kīrtankārs use music to create their vision of the nation, and how audience members experience a kīrtankār's nationalist devotion. I also gained a preliminary understanding of kīrtankārs' nationalist motivations through their assertions in kīrtan, their comments in the framing activities, their interview responses, and their informal conversations with me and with others. Some kīrtankārs recognized that nationalism seems to draw the largest and most enthusiastic crowds, and thus they perform rāṣṭrīya kīrtan because of its commercial viability. Others are drawn to Hindutva because of a feeling of insecurity, in which their understandings of the world and their traditionally dominant social position are felt to be threatened by American neo-Imperialism and state policies of secularism and caste-based affirmative action. In this context, by naming outsiders (Muslims, Christians, Americans, Europeans), Brahmans create an identity by declaring what they are not; and through kīrtan they imagine connections with a Brahman and Hindu past in ways that render it relevant for the present day. This trend did not end when Hindu nationalist parties lost control of both the Indian National Parliament and the Maharashtra State Assembly in 2004. When I was in Pune most recently in 2009, the Akhil Bhāratīya Kīrtan Kula was as popular as ever and the RSS was continuing to rally around the Rāmjanmabhūmi and other hot-button issues, and new Hindu nationalist parties were attracting voters from ever more specific caste clusters. The constancy of Hindu nationalist rāṣṭrīya kīrtan in an era of Congress political hegemony illustrates that a nuanced picture of politics needs to include the activities simmering within cultural and religious spheres only marginally connected to all-India organizations.

This project has led me to approach studies of music and culture devoid of discussions of politics with a new skepticism. Musicians can convince their listeners of political ideas in subtle and incomparably powerful ways. When a listener leaves a kīrtan not realizing that she participated in the performance of harsh stereotypes of minorities or in the devotionalizing of politics, she is unable to fully process the new significations emerging from the kīrtan. But participants at a kīrtan are not blank slates, and many come to the kīrtan already feeling an affinity toward the political and religious philosophies of the kīrtankār, and the experience only serves to strengthen their preexisting sentiments. Listeners at kīrtans are active participants in the creation of a community, and it is the kīrtankār's role to formulate the nature of that community. It may be a community of Hindu fundamentalists or it may be a community of grassroots social activists, but it is in any case both a microcosm of the nation and a moment of inspiration for nationalist action.

NOTES

CHAPTER 1

1. Literally, "Rām's play," Rāmlīla is a dramatic, multi-day performance of Rām's life.
2. Rashtriya Swayamsevak Sangh (National Volunteer Organization).
3. Vishwa Hindu Parishad (World Hindu Council).
4. Marathi is the official state language of Maharashtra, and speakers of Marathi—presumed to share aspects of culture—are also referred to as Marathi. I use the term "Maharashtrian" only when referring to Marathi people in the era of the post-colonial Maharashtrian state.
5. Maratha refers to a Marathi caste generally categorized within the *kṣatriya* (warrior) caste group.
6. Bal Kolhatkar, personal communication, 2000.
7. Rules, knowledge, or scripture.
8. A brief survey of fifteen rāṣṭrīya kīrtankārs under seventy years of age in 2000 revealed that nine are part-time kīrtankārs with middle-class occupations (Dilip Dabir, Narahari Apamarjane, Vijay Apamarjane, Ajay Apamarjane, Yogeshwar Upasani, Manoram Chirmure, Vijaya Dhopeshwarkar, Devidas Pujari, Shyam Hegde), three had abandoned middle-class jobs to perform kīrtan full-time (Moreshwarbuva Joshi, Narayan Hate, Sudhatai Dhamankar), and three do kīrtan either full-time or in conjunction with a related pursuit (Lakshmikant Khadke, Bharat Ramdasi, Narayanshastri Godbole) (Shevde et al. 2000). In contrast, all six of the rāṣṭrīya kīrtankārs performing in the 1920s and 1930s on whom I have detailed information were engaged in kīrtan and related pursuits (*pravacan* [preaching], religious education, etc.) as their primary occupation (Vasudeo Kolhatkar, Dattopant Patwardhan, Pantapratiniddhi, Shivaram Paranjpe, Gadge Maharaj, Kaikadi Maharaj). I am aware of seven other rāṣṭrīya kīrtankārs performing at that time, but sources make no reference to whether kīrtan was their primary occupation (Kolhatkar 1936a: 64–65).
9. "[I]t is to be noted that the mass of the peasantry, although it performs an essential function in the world of production, does not elaborate its own "organic" intellectuals, nor does it "assimilate" any stratum of "traditional" intellectuals, although it is from the peasantry that other social groups draw many of their intellectuals and a high proportion of traditional intellectuals are of peasant origin" (Gramsci; cf. Crehan 2002: 143).
10. 2001 Census of India. http://censusindia.gov.in/Census_Data_2001/India_at_glance/rural.aspx.

11. As discussed by Livingston, creation of national sentiment is only one mode of revivalist thinking (Livingston 1999: 66).

CHAPTER 2

1. See my expanded discussion of Chatterjee's theory in Chapter 1 of this book.
2. Ashok Ranade (1982) has provided an interesting comparison of vārkarī and nāradīya kīrtan in his "Kīrtan Prayogaparaṁparecī Utkrānti."
3. Almost all vārkarī kīrtankārs are men, though I know of a few exceptions. Two of these exceptional women, the late Gayabai Manmadkar and the late Mirabai Shirkar, were disciples of Gadge Maharaj and were active in the nationalist movement. Their kīrtans followed the maverick style of Gadge Maharaj and were only marginally vārkarī. An example of a female vārkarī kīrtankār performing today is Shantabai Maharaj Deshmukh.
4. I found no mention of women kīrtankārs in *Kesarī* newspapers from 1918 through 1932, nor were any women included in a list of twenty-two kīrtankārs in a 1936 volume of *Caitanya*, a monthly journal dedicated to kīrtan and edited by Vasudeo S. Kolhatkar. There were a few exceptional women nāradīya kīrtankārs in the pre-war era, such as Sonutai Kale, a widow who learned kīrtan between 1920 and 1933 from the Maharaja of Aundh (www.dixitfamily.com/sonutaikale.html). In 1977, G. N. Koparkar and the Kīrtan Mahavidyalaya published a booklet called *Mahārāṣṭrātil Kīrtankārāñcī Yādī*, a list of the names and addresses of 401 kīrtankārs, of which approximately 104 (26%) are women. Though most of the kīrtankārs in the booklet are nāradīya kīrtankārs, Koparkar does include a few vārkarī kīrtankārs. Since very few women perform vārkarī kīrtan, the percentage of men is slightly higher than if the sample had included only nāradīya kīrtankārs. Shevde, Joshi, and Khadilkar, of the Akhil Bhāratīya Kīrtan Kula (All-India Kīrtan Group), published a book in 2000 called *Kīrtankār-Pravacaṅkār Parica Sucigraṅtha*, which contains short biographical summaries of most of the Marathi kīrtankārs registered with their organization. Of the 192 entries, approximately 40 percent are women. Most of the nāradīya kīrtankārs I met belonged to the Kīrtan Kula, so I would consider this sample fairly representative.
5. Most songs by Marathi saints are of the abhaṅga genre, which loosely corresponds to bhajan as it is used to refer to songs by saints of northern India. Kīrtankār Vaman Kolhatkar provided this etymology of abhaṅga: "*Bhaṅga* means "breakable" and *a* means "not," so abhaṅga means unbreakable or everlasting." Though abhaṅgas are written in a variety of poetic structures, most abhaṅgas are composed of four lines (each line is divided into two halves), in which the first line serves as a refrain (*dhrupad*), and the remaining three lines function as verses. Two melodies are often used, one for the refrain and another for the verses, as in the sthāi-antarā structure of North Indian vocal music, though some abhaṅgas are sung without a refrain. The last line contains the signature of the saint who composed the abhaṅga. For example, the final line of abhaṅgas by Tukārām begin with "*Tukā mhaṇe*" (Tukā says).
6. Machwe 1968: 3.
7. Maurya 1988: 1, 3.
8. Abbott and Godbole 1982: xiii.
9. Tukārām of Dehu was a poet-saint from the śūdra caste who lived from approximately 1608 to 1649 (Chitre 1991: vii). He is arguably the most important poet-saint for Maharashtrians of all walks of life, and his poetry and/or stories about his life are featured prominently in almost every kīrtan performed today.

Tukārām's abhaṅga, "Sundara te dhyān," marks the beginning of most vārkari kīrtans; another of his abhaṅgas, "Hecī dāna degā devā," marks the end of nāradīya and rāṣṭrīya kīrtan performances; and one of his abhaṅgas is usually chosen as the muḷpad in all sampradāyas of Marathi kīrtan.

10. Read the Vedas, from time to time / Tell the Puranic stories to congregation / Analysis of "Illusion" and "Truth" / Be made wholly with details //19// Protect Brahmanism with respect/ (Tambwekar 61)
11. In the *Das Bodh*, Rāmdās asked the reader to "indulge in a lot of political activity," but not to discuss it with others because political actions are most effective when they are surprising. One should not desire to harm others, but when necessary, violence should be inflicted swiftly and quietly. Rāmdās encouraged militancy when necessary, saying, "Throw away enemies who are engaged in war with you. Advise the king about efficient and effective administration" (Tambwekar 1995: 202–203).
12. *Rasa* as an aesthetic term referring to sentiment or aesthetic essence (literally, it means "juice" or "flavor").
13. According to Namdev scholar Christian Novetzke (personal communication 2002), the term "śāhīr" may be derived from the Persian word *śāhī* (courtly). A śāhīr is someone who belongs to the court, that is, a courtly poet. He adds that the term eventually gained a more general usage, so poets such as Ram Joshi, not associated with any court, became self-proclaimed śāhīrs. Bruno Nettl (personal communication, 2002), a specialist in Persian music, suggests that the term śāhīr in Marathi may be related to the Arabic word śā'ir, which means "poet" (in a general sense) and "śāhīr," which means pen.
14. Digvijay Vaidya, personal communication, 2000.
15. A *paurāṇik* is a Brahman who tells stories from the purāṇas in a seated position, often as part of the daily program of a temple.
16. Religious.
17. The liberation of Ahilyā.
18. Sitā's self-arranged marriage.
19. A character in the Mahābhārata.
20. The killing of Duhāśāsan.
21. These genres are discussed in Chapter 6.
22. A set of invocatory songs. Discussed in Chapter 6.
23. "Emotional songs."
24. Date and name from Harikīrtanottejak Sabhā brochures. An alternative date (1896) is given on page 66 of the April 1936 issue of *Caitanya*. To my knowledge, the first Marathi kīrtan institution was the "Harikīrtanottejak Mandal," founded in Bombay in 1880 to promote Bene Israel kīrtan (Gadkar 1996: 61, Isenberg 1988: 91). The impetus to found this institution was quite different from that of the Harikīrtanottejak Sabhā. Bene Israel kīrtan is a product of the mid-nineteenth century, when members of this Jewish community began performing and publishing Bible stories in Marathi as a way to acquaint Marathi-speaking Bene Israel with ideas from Hebrew scripture (Roland 2000: 330). There was no long-standing tradition of Bene Israel kīrtan instruction as there had been in nāradīya kīrtan, and thus the need to create an institution arose not from the loss of traditional patronage but from the desire to systematically create and teach a new art form. The religious revival that found expression in Bene Israel kīrtan was a product of contact between Bene Israel and mainstream Jewish thought through English and Hebrew education, as well as through contact with Cochin Jews (Roland 1995:

120). The Bene Israel are the largest Indian Jewish community, with a population of about 20,000, but many have now migrated to Israel, where the last twenty years have seen a movement for the revival of kīrtan (Roland 1995: 117).

25. "Mahārāṣṭrātil Kīrtansaṅstha," in *Caitanya*, April 1936: 66.
26. The Bengal Music School, on the other hand, represents a transition from royal to collective patronage, since it appears to have had only one donor, the Rājā S. M. Tagore (Rosse 1995: 30, 111).
27. Vaman Kolhatkar, personal communication, 1999.
28. "Mukhya prerana hotī svātantryāsāṭhi samājprabodhanāc" (Joshi 2000: 12–15).
29. N. G. Joshi, secretary of the Akhil Bhāratīya Kīrtan Sanstha. Personal communication, December 24, 1999.
30. Chatterjee wrote on Ramakrishna and the discourses that surrounded him, but discussed his importance for nationalism primarily as a result of mediation by cosmopolitan nationalist elites (Chatterjee 1993: 35–76).
31. "self-made goods, own religion, and own culture."
32. Modak 1947, app. 1 and 2: 1–20.
33. *Buvā* is a term of respect for an elder male, today used especially for nāradīya kīrtankārs.
34. Vaman Kolhatkar, personal communication, October 2, 1999.
35. Māḷa refers to a garland.
36. eternal.
37. Translation by Vaishali Joshi.
38. Translations of Tilak's speech are by Vaishali Joshi.
39. According to many Hindu texts, the kali yuga is the degenerate, final era in which we currently live.
40. *Kesarī*, Tuesday, May 13, 1919, p. 7.
41. "Kīrtan Sammelan," in *Kesarī*, Tuesday, January 15, 1918; *Kesarī*, Tuesday, May 13, 1919, p. 7.
42. "Kīrtan Sammelan," in *Kesarī*, Tuesday, January 15, 1918.

CHAPTER 3

1. Vaman Kolhatkar, personal communication, Pune, March 21, 2000.
2. Vaman Kolhatkar, personal communication, October 2, 1999.
3. Manjushree Khadilkar, interview with the author, August, 2009.
4. This concept will be discussed in greater detail in later chapters.
5. Vaman Kolhatkar, personal communication, March 2, 2000
6. Translation from Bombay Police Abstracts of 1910, pp. 50–107.
7. This stanza my translation.
8. Svarājya refers to an independent kingdom.
9. This stanza my translation (with last line from largely from Bombay Police Abstracts).
10. Translation of this stanza from Bombay Police Abstracts of 1910, pp. 50–107.
11. Ashok Bhat, personal communication, Wai, October 9, 1999.
12. Ashok Bhat, personal communicaiton. Wai, October 9, 1999.
13. Sūrya namaskār is a rather strenuous series of physical exercises to greet the sun, and Patwardhan performed 1,000 per day, 500 in the morning and 500 in the evening. His goal was to complete 10 million sūrya namaskārs in his lifetime, but at the time of his death, he was 300,000 short of his goal. His *śiśya* (disciple) C. N. Godbole completed the remaining 300,000 sūrya namaskārs in Patwardhan's name after his death (Katgade 1969: 9).

14. Svadeśī was a nationalist project of economic self-sufficiency based on the boycott of British goods in favor of the domestic manufacture of goods using simple, domestic techniques.
15. Govindkrishna Kanhere, personal communication, Wai, October 9, 1999.
16. Govindkrishna Kanhere, personal communication, Wai, October 9, 1999.
17. Govindkrishna Kanhere, personal communication, Wai, October 9, 1999.
18. Patwardhan had great respect for M. K. Gandhi, and Mr. Kanhere characterized him as a "pakkā Gandhian" (perfect Gandhian) because of his insistence on using svadeśī goods and living simply. Patwardhan said of svadeśī that "Gandhi is a big magician. The mills in Manchester are closed because of him" (Govindkrishna Kanhere, personal communication, Wai, October 9, 1999).
19. Supreme God.
20. Translations of Pathak (1980) by Vidya Marathe and Anna Schultz.
21. Ghaisas composed a different pūrvaraṅga to accompany Patwardhan's uttararaṅga; Ghaisas's was on the importance of truth, and he used a few smaller stories to illustrate Tilak's honesty before narrating the story of the old man.
22. In the freely metered musical examples such as this ārya, a quarter note corresponds to a long syllable and an eighth note to a shorter syllable.
23. Māmā means "mother's brother" in Marathi.
24. V. K. Wagh, interview with the author. Bhiwali, July 31, 2000.
25. Dandekar 1988: 233; Ghongate n.d.: 16–18.
26. Satyāgraha can be translated literally as "insistence on truth," but in practice refers to nonviolent resistance.
27. Dandekar 1988: 233; Ghongate n.d.: 16–18.
28. Ahimsa can be translated as nonviolence.
29. www.goodnewsindia.com/Pages/content/transitions/gmAbhiyan.html.
30. C.f. Shirwadkar, pp. 72–73.
31. Barve 1963: 3–4; Vaman Kolhatkar, personal communication, March 2, 2000.
32. Madhukarī is the practice of begging for alms in the form of food; conducted by Brahmans and other students undergoing traditional Hindu religious education.
33. Vaman Kolhatkar, personal communication, March 2, 2000.
34. Vaman Kolhatkar, personal communication, March 2, 2000.
35. Vaman Kolhatkar, personal communication, Pune, March 21, 2000. V. D. Divekar (1990), in his article on rāṣṭrīya kīrtan, writes that Vasudeo Kolhatkar joined the Hindu Mahasabha after independence, but two of his sons deny that this is true. Instead, they argued that he became increasingly distanced from politics after independence.
36. Vaman Kolhatkar, interview. Pune, July 17, 1998.
37. Thanks to Adheesh Sathaye for this insight.
38. Vasudeo Kolhatkar 1933. See also kīrtans by 'sampādakīya (publisher), a.k.a Vasudeo Kolhatkar in each volume of *Caitanya*.
39. Translation by Vaishali Joshi.
40. Vaman Kolhatkar, personal communication, Pune, December 16, 1999.
41. Vaman Kolhatkar, personal communication, Pune, March 2, 2000.
42. Vaman Kolhatkar, personal communication, Pune, October 1, 1999.
43. Vaman Kolhatkar, personal communication, Pune, December 14, 1999.
44. I have heard recordings of Vasudeo Kolhatkar's kīrtan on Subhashchandra Bose and two days of his multi-day kīrtan on Tanaji, and have listened to Vaman Kolhatkar perform numerous songs by his father.
45. A ṭheka is the arrangement of drum strokes associated with a particular tāla (meter).

46. Translation by Vaishali Joshi.
47. See, for example, Smith (2005: 177–179) on nature imagery in civic nationalism and Hutchinson (1995) on ideas of nature in cultural nationalism.
48. Vaman Kolhatkar, personal communication, October 19, 1999.
49. "Examples of rāṣṭrīya kīrtankārs like V. Shi. Kolhatkar," p. 30 in *Kesarī*, March 18, 1930.
50. Vaman Kolhatkar, personal communication, Pune, October 19, 1999.
51. Vaman Kolhatkar, personal communication, Pune, March 21, 2000.
52. Vaman Kolhatkar, personal communication, Pune, October 15, 1999.
53. Bal Kolhatkar, personal communication, Pune, November 1, 2000.
54. During final editing for this book, I learned that the compound is being torn down so that a modern apartment building can be built on the site.
55. Dadamaharaj Manmadkar, personal communication, Pandharpur, November 1999. V. K. Wagh, personal communication, Bhiwali, July, 2000. V. D. Divekar (1990).
56. V. K. Wagh, personal communication, Bhiwali, July 31, 2000.
57. Shirwadkar, p. 69.
58. "Brief Note on the Nature of Activities Carried by Shree Gadge Maharaj Mission, Mumbai," leaflet published by the Gadge Maharaj Mission in Mumbai.

CHAPTER 4

1. Sudhatai Dhamankar, interview, Varje, July 11, 2009.
2. Nāradīya kīrtankārs do, however, routinely travel into rural areas for performances.
3. Vaman Kolhatkar, personal communication.
4. Adheesh Sathaye, personal communication, October 22, 2003. See his dissertation from the University of California, Berkeley, on Marathi kīrtan interpretations of Viśvamitra.
5. Deshingkar 1969: 10.
6. Ashok Bhat, personal communication, Wai, October 9, 1999.
7. Govind Krishna Kanhere, personal communication, Wai, October 10, 1999.
8. Vaman Kolhatkar, personal communication, March 2000.
9. Maratha is a "*kṣatrīya*" (warrior) caste cluster in Marathi-speaking regions.
10. "A folk hero returns to inspire a revolution." Good News India., www.goodnewsindia.com/Pages/content/transitions/gmAbhiyan.html, accessed 10/14/2010.
11. "Mission." Shri Gadge Maharaj Mission Dharmashala Trust. www.santgadgebabatrust.org/index.php?option=com_content&view=article&id=104&Itemid=53?, accessed 10/19/2010. Site no longer available.
12. Ramdas Maharaj Jadhav, personal communication, October 10, 2000.
13. Kaikadi Maharaj, *Mānavāno māṇuskīla jāgā: Sant Kaikāḍībābāṅce Kīrtan,* sound cassette. This kīrtan translated by Vidya Marathe and Anna Schultz.
14. ibid.
15. Manjari Sinha, "Tuned to Excellence," *The Hindu,* August 8, 2008, www.hindu.com/thehindu/fr/2008/08/08/stories/2008080850100200.htm.
16. Similarly, Dadamaharaj Manmadkar, Ramdas Maharaj Jadhav, V. K. Wagh, and Shelar Mama, all belonging to varying degrees to the lineage of those in Gadge Maharaj's circle, employ a vārkarī discourse of bhakti to expound on (*nirūpaṇa karṇe*) abhangas by vārkarī saints.
17. Kaikadis are a Dalit community with traditional occupations of basket weaving and stone cutting who previously spoke the Kaikadi language but now speak

Marathi. There are nine exogamous Kaikadi clans, with the surnames Jadhav and Mane suggesting some relationship to Rajputs and Marathas, respectively (Banerjee 2008: 162–165).

18. Ramdas Maharaj Jadhav, interview, Pandharpur, October 10, 2000.
19. John F. Burns, "Nuclear Blasts Put India's Opposition Parties in a Bind," *New York Times*, May 14, 1998, "India's Nuclear Weapons Program," Nuclear Weapon Archive, 2003, http://nuclearweaponarchive.org/India/index.html.
20. "Maratha Sewa Sangh" booklet published by the Maratha Seva Sangh http://satyashodhak.com/wp-content/uploads/2010/11/about-maratha-seva-sangh-in-english.pdf, accessed June 23, 2012; Hindu Janajagruti Samiti, "Criticism on Hindu Dharma in Khedekar's Felicitation Program" (September 3, 2007), www.hindujagruti.org/news/2923.html, accessed October 22, 2010; Namdev Tukaram Vārkarī Parishad, "warkari association, pandharpur" (June 13, 2008), http://warkariunion.blogspot.com/search?updated-min=2008-01-01T00%3A00%3A00-08%3A00&updated-max=2009-01-01T00%3A00%3A00-08%3A00&max-results=1, accessed October 22, 2010.
21. This genre is also sometimes called *samājik*, or social, kīrtan.
22. Manjushree Khadilkar, interview, Pune, July 15, 2009.
23. Ibid.
24. Manjushree Khadilkar, interview, Pune, July 15, 2009. Translation from Marathi by Jaywardhan Shaligram.
25. Ibid.
26. Mrs. Khare, interview, Pune, July 21, 2000.
27. Ibid.
28. Muḷpad is the song that serves as a foundation for a kīrtan, providing a set of core ideas on which the kīrtankār expounds. It is almost always an abhanga by a Marathi poet-saint.
29. Mrs. Khare, interview, Pune, July 21, 2000.
30. "*Pantapradhān Indirā Gāndhisamor Govinda Khare yānce kīrtan*" [Govinda Khare's kīrtan in front of Prime Minister Indira Gandhi] (*Sakāḷ*, Pune, June 23, 1981). "*Indirā Gāndhice samor nāradiya kīrtan*" [Nāradiya kīrtan in front of Indira Gandhi] (*Taruṇ Bhārat*, June 24, 1981). "*Śrimati Indirā Gāndhice samor kīrtan*" [Kīrtan in front of Mrs. Indira Gandhi] (*Rāṣṭratej*, June 23, 1981). "*Dr. Khare yānce kīrtan*" [Dr. Khare's kīrtan] (*Kesari*, June 27, 1981). "*Hindi tathā angreji me kīrtan saṁpanna*" [A kīrtan was performed in Hindi and English] (*Ājkā Ānand*, June 23, 1981).
31. Several sources have confirmed that Gadge Baba traveled in a government car, and it is a matter of record that he received some government funding to establish schools.
32. In the most extreme case, as carried out by her son Rajeev Gandhi, her population control policies resulted in coercive and even forced sterilization.
33. Charudatta Aphale, interview, Pune, March 15, 2000.
34. Joshi 1982: 28.
35. Charudatta Aphale, interview, Pune, March 15, 2000. Interview was not recorded, but was reconstructed from memory and written notes. Because of this, some wording is paraphrased rather than verbatim.
36. Anonymous, personal communication, December 27, 1999.
37. Front cover of Koparkar, *Kathā Haridāsācī* (1978?).
38. Govindswami Aphale's book (1955) consists primarily of stories of Hindus sacrificing their lives in resistance to Muslim rule. In "*Svadharma nidhān śrey*," he writes

of a Brahman being killed because he doesn't want to give up his "*svadharma*" (own religion/duty).

39. Charudatta Aphale, interview, Pune, March 15, 2000. Interview was not recorded, but was reconstructed from memory and written notes. Because of this, some wording is paraphrased rather than verbatim.
40. Ibid.
41. Ibid.
42. Ibid.
43. Ibid.
44. Anonymous, personal communication, Urbana, Illinois, July 2001.
45. Vaman Kolhatkar, personal communication, October 1, 1999.
46. Gangadhar Koparkar, personal communication, Varje, July 2000.
47. Ibid.
48. This is a conventional practice in kīrtans celebrating the birth of a deity.
49. G. N. Koparkar, interview, Varje, July 29, 2000.
50. Shamsul Islam, "Is the RSS a Cultural and Nationalist Organization? What Does the RSS Archival Material Say?" www.secularindia.net/article28.html.
51. Gangadhar Koparkar, personal communication, Varje, December 2, 1999.
52. Brochure by S.G. Shevde outlining Koparkar's accomplishments on the occasion of the government award, 1996.
53. Ibid.
54. Gangadhar Koparkar, personal communication, Varje, July 29, 2000.
55. Bharatiya Vidya Bhavan, Pune Kendra brochure, Shivaji Nagar, Pune.
56. V.L. Manjul, personal communication, January 2000.
57. Mr. Rairkar, personal communication, Pune, December 2, 1999.

CHAPTER 5

1. Nagpur is a major city in the eastern region of Maharashtra known as Vidarbha.
2. Samādhi in this usage refers to the final absorption of the enlightened self into the Divine at death.
3. From the back cover of S. G. Shevade, Moreshwarbuwa Joshi (Charolikar), and Shrikant Khadilkar, eds., *Kīrtankār/Pravacankār Paricay Sūcigrantha* (Pune: Akhil Bhāratīya Kīrtankul, 2000).
4. Anonymous, personal communication, Nagpur, January 20, 2000.
5. An anonymous classical musician contributed this insight.
6. My translation from Marathi.
7. Koparkarbuva has already been discussed in the previous chapter, so it will suffice to note here that even after the closing of his Kīrtan Mahāvidyālaya, Koparkar continued to attract students and devotees who appreciated his impassioned and scholarly Hindu nationalist kīrtans and pravacans. Since his death in 2001, his śiṣya Sudhatai has continued the tradition by hosting educational events at their Rām temple and by performing kīrtan and pravacan throughout the city and beyond.
8. "Mahārāśtrātil Kīrtansaṅstha," in *Chaitanya* (April 1936): 66.
9. Vaman Kolhatkar, personal communication, 1999.
10. Manjiri Kelkar and Dinananath Joshi, personal communication, Dadar, December 1999.
11. The 2000 Balkīrtan Mahotsav was covered by Marathi Zee TV and featured performers ranging in age from about eight to sixteen.

12. This is according to a pamphlet published by the Akhil Bhāratīya Kīrtan Kula advertising the "Jagātik Kīrtan Sammelan 2002" (The World Kīrtan Conference 2002).
13. This speech was delivered by a non-Brahman scholar of Marathi literature from the lineage of Sant Tukārām, who was invited to speak at the Vāsantik Kīrtan-Pravacan Mahotsav (Spring kīrtan-pravacan festival) in April 2000 organized by the Kula in Pune.
14. "Mission and Vision: Antidote to Self-Oblivion," 2003, www.rss.org/New_RSS/Mission_Vision/Why_RSS.jsp. No longer available online.
15. I am not sure if the song is heard as a Scottish march by its composer, performers, or other audience members.
16. Nayaranbuva Kane, "Akhil Bhāratīya Kīrtan Kula Ghoṣgīt," p. 22 in Shevalkar (2000). The Marathi text is as follows:

    Calā karu harīkathā nācū rangū kīrtanī
    Deśdharma vāḍhavū, sanskṛtī sanātanī //dhru//

    Adeś Shrīharīcā, sandeś Nāradāncā
    Upadeś deū kīrtanī, deś karū bhāgyācā
    Unca unca nācavū, navī guḍhī nabhāngaṇī //1//

    Dharmavīr śūrkathā, kīrtanāt gāūyā
    Dharmāce bīj yā janamanāt lāvūyā
    Kārya hec āmuce, sansmarū kṣaṇekṣaṇī //2//

    Dharma āj nasalā, duṣṭa matt jāhale
    Manāvata sampalī, deś aikya bhangale
    Satyadharma ācarū, jāgavū janīmanī //3//

    Duṣta matī duṣṭa kṛtī, duṣṭa sarva sampū de
    Soukhya janā lābhū de, viśva śānta rāhū de
    Prārthanā aśī karū, kīrtanāt rangunī //4//

17. Translated from Marathi by Anna Schultz.
18. Narahari Apamarjane, kīrtan, January 21 2000.
19. Tāī means older sister in Marathi and is here as a term of affection and respect.
20. V. K. Wagh, personal communication, July 31, 2000.
21. Dadamaharaj Manmadkar, personal communication, Pandharpur, November 13, 1999.
22. Jaytunbi Maqbulbhai Sayyed, personal communication, Pandharpur, October 10, 2000.
23. The *Dipāvalī Strī Śaktī Viśeṣank* (Divali Volume on Women's Strength) of *Kanheri Sandeś* (1999) includes interviews with Jaytunbi Maharaj, Bhagavati Maharaj Satarkar, and Miratai Mirikar.
24. "Ga" is used to refer to a close female friend or relative.
25. Candrabhāg ("piece of the moon") is the portion of the river Bhima that runs through Pandharpur.
26. The bhakta Puṇḍalika is intimately connected with Viṭṭhala. When Viṭṭhala came to appear before Puṇḍalika, Puṇḍalika was so engrossed in worshipping his father and mother that he barely noticed the deity and simply threw him a brick on which to stand. Viṭṭhala was so impressed with Puṇḍalika's devotion to his parents that he decided to remain with him for eternity.
27. www.youtube.com/watch?v=2ufw87hkJKw&feature=related, accessed July 2011. Video no longer available at this address.
28. Smita Deshpande, interview, Pune, July 18, 2009.
29. Vaman Kolhatkar, personal communication, Pune, January 9, 2000.

CHAPTER 6

1. In Marathi, vīna is often used as a general term for lutes.
2. Vaman V. Kolhatkar, personal communication, Pune, October 2000.
3. Khadilkar, Manjushree. Recorded by Mark Nye on October 16, 1999. Kīrtan on Sant Sakhu. Performed in a private home in Pune. Translation by Vidya Marathe and Anna Schultz.
4. In 1998–2000, I would find kīrtan listings in the Marathi newspaper, *Sakāḷ*, but by 2009 they had discontinued classified listings for devotional events.
5. Bal Kolhatkar, personal communication, Pune, 2000.
6. See Ghaisas (1998, 2000) for examples of ślokas used in the Nārad Maṅdir paṭhaḍī.
7. These ślokas were heard at the beginning of kīrtans by Sudhatai Dhamankar (1998), Gangadharbuva Koparkar (2000), and Narahari Appamarjane (2000).
8. Koparkar was an early student at the Nārad Maṅdir kīrtan school.
9. Rāṣṭrīya kīrtankārs from other paṭhaḍīs, such as Dilip Dabir, also use the Śaṅkarācārya śloka, but the particular order of ślokas in Figure 6.3 is characteristic of Koparkar's paṭhaḍī.
10. Karveer Peeth is ancillary to the four main maṭhs.
11. A school in which one learns to memorize and recite the Vedas.
12. Sudhatai Dhamankar, personal communication, Varje, 1999.
13. For example, on December 25, 1999, he addressed a "Dharma Sabha" organized by the Vishwa Hindu Parishad (VHP) and the Hindu Jagran Manch (HJM) in the sensitive Dang tribal area. The function was part of a larger attempt to convert adivasis (tribals) from Christianity to Hinduism. As a result of VHP and HJM efforts, several churches had been burned and attacked in the Dangs the previous year. The re-kindling of those efforts and the convening of the Dharma Sabha resulted in fear among the Christian community and armed protection of many churches (Gonsalves 2000).
14. This is similar to what is called "kīrtan" in Hindi-speaking regions.
15. Manjushree Khadilkar, kīrtan, August 26, 2000.
16. Vaman Kolhatkar, personal communication, October 2, 1999.
17. Like "bhajan" in Hindi-speaking North India.
18. Kīrtan by Charudatta Aphale on Hanuman and Chandrashekhar Azad in celebration of Hanuman Jayanti, Pune, April 21, 2000.
19. Kīrtan by Bhaskar R. Ghaisas on Tilak and Truth., Pune, July 1998. Recorded by the author.
20. In the context of Marathi poetry, *mātra* is used to refer to both the basic unit of poetic rhythm and to the basic unit of musical meter. Here, I am using it in the former sense. Syllables with long vowels such as ā, ī, or ū have two mātra (called *guru*), while syllables with short vowels such as a, i, or u have one mātra (called *laghu*). There are other factors in determining whether or not a syllable is laghu or guru, such as whether or not it contains combined consonants. According to some kīrtankārs, the particular order of guru and laghu syllables is significant when composing *vṛttas* (a general term for genres with specific poetic meters), while others pay attention only to the total number of mātra per caraṇ. Still other kīrtankārs compose vṛttas simply by fitting new texts into popular āryā tunes.
21. Rāṣṭrīya kīrtankār Charudatta Aphale has recently made a set of CDs introducing some of the song genres used in Marathi kīrtan. After his performance of a povāḍā, the narrator comments to the unseen audience: "Friends, you may have

wondered how povāḍā got into kīrtan," in an indication of the continuing connotations of povāḍā's original context.

22. Sudhatai Dhamankar, personal communication, Pune, 2000.
23. J. T. Molesworth and George and Thomas Candy, *Marathi and English Dictionary* (Bombay: Bombay Education Society, 1857).

CHAPTER 7

1. Many thanks to the Society for Ethnomusicology for allowing me to use my earlier article, "Hindu Nationalism, Music, and Embodiment in Marathi Rāshṭrīya Kīrtan" (*Ethnomusicology* 46[2]:117), as the basis for this chapter.
2. The boon of seeing the image of the divine.
3. Rakhumāi is the wife of Viṭhobā (Viṭṭhala).
4. Most North Indian music is separated into two sections: the *sthāi* (refrain; first section) and the *antarā* (verse; second, usually higher section).
5. Richard Bauman (1992) discusses how Icelandic storytellers "contextualize" and "traditionalize" their stories through the embedding of a verse within a narrative. The surrounding narrative contextualizes the verse by providing a framework of interpretation for the listener. Similarly, traditionalization, a type of contextualization, is the use of something archaic to add "a distinctive element of social groundedness and force" (Bauman 1992: 141) and to position the new telling as also "traditional."
6. Moreshwarbuva Joshi (Charolikar) performed a kīrtan on Vasudeo Balvant Phadke using the abhanga "Janmā yeuni kāy kelī" in Pune on August 24, 2000. Yogeshvar Upasani used an abhanga with a similar meaning, "Janmun keles kāy manuja," as the basis for a kīrtan he performed on Yesaji Kanka in Pune on September 18, 2000.
7. In a general sense, gajar refers to a loud clash of musical instruments or a loud shout. In kīrtan, a more specific usage includes the collective repetition of God's name, such as "Viṭṭhala, Viṭṭhala, Viṭṭhala . . . "
8. Prasād is food that has been offered to a deity. After food has been offered to the deity—along with prayers and rituals—it is consecrated and may be eaten by worshippers in an act of communion.
9. Translation by Varada Kolhatkar.
10. Doing good works.
11. Viṭṭhala or Kṛṣṇa.
12. A name of Viṣṇu.
13. Gangadhar Vyas, kīrtan on Eknath. Performed in Pune as part of the Akhil Bhārat īya Kīrtan Kula's *Vāsantik Kīrtan-Pravacan Mahotsav* (Spring Kīrtan -Lecture Festival) on April 27, 2000.
14. Moreshvarbuva Joshi, kīrtan, August 24, 2000.
15. Sudhatai Dhamankar, questionnaire response, Nagpur, January 2000.
16. Ibid.
17. Sudhatai Dhamankar, speech, Tapodham Warje, May, 2000.

CHAPTER 8

1. Many thanks to the Society for Ethnomusicology for allowing me to use my earlier article, "The Collision of Genres and Collusion of Participants: Marathi Rastriya Kirtan and the Communication of Hindu Nationalism" (*Ethnomusicology* 52:1, 2008), as the basis for this chapter. In the earlier version published in *Ethnomusicology*, I used the pseudonym Sanjiv Gogate because of the sensitive

political nature of this topic. Having received the artist's permission to include and discuss this kīrtan recording, I am now using his real name: Yogeshwar Upasani. Recorded by Anna Schultz on September 8, 2000. Kīrtan on Yesaji Kanka. Performed at Bharata Nāṭya Maṅdir in Pune as part of the Rāṣṭrabhakti Saṅkīrtan Mahotsav. Translations by Vidya Marathe, Sharvari Nadkarni, and Anna Schultz.

Intertextuality, a term coined by Julia Kristeva but modeled after ideas from Bakhtin, refers to the notion that texts are structured in relation to other texts, and that they take into account the past, present, and future lives of texts of a similar type (Allen 2000:30–35, Monson 1996:87).

2. *"āp āpalyā gharī āpalyā āvāz pocalā. Tarī puṣkaḷ āhe, sagaḷyāne ṭāḷ vāzvāicā, hātāni ṭāḷī vāzvāici āṇi khaṇkhaṇit Rāmrām ghyāicā. Mhaṇā!"*
3. This is a correction of my earlier article (Schultz 2008), in which I wrote that this is a Tukārām abhanga.
4. Bhārūḍ is a Marathi sung folk drama characterized by social commentary.
5. *Janmūn keles kāy manuja, keles kāy manuja*

   Vādhavile vaya, poṣili khāya, sevuni dahi-dudh
   Viṣay sukh bhogile manuja janmūn keles kāy,
   Manuja janmūn keles kāy
   Eka Janārdani sadguṇa rāhi
6. Vaman Vasudeo Kolhatkarbuva is a notable exception.

CHAPTER 9

1. "Rashtriya geet" by Babunandan Dhobi, Shyam Bihari Gaud, and Yusuf on beatsofindia.com: www.beatofindia.com/forms/rashtriya_geet.htm, accessed on January 1, 2011.

GLOSSARY

A key reference for this glossary was J. T. Molesworth's *A Dictionary, Marathi and English*. 2nd ed., rev. and enl. Bombay: Printed for government at the Bombay Education Society's Press, 1857. University of Chicago, Digital Dictionaries of South Asia: http://dsal.uchicago.edu/dictionaries/molesworth/.

1. Vaman Kolhatkar, personal communication, October 12, 1999.
2. "What's Hindu about the RSS?" *Times of India*, February 13, 2000, http://timesofindia.indiatimes.com/articleshow/16153730.cms.
3. Sudhatai Dhamankar, personal communication, Pune, 2000.

REFERENCES

ENGLISH SOURCES

Abbott, Justin E. and Narhar R. Godbole. 1982. *Stories of Indian Saints*, vols. I and II, a translation of Mahipati's *Bhaktavijaya*, reprint of first editions: Poona, 1933 and 1934. Delhi: Motilal Banarsidass.

Allen, Graham. 2000. *Intertextuality*. New Critical Idiom Series. New York: Routledge.

Anderson, Benedict. 1991. *Imagined Communities: Reflections on the Origins and Spread of Nationalism*. London: Verso.

Austerlitz, Paul. 1996. *Merengue: Dominican Music and Dominican Identity*. Philadelphia: Temple University Press.

Bakhle, Janaki. 2005. *Two Men and Music: Nationalism in the Making of an Indian Classical Tradition*. New York: Oxford University Press.

Bakhtin, Mikhail. 1981. "Discourse in the Novel." In *The Dialogic Imagination: Four Essays by M. M. Bakhtin*, edited by Michael Holquist, 259–422. Austin: University of Texas Press.

——. 1986. "The Problem of Speech Genres." In *Speech Genres and Other Late Essays*, translated by Vern W. McGee, edited by Caryl Emerson and Michael Holquist. Austin: University of Texas Press.

Balasubrahmanaya, N. 1987. "Sankaracharya." In *Encyclopaedia of Indian Literature*, edited by Amaresh Datta, 3804–3805. New Delhi: Sahitya Akademi.

Banerjee, M. N. 2008. "Kaikadi: Dalit Community of Maharashtra." In *Global Encyclopaedia of the West Indian Dalit's Ethnography*. New Delhi: Global Vision.

Bauman, Richard. 1992. "Contextualization, Tradition, and the Dialogue of Genres: Icelandic Legends of the Kraftaskáld." In *Rethinking Context: Language as an Interactive Phenomenon*, edited by Alessandro Duranti and Charles Goodwin, 125–145. Cambridge: Cambridge University Press.

——. 2004. *A World of Others' Words: Cross-Cultural Perspectives on Intertextuality*. Malden, MA: Blackwell.

Becker, Judith. 2004. *Deep Listeners: Music, Emotion, and Trancing*. Bloomington: Indiana University Press.

Bhatt, Chetan. 2001. *Hindu Nationalism: Origins, Ideologies and Modern Myths*. New York: Berg.

Bhave, Y. G. 2009. *Vinayak Damodar Savarkar*. New Delhi: Northern Book Centre.

Bond, Graham Ajit. 1998. "The Kirtan Bhakti of Sri Samarth Ramdas: Renderings from the Dasbodh." Unpublished paper, shared by the author.

Bourdieu, Pierre. 1977. *Outline of a Theory of Practice*, translated by Richard Nice. Cambridge: Cambridge University Press.

Brown, Judith M. 1994. *Modern India: The Origins of an Asian Democracy*. 2nd ed. New York: Oxford University Press.

Brown, Katherine Butler. 2000. "Reading Indian Music: The Interpretation of Seventeenth-Century European Travel Writing in the (Re)Construction of Indian Music History." *British Journal of Ethnomusicology* 9(2): 1–34.

Brown, D. Mackenzie. 1958. "The Philosophy of Bal Gangadhar Tilak: Karma vs. Jnana in the Gita Rahasya." *Journal of Asian Studies* 17(2): 197–206.

Buchanan, Donna. 1995. "Metaphors of Power, Metaphors of Truth: The Politics of Music Professionalism in Bulgarian Folk Orchestras." *Ethnomusicology* 39(3): 381–416.

——. 2006. *Performing Democracy: Bulgarian Music and Musicians in Transition*. Chicago Studies in Ethnomusicology. Chicago: University of Chicago Press.

Capwell, Charles. 1987. "Sourindro Mohun Tagore and the National Anthem Project." *Ethnomusicology* 31(3): 407–430.

——. 1988. "The Popular Expression of Religious Syncretism: The Bauls of Bengal as Apostles of Brotherhood." *Popular Music* 7(2): 123–132.

——. 1991. "Marginality and Musicology in 19th Century Calcutta: The Case of Sourindro Mohun Tagore." In *Comparative Musicology and Anthropology of Music: Essays on the History of Ethnomusicology*, edited by Bruno Nettl and Philip Bohlman, 228–243. Chicago: University of Chicago Press.

——. 2000. "Music and Nationalism." In *South Asia: The Indian Subcontinent*. Garland Encyclopedia of World Music, vol. 5, edited by Alison Arnold, 431–439. New York: Garland.

Cashman, R. I. 1975. *The Myth of the Lokamanya: Tilak and Mass Politics in Maharashtra*. Berkeley: University of California Press.

Chapekar, Damodar Hari. 1910. *Autobiography of Damodar Hari Chapekar*. From Bombay Police Abstracts of 1910, 50–107.

Chatterjee, Partha. 1986. *Nationalist Thought and the Colonial World: A Derivative Discourse?* Minneapolis: University of Minnesota Press.

——. 1993. *The Nation and Its Fragments: Colonial and Postcolonial Histories*. Princeton: Princeton University Press.

——. 1998. "Secularism and Toleration." In *A Possible India: Essays in Political Criticism*, 228–262. Oxford: Oxford University Press.

Chitre, Dilip, trans. 1991. *Says Tuka*. New Delhi: Penguin.

Crehan, Kate. 2002. *Gramsci, Culture, and Anthropology*. Berkeley: University of California Press.

Csordas, Thomas J. 1990. "Embodiment as a Paradigm for Anthropology." *Ethos* 18(1): 5–47.

Cutler, Norman. 1987. *Songs of Experience: The Poetics of Tamil Devotion*. Bloomington: Indiana University Press.

Dandekar, G. N. 1988. "The Last Kirtan of Gadge Baba," translated by Maxine Berntsen and Jayant Karve. In *The Experience of Hinduism: Essays on Religion in Maharashtra*, edited by Eleanor Zelliot and Maxine Berntsen, 222–249. Albany: State University of New York Press.

Date, V. H. 1976. *Meditations of St. Tukarama*. Jodhpur: Marudhar.

Deshpande, Kusumawati and M.V. Rajadhyaksha. 1988. *A History of Marathi Literature*. New Delhi: Sahitya Akademi.

Deshpande, Prachi. 2006. "Writing Regional Consciousness: Maratha History and Regional Identity in Modern Maharashtra." In *Region, Culture, and Politics in*

India, edited by Rajendra Vora and Anne Feldhaus, 83–118. New Delhi: Manohar.

——. 2007. *Creative Pasts: Historical Memory and Identity in Western India, 1700–1960*. New York: Columbia University Press.

Divekar, V. D. 1990. "Rashtreeya Kirtankars in Maharashtra: Their Role in the Indian National Movement." In *Regional Roots of Indian Nationalism: Gujarat, Maharashtra and Rajasthan*, edited by Makrand Mehta. New Delhi: Criterion.

Echenberg, Myron J. 2007. *Plague Ports: The Global Urban Impact of Bubonic Plague, 1894–1901*. New York: New York University Press.

Express News Service. 2003. "Sangh Parivar Pays Tributes to Departed Leader." *Indian Express*, Pune Newsline, July 16.

Fast, Susan. 1996. "Bakhtin and the Discourse of Late Medieval Music Theory." *Plainsong and Medieval Music* 5(2): 175–191.

Feldhaus, Anne. 2003. *Connected Places: Region, Pilgrimage, and Geographical Imagination in India (Religion/Culture/Critique)*. New York: Palgrave Macmillan.

Geertz, Clifford. 1973. *The Interpretation of Cultures*. New York: Basic Books.

Goffman, Erving. 1986. *Frame Analysis: An Essay on the Organization of Experience*. Boston: Northeastern University Press.

Gordon, Stewart. 1993. *The Marathas, 1600–1818*. New Cambridge History of India, II.4. New York: Cambridge University Press.

Gramsci, Antonio. 1971. *Selections from the Prison Notebooks*. New York: International.

Guha, Ramachandra. 2007. *India after Gandhi: The History of the World's Largest Democracy*. New York: HarperCollins.

Guha, Ranajit and Gayatri Spivak, eds. 1988. *Selected Subaltern Studies*. New York: Oxford University Press.

Gurumurthy, Premeela. 1994. *Kathakalaksepa—A Study*. Madras: International Society for the Investigation of Ancient Civilisations.

Guy, Nancy. 1999. "Governing the Arts, Governing the State: Peking Opera and Political Authority in Taiwan." *Ethnomusicology* 43(3): 508–526.

Halliburton, Murphy. 2002. "Rethinking Anthropological Studies of the Body: Manas and Bodham in Kerala." *American Anthropologist* 104(4): 1123–1144.

Hansen, Kathryn. 1991. *Grounds for Play: The Nautanki Theatre of North India*. Berkeley: University of California Press.

Hansen, Thomas Blom. 1999. *The Saffron Wave: Democracy and Hindu Nationalism in Modern India*. Princeton, NJ: Princeton University Press.

——. 2001. *Violence in Urban India: Identity Politics, "Mumbai," and the Postcolonial City*. Delhi: Permanent Black.

Hay, Stephen. 1988. *Sources of Indian Tradition*. Volume 2: *Modern India and Pakistan*. 2nd ed. New York: Columbia University Press.

Heile, Björn. 2004. "Transcending Quotation": Cross-Cultural Musical Representation in Mauricio Kagel's "Die Stücke der Windrose für Salonorchester." *Music Analysis* 23(1): 57–85.

Henry, Edward O. 1988. *Chant the Names of God: Musical Culture in Bhojpuri-speaking India*. San Diego: San Diego State University Press.

Holub, R. 1992. *Antonio Gramsci: Beyond Marxism and Postmodernism*. London: Routledge.

Hutchinson, John. 1995. "Cultural Nationalism and Moral Regeneration." In *Nationalism (Oxford Readers)*, edited by John Hutchinson and Anthony Smith. New York: Oxford University Press.

———. 2001. "Cultural Nationalism." In *Encyclopedia of Nationalism,* edited by Athena S. Leoussi, 40. New Brunswick: Transaction.

Isenberg, Shirley Berry. 1988. *India's Bene Israel: A Comprehensive Inquiry and Sourcebook.* Berkeley, CA: J. L. Magnes Museum.

Jaffrelot, Christophe. 1999. *The Hindu Nationalist Movement and Indian Politics 1925 to the 1990's: Strategies of Identity-Building, Implantation, and Mobilisation.* New Delhi: Penguin.

Jayapalan, N. 2003. *Indian Political Thinkers: Modern Indian Political Thought.* New Delhi: Atlantic.

Joshi, Ram. 1968. "Maharashtra." In *State Politics in India,* edited by Myron Weiner. Princeton, NJ: Princeton University Press.

Kamat, A. R. 1968. *Progress of Education in Rural Maharashtra (Post-Independence Period).* New York: Asia Publishing House.

Khan, Mohammad Shabir. 1992. *Tilak and Gokhale: A Comparative Study of Their Socio-Politico-Economic Programmes of Reconstruction.* New Delhi: Ashish.

Kshirasagara, Ramacandra. 1994. *Dalit Movement in India and Its Leaders, 1857–1956.* New Delhi: M. D. Publications.

Largey, Michael. 2006. *Vodou Nation: Haitian Art Music and Cultural Nationalism (Chicago Studies in Ethnomusicology).* Chicago: University of Chicago Press.

Lelyveld, David. 1996. "Upon the Subdominant: Administering Music on All India Radio." In *Consuming Modernity,* edited by Carol A. Breckenridge, 49–65. Delhi: Oxford University Press.

Livingston, Tamara. 1999. "Music Revivals: Towards a General Theory." *Ethnomusicology* 43(1): 66–85.

Lutgendorf, Philip. 2007. *Hanuman's Tale: Messages of a Divine Monkey.* New York: Oxford University Press.

McKean, Lise. 1996. *Divine Enterprise: Gurus and the Hindu Nationalist Movement.* Chicago: University of Chicago Press.

Machwe, Prabhakar. 1968. *Namdev: Life and Philosophy.* Patiala: Punjabi University.

Mahipati. 1934. *Stories of Indian Saints (Bhaktavijaya),* translated by Justin Abbott and Narhar R. Godbole. Vol. 2, 2nd ed. Delhi: Motilal Banarsidass, 1982.

Maidamwar, G. T. 1998. *Gadge Maharaj: Man and Mission.* Mumbai: Shree Gadge Baba Prakashan Samiti.

Mankekar, Purnima. 1999. *Screening Culture, Viewing Politics: An Ethnography of Television, Womanhood, and Nation in Postcolonial India.* Durham, NC: Duke University Press.

Maurya, R. N. 1988. *Namdev: His Mind and Art (A Linguistic Analysis of Namdev's Poetry).* New Delhi: Bahri.

Mehta, Makarand, ed. 1990. *Regional Roots of Indian Nationalism: Gujarat, Maharashtra, and Rajasthan.* New Delhi: Criterion.

Merleau-Ponty, Maurice. 2002 [1962]. *Phenomenology of Perception.* New York: Routledge.

Monson, Ingrid. 1996. *Saying Something: Jazz Improvisation and Interaction.* Chicago: Chicago University Press.

Mukherjee, Partha Nath. 1999. "Nation-State Reformulated: Interrogating Received Wisdom." *Man and Development* 21 (December).

New York Times. 1897a. "A Member of the Council at Bombay and Other Indian Agitators Arrested," July 29.

———. 1897b. "Damodar Chapekar on Trial," November 3.

Panicker, Prem. 2001. "VHP Temple Date: March 12, 2002." *Rediff*, January. www.rediff.com/news/2001/jan/20kumbh3.htm.

Mishra, Anil Dutta. 1999. "Sarvodaya: A Fresh Look." In *Gandhism after Gandhi*, edited by Anil Dutta Mishra, 37–50. New Delhi: Mittal.

Mitta, Manoj. 2010. "Ayodhya Verdict." *Times of India*. October 3, 2010.

Patil, Anand. 1993. *Western Influence on Marathi Drama: A Case Study*. Panaji, Goa: Rajahauns.

Peirce, Charles. 1955. *Philosophical Writing of Charles Peirce*, edited by Justus Buchler. Mineola, NY: Dover.

Popplewell, Richard James. *Intelligence and Imperial Defence: British Intelligence and the Defence of the Indian Empire, 1904–1924*. London: Routledge, 1995.

Prentiss, Karen. 1999. *The Embodiment of Bhakti*. New York: Oxford University Press.

Puri, Janak, Vivendra Kumar Sethi, L. G. Rajwade, and Chandrawati Rajwade, trans. 1977. *Saint Namdev*. Punjab: Radha Soami Satsang Beas.

Qureshi, Regula. 1991. "Whose Music? Sources and Contexts in Indic Musicology." In *Comparative Musicology and Anthropology of Music: Essays on the History of Ethnomusicology*, edited by Bruno Nettl and Philip Bohlman, 152–168. Chicago: University of Chicago Press.

Ranade, Ashok. 1984. "Keertana: An Effective Communication." *On Music and Musicians of Hindustan*. New Delhi: Promill, 109–140.

——. 1986. *Stage Music of Maharashtra*. New Delhi: Sangeet Natak Akademi.

Ranade, M. G. 1947. "The Late Mr. Vaman Abaji Modak." In *Kirtane va Akhyaane*, edited by Vaman Abaji Modak. Nagpur: Balkrishna Ramchandra Modak. Reprinted from *Subodha Patrika*, Sunday, September 15, 1897.

——. 1961. *The Rise of Marathi Power*. Bombay: Bombay University.

Ranade, R. D. *Mysticism in Maharashtra*. 1988[1933, Poona]. Delhi: Motilal Banarsidass.

Reynolds, Christopher. 2003. *Motives for Allusion: Context and Content in Nineteenth-Century Music*. Cambridge, MA: Harvard University Press.

Rice, Timothy. 1994. *May it Fill Your Soul: Experiencing Bulgarian Music*. Chicago: University of Chicago Press.

Roland, Joan G. 1995. *The Jewish Communities of India: Identity in a Colonial Era*. Brunswick, NJ: Transaction.

——. 2000. "Religious Observances of the Bene Israel: Persistence and Refashioning of Tradition." *Journal of Indo-Judaic Studies* 3 (June): 22–47.

Rosse, Michael David. 1995. "The Movement for the Revitalization of 'Hindu' Music in Northern India, 1860–1930: The Role of Associations and Institutions." Ph.D. Dissertation, University of Pennsylvania.

Roy, Srirupa. 2007. *Beyond Belief: India and the Politics of Postcolonial Nationalism*. Durham: Duke University Press.

Sathaye, Adheesh. 2004. "Visvamitra: Intertextuality and performance of classic narratives about caste." Ph.D. Dissertation, University of California, Berkeley.

Schechner, Richard. 1985. *Between Theater and Anthropology*. Philadelphia: University of Pennsylvania Press.

Scheper-Hughes, Nancy and Margaret Lock. 1987. "The Mindful Body: A Prolegomenon to Future Work in Medical Anthropology." *Medical Anthropology Quarterly* 1(1): 6–41.

Schultz, Anna. 2002. "Hindu Nationalism, Music, and Embodiment in Marathi *Rashtriya Kirtan*." *Ethnomusicology* 46(2): 307–322.

——. 2008. "The Collision of Genres and Collusion of Participants: Marathi *Rāṣṭrīya Kīrtan* and the Communication of Hindu Nationalism." *Ethnomusicology* 52(2): 31–51.

Scruggs, T. M. 1998. "Nicaraguan State Cultural Initiative and 'the Unseen Made Manifest.'" *Yearbook for Traditional Music* (30): 53–73.

Sehgal, Meera. 2007. "Manufacturing a Feminized Siege Mentality: Hindu Nationalist Paramilitary Camps for Women in India." *Journal of Contemporary Ethnography* 36(2): 165–183.

Shirwadkar, Vasant. (no date). *The Wandering Saint: Life and Teachings of Gadge Baba*. Bombay: Shree Gadge Baba Prakashan Samiti.

Singer, Milton. 1972. *When a Great Tradition Modernizes: An Anthropological Approach to Civilization*. Chicago: University of Chicago Press.

Sirsikar, V. M. 1995. *Politics of Modern Maharashtra*. Bombay: Orient Longman.

Smith, Anthony. 1994. "The Crisis of Dual Legitimation." In *Nationalism*, edited by John Hutchinson and Anthony D. Smith, 113–121. Oxford: Oxford University Press.

——. 2005. "Civic and Ethnic Nationalism." In *Nations and Nationalism: A Reader*, edited by Philip Spencer and Howard Wollman. New Brunswick, NJ: Rutgers University Press.

Subramaniam, Lakshmi. 1999. "The Reinvention of a Tradition: Nationalism, Carnatic Music and the Madras Music Academy, 1900–1947." *Indian Economic and Social History Review* 36(2): 131–163.

——. 2000. "The Master, Muse and the Nation: The New Cultural Project and the Reification of Colonial Modernity in India." *South Asia* 23(2): 1–32.

Sugarman, Jane. 1999. "Imagining the Homeland: Poetry, Songs, and the Discourses of Albanian Nationalism." *Ethnomusicology* 43(3): 419–458.

Samartha Ramdas Swami. 1995. *Das Bodh*, translated by W. G. Tambwekar. Bombay: Shri Samarth Ramdas Swami Krupa Trust.

Trumpener, Katie. 2000. "Bela Bartok and the Rise of Comparative Musicology: Nationalism, Race Purity, and the Legacy of the Austro-Hungarian Empire." In *Music and the Racial Imagination*, edited by Ronald M. Radano and Philip V. Bohlman. Chicago Studies in Ethnomusicology. Chicago: University of Chicago Press.

Turino, Thomas. 1993. *Moving Away from Silence: Music of the Peruvian Altiplano and the Experience of Urban Migration*. Chicago: University of Chicago Press.

——. 1999. "Signs of Imagination, Identity, and Experience: A Peircian Semiotic Theory for Music." *Ethnomusicology* 43(2): 221–255.

——. 2000. *Nationalists, Cosmopolitans, and Popular Music in Zimbabwe*. Chicago: University of Chicago Press.

Van der Veer, Peter. 1994. *Religious Nationalism: Hindus and Muslims in India*. Berkeley: University of California Press.

——. 1999. "The Moral State: Religion, Nation, and Empire in Victorian Britain and British India." In *Nation and Religion: Perspectives on Europe and Asia*, edited by Peter van Der Veer and Helmut Lehmann, 15–43. Princeton, NJ: Princeton University Press.

Weidman, Amanda. 2006. *Singing the Classical, Voicing the Modern: The Postcolonial Politics of Music in South India*. Durham, NC: Duke University Press.

Wolpert, Stanley. 1997. *A New History of India*. 5th ed. New York: Oxford University Press.

MARATHI SOURCES

Aphale, Govindswami. 1955. *Āryānce Swāhākār*. Pune: Joshi Bros.

Barve, Sitaram Krishna. 1963. *Bhāratācārya Kolhatkarbuvānce Sannidhyānt*. Pune: Dharma Chaitanya Sanstha.

Bhaakare, Madhukar. 2000. "*Śrī Samarthānce Kīrtanaraṅga*." *Prabhukṛpa* (January): 65–68.

Bokil, V. P. 1979. *Rājguru Rāmdās*. Poona: Master Kamalesh P. Bokil.

Chapekar, Damodar Hari. 1974. *Hrutātma Damodar Hari Cāphekar Yānce Ātmavṛtta. (The Autobiography of Damodar Hari Caphekar)*, edited by V. G. Khobarekar. Mumbai: Mahārāśtra Rājya Sahitya and Saṅskṛti Maṅḍal.

Deshingkar, D. V. 1969. "Haribhakti Parāyan Dr. Dattopant Patwardhan Yānce Saṅkśit Caritra." In *Kai. Dr. Patwardhanbuva Vicārandhara āṇi Śikvaṇ*, edited by Pundalikji Katgade. Belgao: Jivaji Vyankatesh Yalagi.

Dhole, Ramkrishna Govindbuwa. 1925. *Śrīharidās Govindatārak Gīt va Purvāśrami Govindbuwa Hoshing Nāśikkar Yānce Caritra*. Mumbai: Chitrashāla Press.

Eknath. 1936. *Eknāthī Bhāgwat*, excerpted in *Caitanya* (1): 49.

Gadkar, Rachel. 1996. "Āmhī Bhāratvāsī Bene Israēl." *Shaili* 32 (September): 60–64.

Ghaisas, Bhaskar Ramchandra. 1998. *Kīrtana Ciṅtāmaṇi*. 2 vols. Vol. 1. Pune: Harikīrtanottejak Sabha.

Ghongate, R.S., ed. n.d. *Śri Gādge Bābāncī Amṛtavānī: Śevaṭce Kīrtan*. Mumbai: Shri Gadge Maharaj Prakashan Samiti.

Gondhalekar, Raoji Shridhar. 1895. *Kīrtanataraṅginī*. 4th ed. Pune: Moghe and Kemkar.

Inamdar, Vishnu H., Nishikant D. Mirajkar, and Nivruttinath N. Relekar, eds. 1979. *Nāmdevāncī Abhangavāni*. Pune: Modern Book Depot.

Joshi, Baburao. 1980. *Caṅdaśāstra va Saṅgīt*. Kolhapur: Ajab Pustakalaya.

Joshi, Dinanath Manohar. 2000. "Aśī Saṅsthā—Ase Upakram." In *Hirak Mahotsav Smaraṇika*, 12–21. Dadar, Mumbai: Akhil Bhāratīya Kīrtan Saṅsthā.

Joshi, Laksmansastri. 1947. "Prastāvana" In Vaman Abaji Modak, *Kīrtane va Ākhyāne*, 9–26. Nagpur: Balkrishna Ramchandra Modak.

Joshi, R. A. 1982. "Śri Koparkarbuva Vyakti, Yogyata, va Kārya." In *Kīrtanakalāniddhi: Rāṣṭrīya Kīrtankār H.Bh.P. Gangādhar Nārāyan Koparkarbuva Gaurav Graṅtha*, edited by Rāmcandraśāstri Joshi. Pune: Koparkarbuva Satkār Samiti.

Kaikadi Baba, Shri Sant. 1992. *Sukhāci Wāṭ*. Pandharpur: Shantai Prakashan.

——. 1999. *Mānavāno māṇuskīla jāgā: Sant Kaikāḍībābāṅce Kīrtan*. Pune: Anand Music Company. Sound cassette.

Katgade, Pundalikji. 1969. *Rāṣṭrīya Kīrtankār Kai. Dr. Patwardhanbuwa, Vicārdhara āṇi Śikvan* (Rāṣṭrīya Kīrtankār, the late Dr. Patwardhanbuwa: Thoughts and Teachings). Belgao: Jivaji Vyankatesh Yalgi.

Khare, Govinda. 1985. *Ārogya Dhanasaṁpadā*. Pune: Govinda Khare.

Khobarekar, V. G. 1974. "Introduction" to *Hrutātma Damodar Hari Cāphekar Yānce Ātmavṛtta. (The Autobiography of Damodar Hari Caphekar)*. Mumbai: Mahārāśtra Rājya Sahitya and Saṅskṛti Maṅḍal.

Kolhatkar, Vaman Vasudeo. 1995. *Kīrtan: Ase Śikā Ase Karā*. Unpublished manuscript.

Kolhatkar, Vasudeo Shivram. 1933. *Kīrtana-Mandakini*. Part Three: Tilak Janmākhyān. Pune: Vasudeo Shivram Kolhatkar.

——. 1936a. "Bruhanmahārāṣṭra Kīrtankār." *Chaitanya* (April): 64–65.

——. 1936b. "Śrīharikīrtan." *Chaitanya* (April): 2–5.

——. 1963. *Kīrtankalā āṇi Śāstra*. Pune: V.S. Kolhatkar.

Koparkar, G. N. n.d. *Dṛṣṭiskhetrepānt Vaidik Dharma va Tatvajṭān*. Kīrtan Mahāvidyālaya Prakāśan.

——. 1979. *Khiśātil Kīrtan-Śikśak*. Pune: Kīrtan Mahāvidyālaya Prakāśan.

——. 1982a. *Kīrtanadhyāpan*. Mumbai: Kīrtan Mahāvidyālaya Prakāśan.

——. *1982b. Kīrtanācī Prayogakrīya*. Pune: Kīrtan Mahāvidyālaya Prakāśan.

G. N. Koparkar, ed., Narendrabuva Hate, assistant ed., and Govindswami Aphale, assistant ed. 1978? *Kathā Haridāsīcī (Kai. Dr. Patwardhanbuva Janmaśaptābdismaraṇagrantha)*. Pune: Kīrtan Mahāvidyālaya.

Kurtakoti, Shankaracharya Dr. 1929. "Āśīrvād" (Blessing). In *Karmayogi Paṅḍit Jagannāthrāy: Yavan-Vadhū-Udhār,* edited by Mahadev Balkrishna Khaladkar. Saṅgit Aitihāsik Ratnamāḷ, vol. 1. Nasik: Loksatta Publishers.

Manmadkar, Dadamaharaj. 1998. *Vārkarī Sampradāya: Tattvadnyān va Sadyakālin Aucitya*. Pandharpur: Sri H.Bh.P. Guruvarya Vidyavācaspati Dr. Dadamaharaj Manmadkar Satkār Samiti.

Meshram, Satyavan. 1998. *Sant Gadge Maharaj Kal Ani Kartrutva*. Mumbai: Maharashtra Rajya Sahitya ani Sanskriti Mandal.

Modak, Vaman Abaji. 1947. *Kīrtane va Akhyāne*. Nagpur: Balkrishna Ramchandra Modak.

Pathak, Yashwant. 1980. *Nācu Kīrtanāce Rangī*. Pune: Continental Publishers.

Patil, Ramchandra Gopal. 1964. *Tukārām Mahārājāncī Gāthā*, ed. Pune: Viṭṭhala Prakāśan.

Patwardhan, Dattatrey Vinayak. 1950. *Kīrtanapañcak*. Publisher unknown.

Ranade, Ashok. 1982. "*Kīrtan Prayogaparaṁparecī Utkrāntī.*" *Kīrtankalāniddhī Rāṣṭrīya Kīrtankār H.Bh.P. Gangadhar Nārāyan Koparkarbuwa Gaurav Grantha*. Pune: Shri Koparkarbuva Satkār Samiti, 3–5.

Salpekar, Babasaheb. 2000. "A. Bhā. Kīrtan Sammelan, Nāgpūr. Sammelanādhyakṣa H. Bh. P. Śrī Bābāsaheb Sālpekar Yānce Adhyakṣīya Bhāṣaṇ." In *Kīrtan-Sankīrtan,* edited by Ram Shevalkar, 167–175. Nagpur: Akhil Bhāratīya Kīrtan Sammelan.

Sardesai, Govind Sakharam. 1925. "Prastāvana." In *Śrīharidās Govindatārak Gīt va Purvāśramī Govindbuva Hośiṅg Nāśikkar Yānce Caritra,* edited by Ramkrishna Govindbuwa Dhole. Mumbai: Chitrashāla Press.

Sathe, B. M. 1928. *Kīrtan-Kumudinī* (Kīrtan lotus). Pune: Śrī Sarasvatī Maṅḍal.

Shevalkar, Ram, ed. 2000. *Kīrtan-Sankīrtan*. Nagpur: Akhil Bhāratīya Kīrtan Sammelan.

Shevde, S. G., Moreshwarbuwa Joshi, Shrikant Khadilkar, eds. 2000. *Kīrtankār-Pravacankār Paricay Sūcīgrantha* (Part 1). Pune: Kīrtankula Prakāśan.

Tambeshastri, Sadashiv Dhonde. 1910. *Kīrtanamuktahār*. Mumbai: Ramabai Tarte.

Tilak, Bal Gangadhar. 1918. *Bal Gangadhar Tilak: His Writings and Speeches*. Madras: Ganesh.

——. 1976. "Kīrtan va Kīrtankār." *Samagra Tilak* (Tilak's Collected Works), 820–827. Pune: Kesarī Prakāśan.

Vaidya, Digvijay. 1997. Marāṭhī Lāvaṇī – Marāṭhī Sangītāce Prārnatattva. Ph.D. Dissertation, Akhil Bhāratīya Gāndharva Mahāvidyālaya Maṅḍal (Mumbai-Miraj).

GLOSSARY OF MARATHI TERMS

Abhaṅga: Most songs by Marathi saints are abhaṅgas, a genre that loosely corresponds to bhajans by saints of northern India. Kīrtankār Vaman Kolhatkar provided this etymology of abhaṅga: "Bhaṅga means "breakable" and *a* means "not," so abhaṅga means unbreakable or everlasting."[1] Though abhaṅgas are written in a variety of poetic structures, most abhaṅgas are composed of four lines (each line is divided into two halves), in which the first line serves as a refrain (dhrupad), and the remaining three lines function as verses. Two melodies are often used, one for the refrain and another for the verses, as in the sthāi-antarā structure of North Indian vocal music, though some abhaṅgas are sung in a strophic structure without a refrain. The last line contains the signature of the saint who composed the abhaṅga. For example, the final line of abhaṅgas by Tukārām begin with "Tukā mhaṇe" (Tukā says).

Adhyātmik. Spiritual.

Aitihāsik: Historical.

Antarā: In north Indian art song, this refers to the verse, which is usually sung at a higher tessitura than the refrain (**sthāi**).

Ācārya: Spiritual guide.

Ādarśa: Ideal.

Adhyakṣa Chairman or director.

Ākhyān: 1. Story. 2. A story told in speech and song. 3. The written form of #2.

Andhaśraddhā: Blind faith.

Āratī: 1. A ritual in which an oil lamp is waved in front of a deity. 2. The song sung during the āratī ritual—the Marathi āratī is in a triple meter.

Āryā: A short, unmetered song with a particular poetic meter used in kīrtan to narrate important events or describe inner emotions. Moropant wrote almost exclusively in āryās, and the genre is strongly associated with him.

Āṣāḍh Ekādaśi: The eleventh day in the Hindu month of Āṣāḍh. This is the day when vārkarīs convene in Pandharpur to visit the Viṭṭhala temple.

Āśram: Religious retreat or commune.

Bhajan: In Marathi kīrtan, bhajan refers to a devotional song genre comprised of one or two musical phrases and lines of text (usually the name/s of a deity or saint) repeated several times. The short, repetitive melodies promote the participatory performance of bhajans. Bhajans are sung in a variety of contexts—by vārkarīs as they walk to Pandharpur, by neighborhood bhajan groups, in temples, at home during ceremonies, and so on. In other parts of India, bhajan can refer generally to devotional songs or to songs by the north Indian saints that are comparable to Marathi abhanga.

Bhajanī ṭhekā. A series of bols in an eight-beat meter used to accompany Marathi bhajans, abhaṅgas, and other north Indian folk and devotional songs.

Bhakti: A feeling of "devotion" and a set of devotional traditions that provide populist alternatives to the rituals of Brāhmaṇical Vedic Hinduism.

Bhārata Mātā: Mother India.

Bhāvgīt: Emotional songs.

Bol: A sound produced by striking the tablā in a particular manner.

Brahman: The highest caste of Hindus. Traditionally associated with priesthood and education.

Bukā: A black powder applied to devotees' foreheads during some rituals, including kīrtan.

Caraṇ: A phrase of poetry, literally "foot."

Ciplīyā: Idiophones used in nāradīya kīrtan; they are constructed of a piece of wood from which holes are cut out, and in which small cymbals are suspended. They are played by holding two in one hand and beating them together.

Darśan: Seeing the image of the divine.

Dayā: Benevolence.

Deś: Country, nation.

Deśbhakta: Literally, "devotee of the nation." Patriot.

Deśdharma: Religion of the nation.

Dev: God.

Dharmśāḷa. A retreat for pilgrims.

Dhārmik: Religious.

Dhotī: A long piece of cloth tied to create baggy "pants."

Dinḍī. 1. A group of pilgrims devoted to a particular saint who travel to Pandharpur together on the **vārī**. 2. A song genre sung to dādra tāl (a six-beat tāl), comprised of at least two couplets. The same melody is used for each half of the couplet, though the second half is sung up a fifth.

Dhrupad or ***dhruvapad:*** In Marathi, this refers to the refrain of a song, which is usually sung at a lower tessitura than the verse.

Filmī gīt: Hindi film song.

Gajar: Shout or acclamation at a kīrtan.

Gaṇeś: The elephant-headed deity who removes obstacles and loves knowledge and music. He is the son of Śiva and Parvatī.

Gaṇeśotsav: The festival celebrating Gaṇeś.

Gāyan: Singing or song.

Ghī: Clarified butter.

Ghoṣgīt: Continuous, repeating song.

Goṅdhaḷ: A Marathi genre sung in praise of the goddess by male hereditary musicians employed by temples and neighborhoods.

Gurukula: Literally, "guru's family"—a South Asian system of knowledge transmission in which disciples live with the guru (teacher) as his symbolic family members. The student learns through active instruction as well as by absorbing the guru's daily habits.

Haridās: Kīrtankār (literally, servant of Viṣṇu).

Harikathā: A name for Marathi kīrtan that is rarely used today.

Harikīrtan: The term for nāmasankīrtan in rural Uttar Pradesh. Harikīrtan is performed by groups of men, is antiphonal, has duple meters, and gradually accelerates and becomes louder. Henry defines harikīrtan as "antiphonal Vaishnavite songs with short, simple stanzas continuously repeated" (Henry 1988: 139). The goal of singing this type of kīrtan is to achieve a devotional intoxication—sometimes facilitated by the smoking of marijuana—that is itself a form of puja (Henry 1988: 140–143).

Hindustani Music: The north Indian art music tradition.

Hindutva: Literally, "Hinduness"—the guiding principle of Hindu nationalist organizations. Vinayak Damodar Savarkar coined the term in 1922 to describe the Hindu nation, which he believed was composed of people who accepted India as their fatherland and Holy Land.[2]

Iśkārya: Work for God.

Iśvar: God; the ever-present.

Jap: The practice of counting beads while repeating a prayer or name of God.

Jayjaykār: An intoned list of "victory to" various deities and saints.

Jhāṅj: Small, flat hand cymbals played by nāradīya kīrtankārs.

Jñān: Knowledge.

Jñāndev (Jñāneśvar): The first Marathi saint of the vārkarī tradition. Jñāneśvar's works are the earliest extant examples of devotional poetry for Lord Viṭṭhala, the dark Kṛṣṇa.

Jñāy: Logic.

Kathan: Storytelling.

Kaṭāv: A song genre used to list many items in quick succession. It consists of very short musical phrases sung at a fast tempo that, in their unaltered repetitiveness, convey a feeling of infinite sameness or large quantities.

Kendra: Branch of an organization.

Khanjīrā: A secondary percussion instrument used with the mṛdaṅgam in South Indian music. A small frame drum with slits containing small metal discs that rattle when the drum is shaken or struck.

Kīrtan: A type of devotional song and performance with widely varying referents in different parts of India. In Marathi, kīrtan refers to a performance context that includes a mixture of song, storytelling, and religious discourse.

Kīrtankār: A performer of kīrtan.

Krāntikārak: Freedom fighter.

Kuḍtā: A tunic.

Laggi: A quick rhythm in quadruple meter (kīrtankārs often use the first half of keharva tāl or bhajani ṭheka) that repeats cyclically without much alteration. Only open sounds are used, that is, the dagga (larger left hand drum) is not dampened. Full-fledged tāls, on the other hand, are comprised of a combination of open (undampened) and closed (dampened) sounds.

Lāvaṇī: A romantic and/or devotional song genre performed by both śāhīrs and courtesans in a variety of contexts ranging from bawdy tamāśā plays to the more sedate seated performances.

Madhukari: 1. Food donations given to Brahmans. 2. One who subsists by going door to door begging for alms.

Mahārāj. "King." Also a term of respect used to refer to vārkarī kīrtankārs.

Mahotsav: Festival.

Man: Mind or heart.

Maṅḍal: An assembly or committee.

Maṅdir: Temple.

Maṅgalācaraṇ: The opening set of songs and chants in a Marathi kīrtan.

Marāthā: A Maharashtrian kṣatrīya caste.

Maṭh: A spiritual retreat for a living saint or ascetic and his or her devotees.

Māļa: Garland.

Mokṣa: Spiritual liberation, nirvana.

Mṛdaṅg. Double-headed cylindrical drum.

Muḷpad: Main song; the abhaṅga upon which the kīrtankār's discourse is based.

Naman: Literally, a bow of obeisance. Naman also refers to the opening song performed in Marathi kīrtan, which has a verse-refrain structure and lists the good qualities of Rāmakṛṣṇa.

Namaskār: A bow or salutation.

Nāndī: In saṅgīt nāṭak, this is the opening song that serves as an invocation and greeting to the divine.

Nāradāñcī gādī. "Nārad's mat," a space imbued for the time of the kīrtan with the presence of Nārad, the mythological sage whom nāradīya kīrtankārs regard as their founder and patron.

Nāradīya kīrtan: A saṁpradāya of Marathi kīrtan performed by a solo kīrtankār (usually a Brahman) who sings, speaks, and chants. The kīrtankār plays jhānj or ciplīyās and is accompanied by tablā (or pakhvāj) and harmonium. Audience participation is generally limited to the opening, intermission, and concluding parts of the kīrtan; and during all other parts, the kīrtankār intersperses his or her spoken discourse with songs of various genres performed as solos. A kīrtan is separated into two halves of about twenty to forty-five minutes each, the purvaraṅga and the uttararaṅga.

Nāṭya gīt: Songs from Marathi saṅgīt nāṭak.

Navrātra: The nine-night festival for the Goddess.

Nirupaṇa: Spoken discourse. In nāradīya and rāṣṭrīya kīrtan, this is the first half of the kīrtan (also called purvaraṅga), while in vārkarī kīrtan, the entire kīrtan consists of nirupaṇa.

Ovī: One of the oldest Marathi song genres still performed today (Gurumurthy 1994: 67, Joshi 1980: 102–103). There are many ovī structures, but they are all composed of four caraṇ, the first three of which share the same number of mātras, while the fourth has fewer mātras.

Pad: A generic term that can loosely be translated as "song." Pads are metered, are often newly composed, and are not attributed to a saint or other spiritual authority from the past.

Pagaḍi: A silken hat with a tassel on top worn by **nāradīya kīrtankārs**.

Pakhvāj: A double-headed cylindrical drum used for Marathi folk music (also known as **mṛdaṅg**).

Pant-kavi: Learned poets, such as Moropant, Shridhar, and Mādhavmuniśvar of the eighteenth century. They wrote **ākhyāns**, often in the **āryā** meter.

Parameśvar: Supreme God.

Paṭhaḍī: In Marathi, performance lineage.

Pālkhi: A palanquin containing the footprints of a saint. Each **diṇḍī** carries the pālkhi of a different saint on the pilgrimage to Pandharpur.

Pāṇḍuraṅga: Another name for Viṭṭhala.

Pāṭśālā: School, academy, college.

Paurāṇik: 1. A Brahman who tells stories from the purāṇas in a seated position, often as part of the daily program of a temple. 2. Related to the purāṇas.

Pheṭā: Turban.

Povāḍā: A Marathi sung narrative genre eulogizing the heroism of warriors. Povāḍās are composed of long, flexible musical phrases based on a handful of stock melodies. Since povāḍā lyrics are partially improvised, the flexible melodic and rhythmic structure allows the singer to change the melodic rhythm by inserting and omitting syllables without disrupting the metric cycle.

Prasād: A token of food offered to and consecrated by a deity, after which devotees consume it.

Pravacan: Discourse or lecture, usually on a religious topic.

Pujā: Worship or ritual.

Punya: Religious merit.

Purāṇa: 1. Ancient mythological text. 2. A discourse on an ancient text.

Pūrvaraṅga (also called **Nirupaṇa**): The first half of a **nāradīya** or **rāṣṭrīya kīrtan**, in which the kirtankar gives a philosophical discourse expounding on ideas in a selected **abhaṅga**.

Rasa: Taste, aesthetics.

Rakhumāī: The wife of **Viṭṭhala**.

Rāga: A mode used in Indian art music; each rāga is characterized by a unique scale, emphasis on particular notes, a particular ordering of pitches in ascent and descent, mood, and customary performance time.

Rājahans: A song genre that has its roots in drama music and is now a mainstay of rāṣṭrīya kīrtan. One rāṣṭrīya kīrtankār told me that rājahans is used,"to create fervor or say a lot in a short time,"[3] a sentiment echoed by other kīrtankārs.

Rājkāraṇ: Politics.

Rāmdās: A seventeenth-century Marathi saint who broke from the vārkarī sampradāya to worship Rāma, and who advocated combining worldly and spiritual endeavors.

Rāmrājya: Rāma's rule.

Rāmjanmabhumī: Rāma's birthplace.

Rāṇā: King.

Rāṇī: Queen.

Rāṣṭra: Nation.

Rāṣṭrabhāṣā: National language, that is, Hindi.

Rāṣṭrīya kīrtan: Nationalist kīrtan.

Rupāce abhaṅga: **Abhaṅga** celebrating God's form.

Sadguru: True teacher.

Samādhi: State of consciousness characterized by complete meditation; absorption of the individual into the object of meditation at time of death.

Sammelan: Conference.

Sampradāya: Tradition or performance tradition.

Sanātan dharma: Hinduism (literally, ancient religion). Nationalists often use this designation because it does not have the colonial baggage of the term "Hinduism."

Saṅdhyā: Morning, noon, and evening prayers.

Saṅgh Parivār: A coalition of Hindu nationalist organizations and political parties, including the Rāṣṭrīya Swayamsevak Sangh (RSS), the Bharatiya Janata Party (BJP), the Vishwa Hindu Parishad (VHP), and others.

Saṅgīt nāṭak: Marathi musical drama.

Saṅskār: Hindu customs and manners.

Sant: A person generally recognized by Hindus as a saint because of his or her exceptional devotion. The vārkarī saints were poets who achieved samādhi.

Satkār: Token of honor, respect.

Satyāgraha: Literally, "truth force," but in practice refers to nonviolent resistance.

Sādhvī: Female ascetic.

Sākī: A song genre performed in nāradīya and rāṣṭrīya kīrtans, often depicting the emotions or actions of a character making a brave decision. Sākī, sung loudly and at a high tessitura, is said to convey the vīr rasa (emotion of bravery) (Gurumurthy 1994: 71). A variety of tunes were used to sing sākī in the past, but nāradīya kīrtankārs of today use a particular tune in rāga bhairav almost exclusively (Joshi 1980: 91). Sākī is sung to an eight-beat dhumālī tala, and each line begins decisively with a single syllable per tablā stroke.

Sevā: Service, especially as a devotional exercise.

Sevāmaṇḍal: Group of devotees.

Snān: Ritual bath.

Sthāi: In north Indian art song, this refers to the refrain, which is usually sung at a lower tessitura than the verse (antarā).

Sūrya namaskār: Obeisance to the sun.

Sūtradhār: Principal actor of a theater company, the chief narrator of a play.

Svadeśi: A nationalist strategy of using only those goods that are produced in India by Indians for Indians. M. K. Gandhi's interpretation of svadeśi gained extraordinary popularity before Indian independence; he argued that each *individual* should also be self-sufficient, and he thus encouraged all individuals to not only buy clothes from Indian-owned companies but also to spin their own cotton thread with a wheel.

Svara: Note, pitch.

Svarājya: Own country; own nation.

Svayamsevak: Volunteer.

Svayamvar Ākhyān: Story of self-arranged marriage.

Śāhīr: Poet and singer of Marathi povāḍā and lāvanī.

Śākhā: Branch (of an organization).

Śāstrī: Scholar of the scriptures.

Śibīr: Workshops/short-term schools.

Śiṣya. Disciple.

Śivājī: A seventeenth-century Maratha king.

Ślokā: A stanza of poetry.

Śraddhā: Faith.

Śravaṇ: Listening.

Śrote: Audience/congregation.

Tablā: A set of two drums played with the hands and fingers in north Indian music. The slightly conical right-hand drum (called dāyan or tablā) is carved from a single piece of wood, while the left-hand drum (called bāyan or dāgga) is metal and bowl-shaped. Both drums are covered with animal hide. The dāyan can be tuned while the tablā does not produce exact pitches.

Tamburā: A four-stringed lute used to supply the drone in Indian art music. The first string is tuned to the fifth, the second and third strings are tuned to the tonic in the middle register, and the fourth string is tuned to the lower tonic. A buzzing sound is created by small pieces of thread placed under the strings where they meet the flat bridge. Open strings are plucked in succession throughout the duration of the music session.

Tapascaryā: Austerity, penance.

Tamāśā: A bawdy Marathi theatrical genre performed by women (mostly for men) proficient in singing and dancing. The song genre most characteristic of tamāśā is **lāvaṇī**.

Tāl: Meter.

Ṭāḷ: Small, concave hand cymbals played by **vārkarīs**.

Ṭāḷkarī: The chorus of people who stand behind a **vārkarī kīrtankār** playing **ṭāḷ**, singing, and dancing.

Tīrtha: Holy place; a place of pilgrimage.

Tukārām: A seventeenth-century **vārkarī saint** of the śudra caste.

Ṭhekā: The standard sequence of **bols** for a given meter.

Uparaṇā: A piece of cloth worn loosely over the shoulders or around the neck.

Uttararaṅga (also called **ākhyān**): The second half of a **nāradīya** or **rāṣṭrīya kīrtan**, in which the **kīrtankār** tells a story from the life of a **saint**, a nationalist, or an episode from the epics or **purāṇas** that illustrates the philosophical concepts introduced in the **pūrvaraṅga**.

Varnāśramadharma: The duties of one's caste and maintenance of the caste system.

Vāḍā: A Maharashtrian-type of house with a central courtyard; a large, stately house.

Vārī. The annual pilgrimage to Pandharpur to see the image of **Viṭṭhala** in his temple. There are actually two pilgrimages to Pandharpur each year, but many pilgrims only participate in one of them.

Vārkarī. A member of the vārkarī panth. Vārkarīs are not ascetics; they are householders who have made a vow to go on the **vārī** each year, to fulfill the duties of their caste, and to refrain from eating meat.

Vārkarī panth: (Vārkarī sect). A **bhakti** sect based on the literature of the Marathi **vārkarī saints**, who wrote songs in praise of Lord **Viṭṭhala** and who advocated simple methods of devotion that were accessible to all.

Vārkarī kīrtan: A **saṁpradāya** of Marathi kīrtan closely associated with the **vārkarī** tradition.

Vīṇā: A plucked lute used as a drone in **vārkarī kīrtan**.

Viṭhobā: See *Viṭṭhala*.

Viṭṭhala (also called *Viṭhobā* or *Pāṇḍuraṅga*): A Marathi version of Kṛṣṇa whose main temple is in Pandharpur. Usually depicted in black stone with his hands on his hips, Viṭṭhala is the object of vārkarī devotion.

INDEX

abhaṅgas, 23, 26, 34, 35, 48, 69, 85, 89, 107, 140, 145, 147–49, 150, 154, 156, 160–61, 168, 169, 171, 180, 196n5, 197n9
Agnīdās, 28
agricultural reform, 80, 82
Akhīl Bhāratīya Kīrtan Kula, 17–18, 80, 98, 102, 104–6, 111–15, 120, 124, 129, 131, 137, 176, 177, 187, 192, 194, 196n4
Akhīl Bhāratīya Kīrtan Saṅsthā, 39, 98, 105, 109–10, 111, 124, 136
ākhyāns, 27–28, 29, 30, 34, 35, 40, 43, 47, 69, 107, 139, 141. *See also* uttararaṅgas
All-India Music Conference, 36
Ambedkar, Babasaheb, 74
Anjanī, 59
anjanī gīt, 59
anthropology, 4, 8–9, 15, 157, 175, 190–91, 194
anti-colonialism: and Chapekar brothers' actions, 52–56; Chatterjee's theory of, 9, 21, 32–33; and nārādīya kīrtan, 22, 30; and newspapers, 43; and rāṣṭrīya kīrtan, 17, 43, 48, 50, 51, 52, 60, 72–74, 84, 130, 152, 189; and regional culture, 5, 10, 189–90
anti-nuclear theme, at Kaikadi Maharaj Maṭh, 87
Apamarjane, Narahari (N. S.), 99, 119, 122, 138, 142
Apamarjane, Vijay, 142
Aphale, Charudatta, 34, 91, 92, 93–94, 122, 142, 145, 149, 204n21
Aphale, Govindswami, 34, 81, 91–94, 96, 98, 99, 101, 201n38
art music. *See* classical music
āryā, 59, 69, 70, 94, 107, 140, 150, 151
Arya Samaj, 51, 56
Atre, P. K., 64
authenticity, of kīrtan performance, 167–70
Ayerst, C. E., 52
Ayurvedic medicine, 73, 88, 89
Azad, Chandrashekar, 149

Badave, Shreeyash, 25, 143–44, 145, 150
Badodekar, Nanabuwa, 143
Bahiṇābāi, 23
Bakhle, Bhaskarbuva, 34
Bakhle, Janaki, 36
Bakhtin, Mikhail, 174–75, 188
Bala, Honaji, 29
Balaji Viswanath, 28
Barve, Milinda, 34, 145
Barve, S. K., 69–70
Bauman, Richard, 15, 170, 174, 175, 180, 205n5
Becker, Judith, 14, 166
Bene Israel kīrtan, 197–98n24
Bhaakare, Madhukar, 27
bhajan: in nārādīya kīrtan, 23, 48, 140, 141, 145, 146, 150, 154, 171; in rāṣṭrīya kīrtan, 62–63, 83, 84, 85, 124, 141, 145, 156, 159–60, 163, 169, 177–79, 185, 188; in vārkarī kīrtan, 145, 146, 159–60, 168, 170, 171
bhakti, 14, 26, 46, 85, 100, 121, 130, 138, 155–56, 163, 167–69, 171, 182, 185, 200n16

bhangra, 184–85

Bhāratīya Janata Party (BJP), 6, 82, 97, 102, 171, 172, 178, 186

Bhāratīya Jana Sangh (BJS), 97

Bhāratīya Vidya Bhavan, 99, 101

Bhatkhande, V. N., 36, 112

Bhau, Sangam, 29

Bhave, Vinoba, 83

Bhave, Vishnudas, 34

Bhilavdikar, Shankarshastri, 46

Bhilavdikarshastri, P., 37

Bhojpuri language, 189

Bhonsle dynasty, 5, 28

Bhosekar, Govind Ganesh, 109

Birla Foundation, 100

Bose, Subhash Chandra, 93, 139, 152, 190

Bourdieu, Pierre, 157, 170

Brahmans: and anti-colonialism, 54; art and literature of, 27, 28, 47; and Gandhi assassination, 17, 79–80, 82, 91, 101, 189, 192; and music institutions, 36, 99; and nationalism, 10, 11; as saṅgīt nāṭak performers, 34; social identity of, 194

Brahmans, kīrtan activity of, 22, 26, 47–48, 109, 122, 123; and nārādīya kīrtan, 3, 23, 29, 37, 47; and rāṣṭrīya kīrtan, 6, 11, 43, 52, 56, 65, 66, 91, 104, 189

Brahmo Samaj, 39, 41, 48

British colonialism, 5, 9, 10, 21, 30, 32, 43, 48, 52–53, 56–57, 74, 123. *See also* anti-colonialism

Buddhism, 39

Burse, Vasudeo, 137, 152, 172

Capwell, Charles, 13

caste identity: in kīrtan performance, 23; in saṅgīt nāṭak performance, 34; in tamāśā performance, 33

caste system: and kīrtan conferences, 47; and Nehruvian reform, 82; and rāṣṭrīya kīrtan, 12, 43, 58, 60, 64, 67, 74, 75, 192

Chapekar, Balkrishna, 52, 53, 55

Chapekar, Damodar, 52–56

Chatterjee, Partha, 9–12, 21, 32–33, 40, 51, 61, 79, 130, 198n30

Chavan, Yashwantrao, 82–83

Chiplunkar, Vishnushastri, 42

Chitnis, Bhingarbuva, 46

Christianity, 39, 118, 172, 187, 204n13

classical music, 13, 36–37, 107, 112, 139, 142, 161, 192. *See also* rāgas

collision of genres, 18, 170, 175, 180, 183, 185, 186, 187, 193

conferences, kīrtan, 14, 18, 21, 44, 46–47, 48–49, 51, 75, 102–3, 111, 113–20, 167

Congress Party, 6, 12, 82, 87, 97, 101, 189, 194

cosmopolitanism, 11, 12, 16, 21–22, 51, 55, 191, 192

courtly arts, 27–29, 30, 47

cow protection, 7, 43, 56–57, 64, 183

Csordas, Thomas J., 157

cultural nationalism: Chatterjee's theory of, 9–12; and modernist reforms, 32, 33; and nārādīya kīrtan, 22, 48; and publication of kīrtan, 35; and Tilak's advocacy of kīrtan, 21, 22, 43–46

Cutler, Norman, 168–69

Dabir, Dilip, 145

Damāyaṅtī, 28

dance, 25, 29, 48, 99, 119, 160, 163–64, 168, 169, 170, 184–85, 188

Dandekar, Ramchandrabuva, 46

Deshmukh, Shantabai, 125

Deshmukh, Shantabai Maharaj, 196n3

Deshpande, Prachi, 190

Deshpande, Smita, 128

devotional practice, in kīrtan, 22, 25, 44, 141; and devotional embodiment, 166–70, 172–73, 193; and nārādīya kīrtan, 23, 138, 169; and rāṣṭrīya kīrtan, 4, 52, 57–60, 62–63, 71, 85, 145, 147, 155, 169, 171, 172–73, 179, 183, 193; and vārkarī kīrtan, 5–6, 23, 25–26, 85, 138, 168

Dhamankar, Sudhatai, 53, 99, 104, 122–23, 128, 129–30, 143, 156, 158–66, 169–72, 180, 183, 184, 193, 202n7

Dharma Caitanya, in Pune, 73

Dhingre, Madanlal, 139

Dhole, Ramkrishnabuva, 30, 31, 145

dialogism, in kīrtan performance, 174–76, 180, 185
didactic aspects of kīrtan, 26, 27
Divekar, V. D., 5
drama, musical. *See* saṅgīt nāṭak
dress, of kīrtan singers, 47, 127, 137–38, 155

East India Company, 32
education, 11, 17, 18, 32, 36–39, 45, 48, 75, 80, 82, 98–100, 101, 104–10, 112, 120–22, 124, 131. *See also* master-disciple relationship
Eknath, 23, 25, 27, 167, 171, 180, 183
Elizabeth I, 32
embodiment, 3, 14–15, 18, 157–58, 166–71, 173, 193
English language, 11, 41, 44, 45, 46, 52, 90, 94, 98, 100, 174
entertainment, 28–29, 30; kīrtan as, 26, 27, 91, 138, 158
ethnography, 8, 14–15, 18, 135, 190–91
ethnomusicology, 8, 13, 14, 15, 81, 175

Faizapur National Congress, 64
family planning, 88, 89, 90
Feldhaus, Anne, 5
festivals, 42, 43, 54, 111, 120
film music, 93, 184, 185
folk music, 27, 124, 139, 189–90

Gadge Maharaj Mission, in Bombay, 84
Gandharva Mahavidyalaya, 37
Gandhi, Indira, 81, 87, 88, 89–90, 97, 101, 125
Gandhi, Mohandas Karamchand, 11, 12, 17, 50–51, 56, 57, 60, 62–64, 65, 66, 75, 79, 80, 82, 83, 84, 88, 91, 93, 101, 145, 189, 192, 199n18
Gaṇeś, 23, 43, 55, 141, 154
Gayan Uttejak Mandali, 36, 38
gender, in kīrtan performance, 18, 23, 104, 120–30, 196nn3–4
Ghag, Dattadas, 34, 145
Ghaisas, B. R., 38, 39, 57, 58, 108–9, 122, 142, 149, 188, 199n21
ghoṣgīt, 115–16
Goa, 66, 93
Godbole, Narayanshastri, 81
Godse, Nathuram, 79, 101
Goffman, Irving, 14, 179
Gokhale, Gopalkrishna, 10, 11
Gondavalekar, Yashwantrao, 62, 74
Gondhalekar, Raoji Shridhar, 34–35
government policy, kīrtan as organ of, 85–91, 101
government support for kīrtan, 17, 80, 81–82, 86, 87, 93, 98, 101
Gramsci, Antonio, 11, 12, 60–61, 195n9
Gurjar, Chintamanishastri, 38
Gurjar, Dharnidhar Shastri, 37, 38
gurus. *See* master-disciple relationship

Halliburton, Murphy, 15
Hansen, Kathryn, 190
Hansen, Thomas, 79, 96
Hanuman, 59, 147
Harīkirtanottejak Sabhā, 37–38, 42, 98, 104, 105, 108, 110, 111, 121, 124, 131, 197n24
Hate, Narendrabuva, 99
Hedgewar, K. B., 102, 113, 152
Henry, Edward, 189
Hindi language, 46, 63, 88, 89, 90, 114, 115, 174
Hindu Code Bill, 94
Holkar, Ahilyabi, 125
Holub, Renate, 61
Hoshing, Govindbuva, 30–32, 33, 144
Hutchinson, John, 9

iconicity, 15, 153, 156–57
improvisation, in kīrtan performance, 35, 107, 143–44, 148–49, 153–54, 191
Independence, 6, 10, 16, 17, 55, 71, 79, 101, 192
indexicality, 15, 153, 156–57, 159, 161, 170, 175, 177, 179, 188, 193
Indian National Congress, 21, 32, 40, 51, 55, 56, 79
institutions, kīrtan, 14, 17–18, 36–39, 49, 98–100, 101, 102–15, 130–32, 176, 177, 187, 193. *See also* conferences; education
intellectuals, 10–11, 12, 60–61, 195n9
intertextuality, 14, 175, 177, 178, 179, 180, 206n1
Islam, 7, 27, 36, 48, 57, 79, 93, 96, 102, 124, 141, 158, 159, 161, 172, 178, 182, 185, 187, 193, 201n38

Jadhav, Ramdas Maharaj, 86, 87
Janābāi, 23
jayjaykār, 85, 116, 141, 147, 148
Jews, 197–98n24
Jñāndev, 23, 39
Jñāneśvar, 5, 25, 119, 183
Joglekar, Nanasaheb, 34
Joshi, Dinanath, 109
Joshi, Lakshmanshastri, 40–41
Joshi, Moreshwarbuwa, 143, 171
Joshi, Vasudeobuwa, 143

Kaikadi Maharaj Maṭh, in Pandharpur, 86–87
Kaikadis, 200–201n17
Kalaskar, Babanrao, 62, 74
Kale, Sonutai, 196n4
Kane, P. N., 115
Karhadkar, Haribhau, 34, 145
Karhadkar, Rambhau (Ramchandrabuva), 34, 142, 145
karma, 45–46
Karpatriji, Swami, 94
karūṇa rasa, 129, 130
Kashikar, Sakharambuva, 31
kaṭhāv, 59
Kavishvar, Yashvantbuva, 47
Kemkar, Eknāthshastri, 37
Kesari, 59
Khadilkar, Manjushree, 85–90, 101, 122, 136–37, 145, 147, 149
Khadilkar, Shrikant, 88
Khaparde, Dadasaheb, 46
Khare, Govinda, 87, 89, 90, 101
Kher, B. G., 74–75, 83
Khobarekar, V. G., 53–54
Kirloskar, Annasaheb, 31, 34
kīrtan (in general): audience participation in, 22; authenticity of, 167–70; conferences on, 21, 44, 46–47, 48; devotional practice in, 22, 25, 44, 141; dialogism in, 174–76; and dress, 47; and embodiment, 157–58; as entertainment, 26, 27; and government policy, 87–91; government support for, 80, 81–82, 86, 87; improvisation in, 35; institutionalization of, 36–39, 44, 49; instrumental accompaniment in, 141; master-disciple relationships in, 38, 105, 107, 109, 122–23, 141; narrative aspects of, 22, 27–28, 29, 35, 141–55; and nationalism, 8, 40, 194; poetry incorporated in, 28, 29–30; presentational format of, 141–55; publication of, 22, 34–36; and Rāmdās's teachings, 26–27; and reformism, 33, 40; remuneration to performers of, 38, 110; and secularism, 22, 48; theatrical aspects of, 29, 167; Tilak's advocacy of, 16, 17, 21, 22, 43–46, 130, 131, 167; virtuosity in, 22, 29. *See also* nāradīya kīrtan; rāṣṭrīya kīrtan; vārkarī kīrtan
Kolhatkar, Vaman, 38, 52, 53, 70, 72, 80, 105–7, 129, 142, 144–45, 147–48, 167, 196n5
Kolhatkar, Vasudeo, 11, 17, 34, 35, 38, 50–51, 52, 64–73, 75, 80, 92–93, 143, 145, 191
Koparkar, Gangadhar N., 37, 38, 39, 91–92, 94–97, 98, 99, 101, 104, 122–23, 141–42, 158, 202n7
Krishna, 124, 142, 143, 147, 158
Kristeva, Julia, 206n1
Kṛṣṇadayārnav, 28
Kurtakoti, Shankaracharya, 43

lāvaṇī, 28, 29
literature, modern, 32
Livingston, Tamara, 13
Locke, Margaret, 157

Madhavmunishwar, 28, 29
Maharaj, Gadge, 12, 17, 52, 60–64, 73–75, 80–81, 83–86, 87, 90, 101, 191, 193, 196n3, 201n31
Maharaj, Kaikadi, 17, 62, 81, 84–86, 87, 90
Maharaj, Shivaji, 85
Maharaj, Tanpure, 62, 81
Maharaj, Tukdoji, 83
Maharashtra: region of, 5–6; state of, 5, 79, 80, 82–83
Mahipati, 3
Manakeshwar, Anantji, 28
Mane, Yashwantrao, 84

maṅgalācaraṇ, 141, 145, 147
Mani, Yeshwantrao, 61
Manjul, V. L., 100
Manmadkar, Dadamaharaj, 23, 83, 125
Manmadkar, Gayabai, 62, 83, 196n3
Marathi language, 5, 28, 41, 46, 73, 84, 98, 100, 114, 115, 131, 149, 174, 195n4, 200–201n17
Marxism, 12, 60–61
master-disciple relationship, 38, 105, 107, 109, 122–23, 141
Mehta, Makrand, 5
Merleau-Ponty, Maurice, 157
middle class: Chatterjee's theory of, 21; and kīrtan institutions, 36, 37, 44, 48, 110, 112, 130, 131; and kīrtan publication, 34; and nāradīya kīrtan, 30, 101; and nationalism, 10, 13, 21, 30, 32, 33; and religious reforms, 39; and saṅgīt nāṭak, 33
Mirikar, Miratai, 125
Modak, Vaman Abaji, 39, 40–42, 45, 48
modernist reforms, 21–22, 32–33, 45–46, 192
Moropant, 28, 29–30, 59
Mughals, 28, 158, 190
Mukherjee, Partha Nath, 6
muḷpad, 89, 140, 147, 154, 180, 201n28
Mumbai (Bombay), Gadge Maharaj Mission in, 84; kīrtan in, 104, 105, 109–10, 120, 131; kīrtan institutions in, 98
Munshi, K. M., 99
Muslims. *See* Islam

naman, 34, 35, 115, 116, 141, 143–48
Nāmdev, 23, 25, 168
nāradīya kīrtan: audience participation in, 130, 154, 156, 170–71; caste of performers in, 23; and courtly arts, 27, 30; devotional practice in, 23, 138, 169; and embodiment, 3; gender of performers of, 23, 196n4; and government policy, 87, 90, 101; instrumental accompaniment in, 24, 31; and kīrtan schools, 98–99, 104, 124, 131; and middle class, 30; and music institutions, 37, 49; narrative aspects of, 28, 29, 31, 59, 138–39, 149, 150, 160, 171; and nationalism, 16, 22, 30, 42, 47, 48, 51, 104; poetry incorporated in, 28; political aspects of, 22, 27; popularity of, 97; presentational format of, 23–25, 31, 137, 140, 141, 143, 145, 146, 148, 150, 151, 154, 155; and Rāmdās's teachings, 26, 27; and rāṣṭrīya kīrtan, 27, 29, 40, 42, 57, 81, 138–39, 141, 193; remuneration to performers of, 30; theatrical influence in, 33–34; two-part structure of, 30, 31, 150; and vārkarī kīrtan, 47, 48, 138–39, 145, 146, 171; virtuosity in, 30, 31; women as singers of, 120–21, 122, 125, 131
Nārad Maṅdir, in Pune, 37, 38, 69, 92, 94, 98, 104–6, 108–9, 120, 121, 131, 137, 141. *See also* Harikīrtanottejak Sabha
Nārad's mat, 3, 47, 52, 75, 112, 136–37, 150, 176, 187, 189
Narayan, Jayaprakash, 29
nationalism: and abstention from tea drinking, 50, 55, 56, 72; and Chatterjee's theory of, 9–12, 21, 32–33, 40, 51; and cow protection, 7, 56–57; and female kīrtan singers, 129–30; and Gandhi's activity, 11, 17, 50–51, 56, 57, 60, 62–64, 65, 66, 75, 79, 80, 82, 84, 145; and intellectuals, 10–11, 12, 60–61; and kīrtan conferences, 46, 48–49, 102–3, 113–20; and kīrtan institutions, 111–12, 187; and linguistic identity, 115; and middle class, 10, 13, 21, 30, 32, 33, 51; and modernist reforms, 21–22, 32–33, 192; and music institutions, 37, 39, 49, 194; and nāradīya kīrtan, 16, 22, 30, 42, 47, 48, 51, 104; and regional culture, 189–90; and religious reforms, 39–42, 48; and revival of traditional music, 13; and saṅgīt nāṭak, 33; and secularism, 6, 172; and Tilak's activity, 10, 11, 16, 17, 21, 22, 42,

nationalism: and abstention from tea drinking (*cont.*) 43–46, 48–49, 51, 52, 53, 55–56, 57–60, 62, 65, 67, 75, 82, 103, 115, 116, 190; Turino's theory of, 21–22, 51; Van der Veer's theory of, 6–7. *See also* anti-colonialism; cultural nationalism; rāṣṭrīya kīrtan
National Social Conference, 40
Nehru, Jawaharlal, 17, 80, 81, 82, 85, 90, 93
newspapers, 43, 46, 53
Nizampurkar, Lakshmanbuwa, 143
Nizampurkar, Murlidhar, 143
nuclear weapons, 87

oral history, 53, 190, 191
oral tradition, 25, 48, 178
oratory, 42
organic intellectuals, 12, 60–61, 195n9
ovī, 34, 124–27, 150–52, 156, 180

Pakistan, 79
Paluskar, V. D. (Vishnu Digambar), 36, 37, 85, 112
Panchayat Raj, 83
paṅth-kavis, 29–30, 47
Paranjpe, S. M., 46
Parshuram, 29
participation, audience, 22, 23, 60, 62–63, 84, 85, 112, 119, 130, 140, 141, 145, 146, 149, 154, 156, 163, 168, 170–71, 177–78, 179, 184, 185–86, 187
partition, national, 16, 79, 80, 90, 101
Patel, Vallabhai, 86, 93
paṭhaḍī, 18, 135, 141, 143, 145, 147
Pathak, Yashwant, 29, 42–43, 57, 81
Patil, Nana, 124
Patwardhan, Dattopant, 22, 49, 52, 56–60, 62, 64–65, 68, 80–81, 92, 143, 198n13, 199n18
Peirce, Charles, 14
Peshvas, 27, 28, 29, 47, 123, 145
Phadke, Vasudeo Balwant, 29, 53, 139, 171
Phandi, Anant, 29
pilgrimage, 5–6, 12, 17, 73–74, 84, 86, 99, 124–25, 158, 177
poetry, 27–28, 29–30, 59, 168–69, 204n20
political relations: and nāradīya kīrtan, 22, 27; and rāṣṭrīya kīrtan, 4, 17, 26, 27, 47, 49, 53, 67, 95–97, 166, 171–72, 186, 189, 191, 192, 193, 194. *See also* government policy; nationalism; reformism; socialism
Poona Gayan Samaj, 36–38
popular music, 92–93, 103
post-Enlightenment ideology, 10, 11, 21, 32
povāḍā, 6, 27–28, 29, 43, 47, 59, 92, 107, 123, 124–25, 128–30, 141, 153, 156–57, 180, 182–84, 186, 188, 204–5n21
Prabhakar, 29
Prarthana Samaj, 39–40, 48, 51
Prentiss, Karen, 168
publication, kīrtan, 22, 34–36, 40, 43, 49
Pune: Dharma Caitanya in, 73; nāradīya kīrtan in, 25, 87, 104, 171; Nārad Maṅdir in, 37, 38, 69, 92, 94, 98, 104–6, 108–9, 120, 121, 131, 137, 141; Peshva government in, 28, 47, 145; rāṣṭrīya kīrtan in, 17, 81, 91, 92, 111, 120, 156, 176, 194
pūrvaraṅgas, 24–25, 27, 30, 46, 107, 109, 139, 140, 147–50, 155, 158, 180–82, 185, 186; and rāṣṭrīya kīrtan, 57, 58, 68–69

Quit India movement, 39, 63, 74, 83, 124

radio, 88, 89, 92
rāgas, 26, 35, 94, 107, 115, 138, 141–45, 148, 149, 152, 154, 161
Rajaram, 28
Rajputs, 70, 190, 201n17
Rāma, 23, 57, 94, 95, 142, 145, 147, 178
Rāmdās, 26–27, 47, 73, 147, 148, 183, 197n11
Ramjoshi, 29, 30
Ram Rajya Parisad, 94, 95, 96
Ranade, Ashok, 27
Ranade, M. G., 10, 11, 40, 41–42, 55, 56
Rand, Charles Walter, 52–53
Rashtriya Swayamsevak Sangh (RSS), 4, 17, 79–80, 96, 97, 101, 102–4, 111, 113–14, 120, 129, 132, 152, 171, 179, 186, 187, 194

rāṣṭrīya gīt, 189
rāṣṭrīya kīrtan: anthropological approach to, 4, 8–9, 190–91, 194; and anti-colonialism, 17, 43, 48, 50, 51, 52, 60, 72–74, 84, 130, 152, 189; audience participation in, 60, 62–63, 84, 85, 112, 119, 154, 156, 163, 171, 177–78, 179, 184, 185–86, 187; and brahmanism, 6, 11, 43, 52, 56, 65, 66, 79–80, 91, 104, 189; and caste system, 12, 43, 58, 60, 64, 67, 74, 75, 192; and community organizations, 102–4, 111–12, 120; and conservatism, 10, 40, 42, 48, 51, 91, 183, 186, 189; and courtly art forms, 27; devotional aspects of, 4, 52, 57–60, 62–63, 71, 145, 147, 155, 156, 169, 171, 172–73, 179, 183, 193; and dialogism, 174–76, 180, 185; and Gandhi's activity, 56, 57, 60, 62–64, 65, 66, 75, 84, 85, 88, 93, 101, 145; and government policy, 85–86, 87–91, 93, 101; and government support, 17, 80, 81–82, 86, 87, 101; and indexicality, 157, 193; instrumental accompaniment of, 70, 177, 185; and kīrtan conferences, 14, 46, 51, 75, 113–20; and kīrtan schools, 14, 80, 98–100, 101; and modernist reforms, 50, 51, 192; narrative aspects of, 6, 27, 29, 42, 43, 49, 50, 51, 52, 53, 57–59, 68–71, 91, 128–29, 135, 139, 148–49, 152–54, 158–66, 171, 174, 180–87, 188, 193; and nationalist elite, 10, 17, 43, 49, 50–51, 52, 62, 66, 69, 71, 75, 80, 92, 190, 191, 192; philosophical aspects of, 67–68, 80, 105, 142; poetry incorporated in, 59; political aspects of, 4, 17, 26, 27, 47, 49, 53, 67, 95–97, 166, 171–72, 186, 189, 191, 192, 193, 194; popularity of, 42, 52, 80, 81, 92, 97, 103–4; and popular music, 92–93; presentational format of, 52, 112, 136–38, 141–43, 145, 147, 149, 151–53, 158–66, 171, 176–88, 193; publication of, 43, 49; and Rāmdās's teachings, 26, 147; and religious reforms, 40, 51, 52, 69; and rural relations, 12, 17, 60, 64, 73, 80–84, 90, 101, 189, 192; and Savarkar's activity, 66–67; as subtype of nāradīya kīrtan, 27, 29, 40, 42, 57, 81, 138–39, 141, 193; survey of performers of, 195n8; theatrical aspects of, 15, 34, 157; and Tilak's activity, 42, 43–46, 48–49, 51, 52, 57–60, 62, 65, 67, 75, 89, 92, 116, 139, 149, 152, 191; two-part structure of, 57; and vārkarī tradition, 6, 61–62, 85, 87, 138–39, 158–61, 170–71; women as singers of, 87–89, 120, 121, 124–25, 128, 129–30, 131, 147, 156, 158–66, 170–72, 188; and working class, 60–61, 80
rāṣṭrīya kīrtan, singers of: N. S. Apamarjane, 119, 142; Charudatta Aphale, 93, 149; Govindswami Aphale, 81, 91–94, 98, 99, 101; Narahari Appamarjane, 99; Sudhatai Dhamankar, 53, 99, 104, 122–23, 129, 156, 158–66, 170–72, 180, 183, 184, 193; B. R. Ghaisas, 39, 57, 59, 149, 188; Yashwantrao Gondavalekar, 62, 74; Narendrabuva Hate, 99; Moreshwarbuva Joshi, 171; Tanpure Kaikadi, 81; Babanrao Kalaskar, 61, 74; Manjushree Khadilkar, 85–90, 147; Govinda Khare, 87, 89, 90; Vaman Kolhatkar, 80, 105–7, 129; Vasudeo Kolhatkar, 11, 17, 50–51, 52, 64–73, 75, 80, 92–93, 191; Gangadhar N. Koparkar, 39, 91–92, 94–97, 98, 99, 101, 104, 141–42, 158; Gadge Maharaj, 12, 17, 52, 60–64, 73–75, 80–81, 83–86, 87, 90, 101, 191, 193; Kaikadi Maharaj, 17, 62, 84–87, 90, 101; Tanpure Maharaj, 62, 81; Yeshwantrao Mani, 61; Gayabai Manmadkar, 62, 81; Vaman Abaji Modak, 40;

rāṣṭrīya kīrtan, singers of: N. S. Apamarjane (*cont.*) Dattopant Patwardhan, 49, 52, 56–60, 62, 64–65, 68, 80–81, 92; Jaytunbi Maharaj Sayyid, 124–25, 129, 188, 193; Ramchandra Shelar, 61, 74, 81; Mirabai Shirkar, 62, 73–74; Shrikrishna Sinnarkar, 99; Yogeshwar Upasani, 156, 174, 176–88, 193; Vishwanath Wagh, 61, 74, 84
reformism, 16, 17, 21, 32–33, 39–42, 48, 50–51, 52, 55, 69, 192; and agriculture, 80, 82; and education, 80, 82, 99; and modernist reforms, 21–22, 32–33, 45–46, 192; and Nehru government, 80, 82, 85–86; and religious reforms, 32, 33, 39–42, 48, 50, 51, 52, 69
regional culture, 5, 16, 189–90
resolutions, at kīrtan conferences, 46–47
Rosse, Michael, 37
Roy, Rammahun, 39
Roy, Srirupa, 81
Rukminī, 28
rural relations, 79, 82–83; and rāṣṭrīya kīrtan, 12, 17, 60, 64, 73, 80–84, 90, 101, 189, 192
Ruskin, John, 83

śāhīrs, 27, 29–30, 47, 91, 197n13
sākī, 35, 69, 92, 94, 107, 150, 151–52, 153
Salpekar, Babasaheb, 116–18
Sambhaji, 28
Sammelans.
see conference, kīrtan
saṅgīt nāṭak, 22, 29, 31, 33–34
Śaṅkarācārya, 141–42, 145
Sanskrit, 6, 11, 28, 29, 46, 52, 65, 91, 92, 95, 98, 105, 108–9, 122, 130, 131, 141, 142, 149, 171, 177
Sant Namdeo-Tukaram Warkari Parishad, 87
Sarasvatī, 141
Sardesai, Govind Sakharam, 30, 35
sarvodāya movement, 83
Satarkar, Babamaharaj, 125
Satarkar, Bhagavati Maharaj, 125
Sathaye, Adheesh, 80
Sathe, Balasaheb, 35
Savarkar, V. D., 10, 11, 66, 93, 116, 139, 147, 152, 191
Sayyid, Jaytunbi Maharaj, 124–27, 128, 129, 130, 188, 193
Schechner, Richard, 3, 14
Scheper-Hughes, Nancy, 157
schools. *See* education
secularism, 6, 22, 48, 79, 80, 91, 96, 97, 172, 192, 194
Seva Sangh, 87
Shahu, 28
Shelar, Ramchandra, 61, 74, 81
Shirkar, Mirabai, 62, 73–74, 124, 125, 196n3
Shirwadkar, Vasant, 64
Shivaji, 6, 28, 29, 43, 45, 59, 139, 147, 152, 158–66, 169, 171, 172–73, 182–86
Shiv Sena, 82, 97
Shridar, 28, 29
Shridhar, 28
Sikhs, 90, 114
Singer, Milton, 131
Singh, Rajendra, 102, 113, 179
Sinnarkar, Shrikrishna, 99
Sītā, 28
Śiva, 23
ślokas, 54–55, 69, 140, 141, 142, 143, 147, 149, 150
Smith, Anthony, 10–11, 55
socialism, 17, 60–61, 81, 86, 91, 192
sugar industry, 82

tamāśā, 28, 29, 30, 33
Tambeshastri, Sadashiv Dhonde, 35
Tamils, 114, 168–69, 190
tarāna, 144
tea drinking, abandonment of, 50, 55, 56, 72
television, 93
theater. *See* saṅgīt nāṭak; tamāśā
Tilak, Bal Gangadhar (Lokmanya), 10, 11, 16, 22, 42, 43–46, 48–49, 51, 52, 53, 55–56, 57–60, 62, 65, 67, 75, 82, 89, 92, 103, 115, 116, 130, 131, 139, 149, 152, 167, 190, 191, 1721
trance, 15, 113, 156, 166–68, 170
Trimbakkar, Anyagosavi, 145

Tukārām, 23, 26, 148, 149, 154, 158–65, 167–68, 169, 170, 171, 172–73, 180, 183, 196–97n9, 196n5
Turino, Thomas, 7–8, 14, 21–22, 51, 157

Upasani, Yogeshwar, 156, 174, 176–88, 193
Urdu language, 174
uttararaṅgas, 24–25, 27, 30, 46, 129, 149, 150–54, 155; and rāṣṭrīya kīrtan, 57, 58, 69, 70, 95, 139, 149, 156, 158, 182, 193. *See also* ākhyāns
Uttar Pradesh, 189

Vaidya, Chintamanrao, 46
Vāmanpaṇḍit, 28
"Vande Mataram," 56
Van der Veer, Peter, 6–7
vārkarī kīrtan: audience participation in, 23, 154, 158, 168, 170–71; caste of performers in, 23; devotional aspects of, 5–6, 23, 25–26, 85, 138, 168; gender of performers of, 23, 124, 125, 131, 196nn3–4; and government policy, 87; instrumental accompaniment in, 23; and kīrtan conferences, 118–19; and kīrtan schools, 124; and nāradīya kīrtan, 47, 48, 138–39, 145, 146, 171; and Nehru government, 81; origin of, 5, 6; presentational format of, 23, 119, 145, 146, 149, 154, 155; and rāṣṭrīya kīrtan, 6, 61–62, 85, 138–39, 158–61, 170–71
Vārkarī Śikṣan Saṅsthā, 124
Vayu, 59
Vedas, 10, 68, 91–92, 105
vīr rasa, 124, 127–30
virtuosity, musical, 22, 29, 30, 31, 138
Vishwa Hindu Parishad (VHP), 4, 97, 102, 104, 111, 171, 179, 186, 204n13
Viṣṇu, 137
Viṭṭhala, 23, 26, 145, 147, 149, 203n26
Vyas, Gangadhar, 171

Wagh, Vishwanath, 61, 74, 84
widows, rights of, 39, 41, 42
women: and kīrtan schools, 18, 104, 108, 120–22; as kīrtan singers, 23–24, 87–89, 120–30, 121, 131, 147, 156, 158–66, 170–72, 188, 196nn3–4; and rights of widows, 39, 41, 42; in tamāśā performances, 29
working class, 60–61, 80, 82